As I sit and write this, looking back on a
that life changing moment that made m
to put it into perspective. The death of m
birthday. That changed everything.

I graduated high school in 1980, B student. Quite average. I loved sports. I had every season covered. Fall- tennis team, Fall- Winter- Volleyball, Spring- softball. I had no desire to leave to go to college, I never really thought in terms of a career, I just always wanted to be a mother. First and foremost. I started my first job after I turned 16. I was a cashier in a drug store, then moved to fast food. I liked the independence it gave me and the ability to pay for my own gas and incidentals. I soon moved over to retail. Barbara Moss was the first retail store I ever worked at. I loved it! I loved retail, much more up my alley! But the right thing to do was enroll in my local community college. My father was a detective. He started with the New York State Police, moved through the ranks, ending as an investigator with the OCTF (organized crime task force) He didn't talk much about it but it was interesting. He was forced to take an early retirement after a massive heart attack and subsequent surgery made it impossible to work. A career he loved, done at 46. One of my professors who had a close relationship with the NYS Police surprised and made me so proud as he introduced me to the class as the daughter of one of the greatest troopers he ever met. My father, had other ideas for me. At that time, there were hardly any women police officers around. I actually graduated with the first woman that was hired in a nearby city. But he didn't like it. He didn't want me to do it. So, I ended up taking the Juvenile end instead of the actual police work. That was brutal. My love for children and learning about the brutal beatings and case studies, I knew I couldn't handle it. I'd end up in jail myself. No way could I restrain myself from these animals. I finished my first year, not really looking forward to my last year. That's when it all came crashing down. My father, in 1976 suffered 3 massive heart attacks. Knowing all they know now, he probably would have been alive longer. But the damage was done and he was given less than 10 years to live. He did live, everyday. His way. There were times I would get so angry at him. He smoked, he quit for a while but started up again, he made us go to church and I would always get caught sneaking out after communion with my friends, I was allowed to sit with them instead of family. He just knew too many people. I couldn't understand why he didn't change everything to live longer. Didn't he want to? Honestly, I never asked him. Maybe I was too afraid of the answer. Faith was always a part of my upbringing. I believed, but I was also 18. The " invincible age"! I knew religion was there but was it a huge part of my life? No. Not yet. I could not have prepared myself for the amount of time my faith carried me.

August 1981. Enjoying the summer. My parents and grandparents a few years before sold our family camp on Oneida Lake. Instead putting in an inground pool. Coming from the generation that grandparents lived in the same house, my maternal grandparents lived in a ground level flat that opened to our family pool. My grandparents, both sides, so sweet, but we were always closer to my mother's parents. Earlier that week, my father called me into the living room, serious conversations only took place in there. I remember sitting down, finding this extremely weird because this was not my father's normal behavior. He just looked at me and said, " You, you out of everyone will have everything you want out of life." I was confused, I kind of laughed it off and said, "ok." I didn't know what else to say. I mean, I'm 18, I work nearly full time, in school, not happy with my direction and then I just walked out, kind of forgot about it and went on with my day. Those words would stay with me all my life.

I can't really say that I remember the details of that particular Monday, August 3rd, except for that it was extremely hot day. My mother was aggravated because it was my father's regular golf day, but being that hot, she worried about his heart. This is all before cell phones and so the day continued as normal, and we wouldn't find out the truth for a few more days, that he had a very bad day and wouldn't go to the doctor. I went to bed, my room directly across from my parents and in my slumber, I never heard him slam the garage door down or the conversation that took place between my parents. I never knew that as my mother got into bed that night, my father, laying on her side of the bed,(after surgery he was unable to sleep on his side so after 25 years he changed sides) he says to her " I'm giving you back your side of the bed."

It was a thump that was unmistakeable. It was a dead fall. Sitting up in bed, looking at the clock, 2:58 am, I hear my mother screaming, " oh my God, Joey get up, get up." I ran into my parent's room to see my father laying on the floor. Instantly I remember the CPR procedure from the course I took in case this happened, never believing I would have to or even remembering how to. But it kicked in. Starting on mouth to mouth, the chest pumps, functioning, as my mother in the doorway screaming and someone, I couldn't even guess who, called the ambulance. Jody and Billy and I lived home, my other 2 sisters, Eunice and Corinne, 5 minutes away. Everything happened so fast. His heartbeat wasn't life sustaining I was told. I held his hand, he squeezed it, begging him not to die, as I saw life excrete itself from him. He was gone. My father was gone. I was daddy's little girl and he was gone. August 4th, 1981.

The wake and funeral was endless. It was mentally exhausting. My father's family, very large, and my father, well respected and very well known and it seemed like the world showed up. The wake went on for 3 days. Lines and lines of people. 51 years old and gone. He was honored with a 3 gun salute and policemen from every agency in the area led the procession. It was quite an honor and I was so proud to have my father respected like that. But I knew my life was different. My father, my security. He was such a big man. I always felt so safe. I was scared inside. Who would watch over me now?

It was during this time that I actually held rosaries for a purpose. There had to be a reason? But why? I needed him more than God did, didn't I? As the days went on, once it was over, once we all came out of shock. Once everyone goes away, and " normalcy" returns. When your mind begins to wander and the tears roll down your face and you don't even realize it. I used to walk and walk around the block with my friends. I remember walking around and around the block. Talking, crying and then, remembering his words, " you, you out of everyone, will have everything you want out of life." Oh my God! Did he know he was going to die? Then I find out that he gave my mother her side of the bed back! I was convinced. He knew! Then, for the first time, but certainly not the last, the scent of his cologne hit me directly in the face. I stopped cold. My friends on both sides of me. " Do you smell it????" They had no clue. That scent would visit me over the years when I least expected it.

I had been dating my boyfriend, Paul, since high school. Senior year to be exact. His dad was diagnosed with cancer after my father died, within months, he was gone too. It was horrible to see how cancer just broke him down. He wasn't a tall man, but very stocky. Watching the cancer eat away at him was brutal. In a matter of months he went from walking to being unable to and having Paul carry him from the couch to the bed. That pulled us closer, both having lost our dads within 3 years. He told his father on his death bed that he was going to ask me to marry him. And we did. October 5th 1984, I married my high school sweetheart. What a mistake. I knew it going into it. I knew it on my wedding day. As I walked down the aisle in St. Anthony's Church, somehow, my foot became wrapped around the tape holding the runner down just as I was to take the step to the altar. My maid of honor literally had to get on her hands and knees and unwrap the tape. I was unable to move. My father, I know, was sending me a message. My friends tried so hard to stop me. He was jealous and controlling. But in my naïve state of mind, I thought that LOVE CONQUERED ALL! I loved him and thought once we were married, he would stop. Understanding that I was his. It didn't work out that way. It ended after 3 months. I found out he was cheating, while he was accusing me. One night he didn't come home. When he walked in the next morning, I threw him out. High on Valium, He came at me, loaded a shotgun and put it to my head, my little 6 year old niece, who lived downstairs, unknowingly walked through the door at that moment. I was so afraid for her that I turned on him screaming, thankfully she got scared and ran out. But in his condition, I'm lucky he didn't kill me. He was ranting and accusing. He dropped the gun and picked up a knife. Holding me against him, he put the knife to my cheek and cut me. My sister called the cops and his best friend. Upon their arrival, they removed him from the house, I was called every name in the book. He was outside on the lawn calling me horrible names. I had to get out. He left for a few days, and came back, crying, sorry for all he did. Like a fool, I took him back, until I caught him cheating again. That was it. 5 days before Christmas 1984, I threw him out. I was going to be divorced at 22. I walked back into my mother's house, suitcase and my cabbage patch doll, Newton Logan. A gag gift from my grandmother the year before because I loved my nieces cabbage patch. As much as I wanted a baby, the smartest thing I ever did, was not becoming pregnant.

Those months after were tough. I was so lost. I wanted my name back. It took 9 months. He refused to sign papers. All I wanted was to forget about it. Even though I knew it was the right thing to do, it had an effect on me. I lost about 15 lbs and had to endure him following me. Everyone was afraid of what might happen. I just wanted to be left alone. I was so angry. He made a joke of marriage. I wore my mother's wedding gown and prior to my father's death, he had received a bottle of Dom Perignon, 1968. His will stated that it be opened at my wedding. All that was important to me, was a joke to him. My anger would last for years over that bottle.

Chapter 2

By 23 I was divorced. I ended up staying in retail. And I loved it! I couldn't go into Criminal Justice. My heart wasn't in it. Knowing my father didn't want me to go into law enforcement, and honestly, I hated college. Retail was perfect for my hyper self. Constantly busy and moving around. I was not the type of person to sit behind a desk all day. I worked my way up to store manager/ training manager of Tops n Bottoms, a men's/ women's store in Sangertown Square mall. It is here that the hunt for the perfect man came to an end.

By the time I was 26, I had dated every idiot in the city and the surrounding areas. I was honestly to the point of giving up dating all together. It was exhausting! Managing a men's/ women's store that was very popular gave me access to meeting a lot of guys. I had enough. But isn't that when it happens? When you realize you don't need someone to make you happy? I made good money, I had friends, I had a career I enjoyed. I was happy. Then one day, my assistant comes to me and says there is a really cute guy at the new Taco Bell that opened in the food court. We ended up ordering lunch or dinner there a lot because they were one of the only places that delivered. So a few weeks go by and I still didn't know who she was talking about. As it turned out I had more day hours and he had more night hours so our paths never crossed. I would go during lunch and this older guy would just stare at me, laughing I went back to my assistant to describe him thinking this couldn't be the guy???? Nope! So on an Iron day, (retail for and open to close) I was walking across the food court, towards the Taco Bell, heading back to TnB, and I'm looking, looking, profile view, not bad, could this be him? He has a 60's hair cut but he's got potential, I'm thinking to myself. I would later come to realize how spot on I was! So a few more days go by, my assistant is insisting I go meet him. Well at Taco Bell the conversation was all about Tops n Bottoms. So that day I choose to order with, naturally delivery. I was speaking to Adam I later found out and the conversation goes like this…" Is this the manager with dark hair?" Me, "Well everyone in the store has dark hair." " But are you the manager?" " Yes I am." " Well our manager wants to meet you." Long story short, I stopped down to say hi one slow Saturday afternoon in February. He comes out, cute smile, deep voice and gorgeous green/ gray eyes. My fathers eyes. The eyes always get me. We talk for a while and he finally invites me to a party for season ticket holders for the AHL Hockey team in Utica. The UTICA DEVILS, farm team of the New Jersey Devils. I politely decline explaining that I just broke up with one of them and I didn't think it was a good idea. Then, BAM! " ARE YOU A PUCKETTE???" A PUCKETTE is a common name for the girls that chase the hockey team. I looked at him in disbelief and said," No, but are you an asshole??" I walked away, dad's eyes or not, see ya later!

Monday morning started normally, then by lunch time, the asshole with the green eyes shows up at my store. He apologizes but I'm really over it now. My assistants, pushing me, literally, pushing me out the door, forcing me to go to lunch with him. The best thing they ever did. We talked and talked, having a lot in common, more than we realized actually, as the guy I was " kind of" dating walks in, giving me filthy looks behind Bob's back and the waitress that Bob " was kind of" dating giving him filthy looks behind me. I can say this now with no fear of retribution from Tops and Bottoms, that my hour lunch turned in to a 2 hour lunch and with a date for that night. It was very clear to me very early on that he was going to be the man I married. From deep into my soul, I knew, instinctively, that he would take care of me forever.

We were inseparable. We were so alike yet so different. Morals, values, politics we meshed perfectly. Other than that, we were like Felix and Oscar. But our differences balanced us. We were both ready to make that long term commitment. February 28, 1989. Our first date. Later that year, fully committed, we bought a house, planning our wedding in May of 1991, everything was in order. Bob loved the restaurant business, but he wanted more. He would soon leave Taco Bell for a position with WENDYS RESTAURANT. A franchise owned locally with the potential for a multi unit manager position.

We got married on May 25, 1991. I continued at Tops and Bottoms and Bob, was still managing the Taco Bell. We had our house, we made good money and now, all there was left was for me to become a mom.

It was August, 3 months after we got married and I'm at work. It was a Tuesday, I remember clearly, because markdowns came in every Tuesday. I was so aggravated with myself all morning, for no known reason I was jumpy and short tempered. . I was barking at everyone that came near me. Not a good way to work in retail! I stopped my markdowns and almost kiddingly said to my assistant, I'm going to CVS for a minute, either I'm pregnant or I'm dying cause something isn't right with me.

I WAS PREGNANT!!! The first of 4 unplanned pregnancies! I cried. I was so happy. I was scared. How do I tell Bob? I can't over the phone. He now worked in a different mall across town. He was there til 10 pm. I was out at 5. I couldn't wait. I can't wait to open Christmas presents, I certainly can't wait until 10 pm! I wanted kids right away but he wanted to wait a bit. Surprise!!!! I got through the day and went to the other mall. Thankfully they weren't busy. This wasn't the perfect scenario that I had in my head forever, on how I would tell my husband we were going to have a baby, but, I was too excited to wait. I blurted it out almost immediately. " I'M PREGNANT!!!!!" Well, thank God his assistant was standing behind him because I thought he was going to hit the floor! He slapped him on the back! 'Congratulations, man, that's awesome! " My joy quickly turned to tears as I saw his face. He wasn't happy. Now I know it probably wasn't very fair of me to spring it on him like that, something I did 3 more times after too, but he recovered. He grabbed me and hugged me. When he came home that night, he apologized for his reaction. He told me as he got into the car to come home that night, a song was on, "WINDS OF CHANGE" by the Scorpions. A song about the future generation. He listened to the words. Bob loves, loves, loves music. So the words were what he needed to become as excited as I was. Bringing a child into the world. I was so excited. Finally, at 30, my baby was on it's way!

My first visit to the doctor's office was a few weeks after I found out. I couldn't wait. I ran out and bought the book," WHAT TO EXPECT WHEN YOU ARE EXPECTING" and read chapter by chapter. I was so fascinated by creation. I loved my baby instantly. What they say is true. I felt that bond immediately. The doctor went thru the check up like he did with so many other women. The sonogram was done and I couldn't see anything! Not that there is anything really to see. I was 5 weeks pregnant. But the news that rocked my world and made me cry was the sonogram due date given to me. April 9. My father's birthday. Now what are the chances of that being a coincidence? My father was around me. It was easy to pick a name. He would be named after both of our fathers.

As it turned out, he was born not on my father's birthday, but on April 13, 1992. Bob wanted me to hold off for just one more day to be induced. April 14th, I came to find out it had nothing to do with taxes, but everything to do with his favorite guitar player from the band DEEP PURPLE. I was well prepared for the trip to the hospital. My bag was packed. Bob's bag was packed....meaning I had to worry about if he would eat all day so I had to make sure his snacks were packed. Opening day of baseball just happened to fall on April 13th that year. Bob played in roto baseball (fantasy league) was good enough to wish me happy opening day! Would I make it thru the day without killing him? He had a few near misses that day. As I lay in the hospital bed, in the early stages of labor, all in my back, and I had bad discs from a fall back in the 80's, the monitor that is wrapped around your stomach was showing minor contractions. The nurse had explained to Bob earlier that day that as they got stronger the monitor would spike and I would have trouble talking. As I'm laying there, in full back labor, Bob looked at me and said," Hey Lor, these contractions are going to get a lot worse, you gotta tough this out a little more." OHHHH, if looks could kill. The nurse came in, Bob had his private conversation with her, she walks over to me and I explain to her that it's all in my back. The nurse moves the monitor around and with the next contraction it's spiking!!! That was a close call for Bob. He started learning not to say everything that was on his mind.

Our son was the first baby born on my side in several years. My sisters, eight and ten years older than I had their kids in the 1970's. I watched my niece and nephews so much as babies, I started out with more knowledge than most new mothers. This was the first grandchild on Bob's side. He was an only child. So to say that the site of a newborn didn't intimidate him was an understatement. But he learned quickly, getting over his fear and before he had a chance to say no, he learned to change diapers. Oh no, we were in this together. He was going to enjoy as many diapers as humanly possible. I loved being a mom. It just fit. Six months later, I left work to stay home, I didn't care about vacations, clothes, nothing. I just wanted to be home.

When I found out I was pregnant for the second time I had so many fears. Maternally, it was all the same. I felt that strong bond immediately. But would I have enough love for 2 children? How foolish that sounds as I write this but I was so worried! Little did I know how much love you have in your heart. As soon as she was born, that fear was gone. My question was answered. Going to the doctor for the first visit, excited to learn of the due date, not so thrilled about being pregnant all summer. I fully planned on submersing myself in my mother's pool. As the sonogram was done, the date was given to me. My due date was August 5th. The day after the anniversary of my father's death. Once again my father was with me.

I was not a pretty pregnant woman. I have known some women that literally thrive in pregnancy. Their skin glows, they are luminous! Not me. My face broke out horribly and the pattern continued, I gained 50 lbs., just like the first pregnancy. She was a big baby, the biggest of the four. I never thought I would get through the last month. Her heel would push on my ribs all day long. Being as big as she was, and with my back condition worse. A cesarian section was scheduled. Alexandra Nicole Markason was born 2 weeks late on August 19, 1994 at a whopping 9lb 10oz.

After going through two very normal pregnancies, now fully knowing what to expect, the miracle of it all. This was absolutely amazing! How does a fetus start out a cell, that splits, and splits and splits. A visible heartbeat at 7 weeks. It's own blood supply. Life supplemented by a cord. A womb, deep inside of a woman. God did this. This is God's creation. It's overwhelming when you really stop and think about it. Now, in this day and age, videos can take you through the 9 months of pregnancy, right in the womb. It was after the birth of our children, the connection to my father, twice, that is no coincidence. Time after time, I would walk into my childrens' rooms, only to smell Aramis, the cologne my father used to wear, on my childrens' heads. I knew my father was in Heaven, and I knew he was with me, always. I would pray to him and for him. I would talk to him. I missed him everyday of my life. I still do.

As I got older, my faith was just there. I was brought up with it but my life experiences so far just deepened it. I am so thankful I had my faith to carry me through pregnancy number 3. I could not imagine life without faith.

Once again, my pregnancy came as a surprise! Our starter home now starting to bust at the seams. 3 bedroom, raised ranch, it was time to move. The market was down and we listed it but nothing. We tried different realtors but we just couldn't sell. We took it off the market for a while. Our oldest was now in kindergarten. Ali was 3 and we really wanted to move out of the city and the school district. But we were stuck. I was 30 weeks along when I noticed the change of movement. I called my doctor and he brought me in immediately. He could not find anything wrong. This entire pregnancy was different. Instead of gaining 50 lbs, I only gained 19 lbs. Keeping me under a close eye, and me with a bad, bad feeling, just tried to keep myself calm. At 34 ½ weeks I went into labor. I was hospitalized and they were able to stop labor. Giving me the option to stay or go home, I opted for home. Promising to rest. Given the meds to take if, God forbid, labor started again. It did. In the 3am hour, I took the pills once again, it didn't help. Contractions were far enough apart that I decided to let Bob and everyone else sleep as long as possible. It was obvious that she was fighting to be born. At around 5 am I woke Bob up. " You better get me to the hospital. Contractions started again." He rolled over and said, " Take the pills, Lor!" Ugh! Sometimes I just wanted to hit him over the head! "I DID! 2 HOURS AGO!" We made it to the hospital around 6. By that time I was contracting hard and fast. Family came over to watch the kids. Once I was in, I was immediately prepped for emergency surgery. Earlier in the pregnancy we had made the decision to have my tubes tied. Now. With all this happening. The doctor questioned my decision. " No!" Bob looked at me horrified! "What?????" He couldn't understand my thoughts, I could not make a life changing decision right now. As I was wheeled into emergency surgery, Bob was right next to me. This was baby number 3, he knew his job. Counting fingers and toes as soon as the baby was on the table being cleaned up. But nothing that simple was going on. As soon as I was opened, merconium was all through my uterus. I saw Bob's face, I knew something was wrong. " What's wrong?" He wouldn't answer. She was covered in merconium. Looking like a pea soup, my baby was covered in it. She was in fetal distress. Taken out and rushed to neonatal ICU, I never had a chance to see her, to hold her. Nothing. She was placed in an incubator. I couldn't hold her. Regina Maria Markason, born on September 11, 1997. A real 9-11 baby. I couldn't take it all in. Bob wouldn't tell me everything. He would tell me slowly, in spurts. She was 5 ½ weeks premature. Her head was too small, her liver and spleen were enlarged. She wasn't making platelets. Cytomegalovirus, CMV. Supposedly, I contracted this virus, as simple as a cold, supposedly in my first trimester. A virus that is common and the only time is dangerous is when a pregnant woman contracts it. 30 % mortality rate. If she lived, she could be facing mental retardation, deafness and blindness...If. She. Lived. If she survived the first month, bone marrow transplants would be necessary. I cried. I prayed. Bob cried. Bob prayed. Our families prayed. She survived those first days, in an incubator. Me, all the way down the hall, as far away from the nursery as possible. Listening to those baby carts coming down the hall and knowing Regina wouldn't be in one of them, coming down to me was crushing. It didn't matter how far away they put me, I was going to walk miles to get to her. I had complications as well. The day after the c-section, I'm still wearing a catheter. I wasn't peeing urine, but all blood. I didn't care about me. I didn't even think about me. They were sending me for scans. They couldn't figure out where the blood was coming from. I prayed constantly. " Please God, just don't take her,   I will handle anything you give me but please don't take her from me." That was my mantra. Over and over again. I will never forget as long as I live, sitting in my room, talking to my father, like he was sitting right next to me," Please daddy, please, help me" and then I would smell it. His cologne. It was in my nose. Strong. Unmistakeable. The bleeding stopped. It just stopped. They never figured out where it was coming from.

Those next hours and days were brutal. I had to go home without her. In order to jump start her platelets, they transfused platelets into her. She was born with 23,000, she would bleed out at 15,000. With 3 transfusions done over a one week period of time. It wasn't working. Locally, our hospital couldn't help. She needed to be transported to a bigger hospital. During this time, I was given a fax number to a Sister Briege Mc Kenna. She was a nun, living in Florida with the Blessing to heal. Having read up on her, she always said that God heals, she was just the vessel for the healing. I faxed her my story about Regina and asked her to please pray for her. Regina, born on September 11, transported to Upstate Medical Hospital in Syracuse a few days later. Now, our baby was an hour away from us. Upstate wasn't going to attempt anymore transfusions. They didn't believe it would help. It was September 19, Friday, my birthday. Those days are still blurry. Bob and I would drive out every day for a few hours. I couldn't take it anymore. Bob was given extra time off from work, but needed to go back on Monday the 22nd. Bob, now was a multiunit manager, having to over see 4 restaurants. Sam, the franchise owner, was very good in times of illness, but there was nothing we could do, nothing the doctors could do. " Pray" , they told us. By that time I had just about enough. It was absolute hell leaving her there. I was exhausted, both physically and mentally. A week out of surgery and I never sat down. Bob and I drove out on Sunday. He had quit smoking a few months earlier and I know he left the ICU to go have one. But he later told me he just went outside and lost it. I sat there alone, with her in my arms, surrounded by machines, and so many other babies. Listening to the wails of these other children. Sometimes the cries were horrifying. We found out at some point during Regina's stay that some were crack babies. That made me so angry. These babies, starting out like that, sitting there, I would say little prayers for these angels. I placed my Regina in her bassinet, thinking of Sister Briege, maybe God could use me as his vessel? It was one of those random thoughts that you just figure what do I have to lose? I cupped my hands around her middle. She was so tiny that my hands touched. I was crying, praying, "Please, dear Lord, heal her. Please, through my hands, heal her." My hands started to get hot, really hot. So hot that I took my hands off of her and looked at them. I didn't know what happened. Not yet, anyway. Bob came back in, I never said anything to him. We stayed for a bit more and left. Bob had to return to work the next day. Luckily he would be in Syracuse so he could stop in to see her. Monday morning came, I was getting ready to drive out by myself to see her. I was so angry that morning. I had quite enough and I wanted her home. Bob and I had a huge fight because I insisted I was taking her home. I put the car seat in the car. Bob said I was being unreasonable. I know I was but I got in my car and drove that hour drive. Every day was the same, I came to learn. Testing, then waiting for the reports. I just sat there, nurses buzzing around, waiting for the doctor to come in, a report was placed on the bottom of her bassinet. I looked at it. It was the platelet count that was done every morning. My poor baby had to endure being poked with a needle every morning for bloodwork. As I looked at the report, I questioned what I was seeing. The doctor, now visible to me but busy with another child. I interrupted her. " Am I seeing this correctly?" Her platelet count on the report said 239,000. The doctor took it, looked at it and said," she can go home!" I don't think it registered in my brain when she said it. It was like slow motion, it was a surreal moment. I didn't know what to do first. I think I screamed. Not a good thing to do in any ICU department. I called Bob, talking so fast that he couldn't understand what I was saying. He couldn't believe it or the fact that I actually took the car seat with every intention of bringing her home. Did we have a miracle? Did God use me as his vessel to heal her? We believe so.

It wasn't as though we could just whisk Regina out of there. When she was brought in, a team of doctors converged on her. Now, they all needed to evaluate her. Her hematologist was very good to us. He was the sweetest man, he told me that I reminded him of his sister, if and whenever we needed to speak to him, call him, anytime. When we did call his number and we were patched thru to him immediately. We had never experienced that with doctors before. After his evaluation he approached us, he was shaking his head, he looked at us and smiled. He said," you need to know that we have never had a baby just come out of this. We need to see her weekly, to monitor her liver and spleen." They were still enlarged, but functioning) " But God answered your prayers." Then we took her home.

Weekly trips to Syracuse only went on for a few weeks. She was doing beautifully. Weekly trips became monthly, and just before Christmas 1997, we received the best gift ever. No more trips to Syracuse. During that time her liver and spleen would shrink down to normal size. She was healing. She was healed. We had our miracle. Sometime during all of this, I received a handwritten letter from Sister Briege McKenna saying that she was at the Shrine of the Little Flower, St. Therese, in Lisieux, France. Along with her note was a Blessed miraculous medal. The history behind St. Therese of Lisieux was interesting, her calling and conversations with Jesus came on Christmas Eve, 1886 at the age of 4, and she died in 1897. 100 years before Regina was born. If there was any question whether we had our miracle, it was hushed when we took her 6 month picture and you can see the cross on her hand, clear as a bell.

The new year had us starting out as sardines in this house. Kids ages ranging from 6 to 1. Regina was totally healthy, receiving that clean bill of health right before Christmas 1997. We decided to remodel the downstairs from Bob's mancave to a playroom, extra bathroom and office. By February it was done. It was then that I walked downstairs into his office, crying because I found out I was pregnant again. The ink wasn't even dry on the check for the remodel. Once again we were out of room.

I was so afraid of this pregnancy. After Regina I was so paranoid. I always did everything I could during pregnancy to ensure a healthy baby. Would it happen again? I prayed so hard during that time. I was glad I had made the decision not to have the tubal ligation, but I wasn't prepared for another baby. I know I would have eventually called and scheduled it. But I never had the chance. A month or so before I found out I was pregnant, I started blowing up like a balloon. By the time I was 3 months pregnant, my weight was at the same it was when I delivered our other children. What the hell was going on? I later found out that it all started during my pregnancy with Regina. I went from hyperthyroidism to hypothyroidism within a few months after, but that diagnosis wasn't made until 9 months after Zach was born. With the exception of the weight gain, everything else was normal for this pregnancy. But it still made for the longest 9 months. Zach was a scheduled c-section. Slated for the first week of November. My parents wedding anniversary would have been on the 3rd of November. Once again, another birth associated with my father. We decided on the 5th, for no other reason than I wanted him to have his own day. Then I find out that November 5th was St. Zachary's day! I had never heard of St. Zachary!

There was no way around it. We had to list this house. We were so overstuffed. I had our oldest two in bunk beds in one 10x10 bedroom. Regina was alone in the 2nd bedroom and we had no other choice but to put Zach in a crib in our room. We did everything we could to make the house attractive. For the past few years I got very good about throwing things out or having garage sales. First rule of thumb when selling is reduce all the clutter. Honestly, for as packed as we were, there was literally no clutter. The market was still down but luckily we were able to sell within a few months. We took a beating, selling for less than we paid, even though with the nasty storm that came through in July of 1992, straight line winds they called it, bull, I watched the trees bend, hail through my windows and the tree landing on my car roof. Insurance paid for new siding, windows and a roof. It didn't matter, we sold it at a loss of almost $6000.00. But while we lost there, we gained buying. We found a gorgeous ranch in terrible need of updating in the same Whitesboro neighborhood Bob grew up in. He loved that house growing up and delivered newspapers there as a child. We were able to swing a 30 year mortgage and paid $40,000 less than the asking price. Bob, just receiving a promotion to company operator after the other multiunit manager was found to have embezzled $25,000.

Chapter 3

We closed and started moving in on May 25, 1999. Our 8th anniversary. I was exhausted. But why shouldn't I be. Moving, 4 kids, Bob was working a ton of hours. My back was killing me. During my pregnancy with Zach, I developed this bump on my leg. I retained a lot of fluid in my legs with that pregnancy and what never went away was this golf ball type lump on the front of my leg a few inches above my ankle. Right on the bone. I couldn't stand how I felt. I was exhausted, my hair was falling out. My skin was horribly scaly. My nails were breaking. I couldn't lose an ounce of weight. But worst of all, the exhaustion. I could never get enough sleep. I felt like I was narcoleptic. If I sat down, I would fall asleep. Everyone just assumed, like I did that it came with the territory. No one could figure out what that was on my leg. It was like the fluid pooled there and was trapped. I hated myself. I was so ugly, tired, not in control of my life and I had this stupid thing on my leg. I always was told that I had beautiful legs. So the last good thing I had was ruined. I went to the doctor to have it removed. The doctor looked at it, I told him how it appeared. He wasn't sure what it was. He wanted to biopsy it. I went back the following week for the results. He started with questions. " Have you ever had any thyroid issues?" I answered that I wasn't aware of any. He continued," Are you tired, have any weight gain, hair loss, itchy, scaly skin?" I answered yes to everything. He concluded that the bump on my leg was a goiter. He sent me to my primary doctor. My primary did my bloodwork and concluded that my thyroid was " a little low." Well, that's like being a little pregnant. Either you are or you aren't. He started me off on synthroid a very low dose and every 5 weeks I would have blood work to see how it was working. It wasn't. I insisted on a specialist, he told me I didn't need one. I love how these doctors argue. They don't like having patients tell you what they want. They don't like being challenged. I went through every specialist in the area. I felt like hell. No one helped, no one listened, no amount of this medicine was helping. The doctors didn't want to hear it. I was in a downward slump. Every visit I would complain, I can't lose weight, I'm exhausted. This medicine isn't working. I hated myself. I spent every day just surviving. From 1998 to 2009 I was on SYNTHROID. Bob's hours were long and hard, on his feet all day. I felt like a single mother. He did what he had to do to support us. He was a good father and husband. I would always tell our girls that they needed to grow up and marry a man like daddy. I would always tell our boys that I would be so proud of them if they grew up and was the man that their father is.

My thyroid battle continued. I gave up trying to fight it. No doctor listened. I had remembered the promise I made to God after Regina was born. That I would take whatever was given to me if God would not take her from me. Well, he fulfilled his end of the bargain and now I felt it was my turn. I guess this was it. So I accepted my fate.

Looking back, those were tough years. But I had no idea what was around the corner.

I was Blessed with a core group of friends. Through the years, we may have drifted a bit, but we always had each other's back. It was a good feeling knowing they were there because unfortunately my relationships with my sisters were never that strong. I knew dysfunctional families existed but It wasn't until I became older did I realize I grew up in one. It was during my pregnancy with Zach, one of our core group, Debbie, found out she had breast cancer through a mammogram and biopsy. She was 38 at the time. Debbie was an extremely smart, a well read woman, a CPA, and she was fully involved in her treatment. She researched everything. Once conferring with her medical oncologist, Dr. Jones, and the surgeon, Dr. Logan, she decided on a lumpectomy and radiation for her treatment. Always loaded with questions, very little information, if any, got by her. She was adamant about all of us having a baseline mammogram done. She told us how she was in the car one day, the radio was on and a commercial for mammograms came on. She thought it was a good idea after hearing it and made an appointment. And they found breast cancer. A silent killer. No bumps, lumps, signs or symptoms. It saved her life. And naturally, we all promised. Two of our other friends, Bernadette and Lisa, sisters, had buried their mom a few years before, she went 8 years in remission from breast cancer and then ovarian cancer hit. My intentions were good, I knew having a baseline mammogram was important but now with my fourth child on his way, knew I would end up putting it off until my obstetrician actually scheduled it.

Well it had to be all of two years later, if I can recall correctly, one night in the shower for some reason I decided to do a breast exam. It's not like I did this on a regular basis, but I knew the basics of it all. In the shower or laying down, raising your arm over your head. Starting on the outer breast , with your index and middle finger, follow the shape of your breast pushing lightly in a circular motion, until you get to the nipple. Squeezing gently top and bottom and side to side. As I did, something black came out. I panicked!! I squeezed it again, more came out. Jumping out of the shower, scared as all hell, I immediately got on the computer. Web Md. I typed in the symptom. BLACK DISCHARGE FROM NIPPLE. It came up stage 4 cancer. OH MY GOD! OH MY GOD! I became hysterical, immediately! I called down the hall to Bob, he heard the panic in my voice. Crying and completely hysterical, Bob, unable to understand what I was saying and he was trying to just get me to breathe and calm down. I finally calmed down enough to explain my findings. I had myself dead and buried, already! " We don't know anything yet. Call the doctor in the morning." He was always good when I panicked. I had to calm down, there was nothing I could do until morning. Morning couldn't come fast enough, and the night was forever. Every scenario went through my head. I'm not going to see my kids grow up. I'm not going to grow old with Bob. I won't see my grandchildren. Sleep came only from exhaustion, nothing restful about it.

9 am came. I couldn't call fast enough. Trying to talk through my tears, I explained to the nurse what I had found. They called me in immediately for an exam. Nothing was palpable. Dr. Silver wanted an immediate mammogram. I was able to get an appointment very quickly, because at this point, Dr. Silver didn't actually know what we were dealing with. After my mammogram, I was to have a follow up appointment with a breast surgeon, Dr. Logan. Debbie's doctor. It was at this point that I wished I had heeded Debbie's advice for a baseline mammogram. A baseline mammogram is just your first ever mammogram. It is referred as a baseline so doctors have a starting point when women, after the age of 40, start getting yearly mammograms. They can follow any changes in the breast tissue. Over the years, Breasts can and will change, weight loss or gain, surgeries. But having the baseline is their picture for reference. The risk of breast cancers increases in women as they age. Now, sitting here, not knowing

my fate, I was so angry with myself. If only....shouda, coulda, woulda. What if it is? Could I have found it sooner? The range of emotions were swirling around in my head. I couldn't take the wait. The wait is the worst. I said my prayers. I talked to my father. I just wanted to see this doctor. Finally! Our visit! Bob and I went in to meet with the doctor. He was a huge man. Well over six feet, bald and hands that just enveloped mine. Dr. Logan. Debbie's other doctor. He was very soft spoken in a very confident way. He looked like a cabbage patch doll. A gentle giant. He was patient and kind. I don't ever remember having a doctor like this. I felt very safe and secure. He looked at my mammogram and without hesitation said," you don't have cancer. You have a blocked milk duct in your breast. You are just fine." Hearing those words, the tension in my shoulders released as the weight of the world fell from them. " We walked out of there so relieved. God works in mysterious ways! What had happened was I was now on life saving course. I was on a schedule for yearly mammograms. Taken a few years late, but better late than never.

They hurt. I hated mammograms. If this wasn't necessary, I guarantee not one woman would go through it. One breast at a time, placed on a clear platform with a bead placed over your nipple for the point of reference. As you stand there in the most uncomfortable positions, waiting for the top plate to come down upon your breast and flatten it like a pancake. It's especially fun if you are in the middle of your menstrual cycle! TALK ABOUT PAIN! I'm telling you, they tell you to hold your breath, which is really not necessary because you can't breathe because of the pain ANYWAY! Over the years the wait time has improved. Now, they can immediately send it off to the radiologist to read. Sometimes, a picture may not be clear enough, or something is questionable or they need another angle, and they call you back in. Unless you have a breast cancer history, they do not read your films immediately. If you have had cancer or have had questionable mammos they will read it and you will get your results. It is, without a doubt, the longest 20 minutes of your life.

It was the summer of 2004, and the dysfunction of my family continued. By this point I had gone back and forth a hundred times speaking and not speaking with members of my family. It was endless. I didn't want to be a part of it anymore. Bob was disgusted. I didn't want my kids around it anymore. Unfortunately it came time to break ties even with my mother. That was not an easy thing to do. After my father died, I was very close to my mother. She walked on water as far as I was concerned. She was a brilliant woman. A beautiful woman. A woman who spoke her mind and could be fiercely loyal or your worst enemy. She held an elected position on the local School Board for 20 years. An advocate for the kids, always. The teachers unions hated her. But she wasn't out to make friends. She was black and white. Either you loved her or you hated her. Along her 20 year ride, she helped numerous people. She also bought coats, boots, gloves and hats every winter, without anyone knowing it. Making sure the poorest in the school that we attended was warm. No one ever knew. She had her good side. She liked to control people, though, and she was brilliant at it. Some never even realized that's what she did. When I realized that is what she was doing to me, we had a huge falling out. There came a time where I had realized that my brother, Billy was addicted to drugs. My mother didn't want this out, although everyone knew, we lived in a city but it was still small town. When I tried for an intervention, I was blackballed from her world. Then I saw what so many other saw and had to deal with. The vengeful side. I couldn't believe this was happening to me. She was telling people that I was on meds with my thyroid and depression and I was off the wall. My mother in law questioned my husband privately when she called the Parrish Priest from the church we got married in and our children attended religious education. He approached my mother in law, asking if I was ok. I was mortified. I couldn't believe what she did. That was it. The final straw. She never loved me, I realized. She controlled me. And when I was no longer controllable, I was no longer necessary. That realization broke my heart. There was no getting through to her. So many of her family didn't speak to her. Now I understood why. It was obvious to me that her intentions were to control my brother. If he remained on drugs, he would need her, if he became sober, he wouldn't. Co dependency I believe this is called.

During that summer, issues arose with my grandmother, my mother's mother. She was over 90 and spunky! Able to walk without help and still mentally sound, my two older sisters and I agreed to take her monthly so everyone could take care of her. My mother hated her. That I could never understand. My grandmother was the sweetest person alive. She truly loved everyone. Within a few days of her supposedly living with my sister, I get a call that she was placed in a nursing home. I went off the wall. All these lies where being told so she would be admitted. She was unscrewing the bathroom pipes, feces all over the wall. I called both my sisters on 3 way calling and got into a huge war. After all that my grandmother had done for them, for all of us, over the years. I was heartbroken. The following day, I started visiting her everyday. The kids and I would spend a few hours with her. The kids were so sad. She was depressed. She would tell me that she would sit in the window and count the red cars that drove by . It broke my heart. I met with the social worker who now, after observing my grandmother, came to realize that all that she was told were lies to get her in. She was placed in as emergency status, based on what my sisters had told them. I decided that I wanted to take her out. She could live with us. I went to the nursing home's social worker. She was a bit angry at the lies she was told. Knowing full well that beds there were given in a first in need basis. But now, paperwork, social security, all this red tape was being processed. She asked if I would be willing to wait a month. And if I just took her at that point, with no one else knowing, no one could stop me. Yes! I was planning a jail break! Her social security had been turned over to the nursing home. When they signed her in the admitting office had made it a point to say, legally that the social security now belonged to the nursing home, and if her account was touched, they would prosecute whomever. I told nonnie what the plan was. Damn them, accusing her of her mind being gone! She kept that secret for 3 weeks! The first of September we broke her out. The plan was simple. My sister Jody and I would walk in, normally, like we were visiting. We took her outside, which was allowed, and sat with her. Gina, my girlfriend, drove up and we put her in the car. Jody and I walked back in and told the floor nurse that we were bringing our grandmother to my home. We walked into her room and took the few things that were hers along with her clothes and we left. Back at my house, Jody sent an email to our other 2 sisters and our mother to tell them nonnie now lived with me. As she did that, I went down to the bank with nonnie to withdraw and reopen another account. She should have had 2 months of social security in her account, instead, there was only one month. My sister Corinne had taken it out during the time nonnie was still in the nursing home. August's check being earmarked for the nursing home. The check they said they would prosecute over. They took her money. Unbelievable. Robbing your own grandmother. I made the sign of the cross on all of them. I was done. I called the nursing home immediately, and explained the situation. They insisted I hand over September's check. I refused. I argued with them that they had made it very clear that August's check was earmarked for them and if it was withdrawn they would prosecute. That's exactly what I wanted. They didn't want to. They now considered this a family matter and my 93 year old grandmother would have to have her arrested. This would never happen. My grandmother would never do that. She was so sad, she couldn't believe what her own family had done. I made sure that the nursing home was compensated for the July days and the first 2 days in September, hoping to pressure them into prosecuting them. It never happened even though the bank had produced a picture of my sister Corinne at the ATM, withdrawing money. There comes a time when you just cannot take it anymore. I made the sign of the cross on all of them. I was done. Again.

September was very hectic. Trying to get into a routine with my grandmother. She was so sad that her own family did this to her. I had an organization that aided the elderly and their sole purpose was to keep them out of nursing homes if at all possible. Getting set for that was exhausting. Visiting nurses, paperwork, you name it, that first month I was ready to tear my hair out. Shuffling the kids around. The boys now shared a room, so did The girls. Zach, happily gave up his Scooby doo room for nonnie. It was the end of September and I was playing catch up all month. I ended up canceling my mammogram that month and rescheduling for December 1st. I really didn't want to wait that long but they were booked solid. December 1st came and I went to my appointment. Checking in, the receptionist was obviously having a miserable day and taking it out on everyone she could. I was the latest victim. "You don't have paper work? You don't have your referral, I can't let you go in!" I really just wanted to walk the hell out of there. I had too much going on, but the little voice in my head said with your luck, you'll have cancer!! I ripped back into her," Can't you just call the doctor, he scheduled it last year, they can fax you over one!" Seeing that I wasn't backing down, they called my gynocologist. Other than the pain from the mammogram itself, I wasn't nervous at is point. Once Dr. Logan told me I was clean a few years back I honestly didn't give much thought to it, other than knowing it was very necessary, like a Pap smear test, to have done. Grin and bear it! Well as luck would have it I had missed my yearly exam and now they were saying you need to come it. When it rains it pours, right???? Ugh!! I promised to be in the next morning but please, fax the referral over, please???? They did, in and out, no second pictures to be taken. Thank God! One and done!

The next morning, December 2nd, as promised, I went to my obstetrician/ gynocologist appointment. As I was ushered in, weighed and blood pressure taken, the nurse notices a post it on the front of my folder. She read it out loud, obviously not seeing it before this. " You need a biopsy" , she said. My jaw dropped. "WHAT? WHAT?" She repeated," You need a biopsy. " There is a questionable spot that they want to check!" I started shaking. I needed answers. " What does that mean?" By now, she realized she did the wrong thing. She had not realized I didn't know and I know she felt terrible for springing that on me as she did. She left the room as quickly as she could, promising the doctor would be in soon…. She left me! She left me alone in the room. How could she do that? The table starting spinning. I think I started crying. I know my blood pressure went sky high because I could feel myself sweating and my heart was pounding what seemed to be out of my chest. I tried to call Bob. I couldn't hit the buttons right. The office didn't have good reception and I couldn't get a signal. I was in panic mode. I couldn't breathe….oh dear Lord, help me! The doctor walked in after what seemed to be an endless wait. My chest was heaving. My doctor, Dr. Silver, was always very calm. He walked in and said, " I want you to go to the imaging center and pick up your images, and go see the breast surgeon, Dr. Logan again. I felt like I was being pushed out. I knew I should have asked questions but I couldn't find my tongue. He continued on with my yearly exam. I laid there trying not to cry. Trying to keep it together. All I wanted was Bob. I needed to talk to Bob. Everything was set. I left there shaking. Once in the car, I tried Bob. It was as though I had Fred Flintstone fingers. I really couldn't hit the buttons. I sat and cried. I was so scared. I finally got through to him, I had 9 stores to choose from, it seemed like it took forever. . Talking through tears I told him the news. He was in Syracuse, did I want him here? No, he had a job to do and I knew nothing yet. I told him I'd call him back. We exchanged I love yous and I walked into the imaging center, face to face with the same miserable woman from the day before, and she was breaking my chops….ARE YOU KIDDING ME???? " I told her, calmly, and trust me, calmly isn't a word in my vocabulary, " I was told to come and pick up my films." Her reply? " You are going to have to wait until they are located, have a seat." I had all I could do not to lunge at her throat. I walked out to the lobby, called Dr. Silver's office and told them them the problem I was having with this receptionist. I barely had the chance to hang up the phone as the receptionist's phone rang. By the time I walked back into the waiting room, I was being called up. All I could think was THIS IS BAD! No one moves that fast. I had that nasty feeling in the pit of my stomach. It was back to Dr. Logan's office once again.

Dr. Logan was able to get biopsy was scheduled for the following week. We had to meet with him again, late in the afternoon, this is how he scheduled new patients. While I wasn't technically "new" I hadn't seen him in 2 years. Now we were here with some certainty. The only problem was that on that same night was Ali's school Christmas concert. I was sure we were going to miss most of it. Parental guilt. Honestly I was hoping that we would walk into Dr. Logan's office and miraculously say that everyone was wrong! He explained to us both that they were sure it was cancer. He was very familiar with the pattern and referred to it as " twigs and branches." He explained that my cancer was DCIS. Ductal Carcinoma in Situ. We just sat in silence trying to take it all in. He explained, "DCIS is the most common breast cancer, and at this point I was stage 0." Ok, if I have to be a stage, I'll take 0, I kept thinking to myself. But the biopsy would help us determine if there were any signs of evasive cancer. Meaning, some forms of DCIS will mutate into evasive cancer and that is what breaks out of the breast and hits the lymph nodes. But until the biopsy, we know nothing else. He advised us to try to remain calm. Things were moving as quickly as possible. You couldn't convince me of that. I wanted everything done as fast as yesterday. The waiting, like with everything else in life, is the hardest to bear. As expected, we walked out of there late. Bob got home to sit with the rest of the kids and I got to the school as fast as possible. Ali, like me, wore her emotions on her sleeve. And I could clearly see from all the way back of the auditorium the sadness in her face. I felt horrible. We told her that I had an appointment I couldn't miss and we left it at that. Frantically I started waving, hoping she'd see me. She did! She smiled. It was one of those horrible mother moments that I felt that I put myself in front of my child. On top of everything else, I didn't want to feel guilty too.

Up until the biopsy, we made a decision not to talk to the kids. It didn't make sense to have them all upset and worry. I knew there was no way that I could put it past them. Eventually I would have to say something, they would know something was wrong, I was too emotional of a person. And now, with us missing the majority of the concert, this wasn't going to be easy. Ali and I got home. She cried from the minute she got into the car. She thought we didn't love her. We didn't care. Why else would we miss the concert? Bob and I just looked at each other, we didn't have any words. That, actually made it worse. We weren't denying anything. We just didn't have the words. I couldn't take it anymore. We sat the kids down. I told them that I had to have a big test and the doctor needed to talk to mom and dad. Ali stopped crying for a moment with the saddest eyes I ever saw, said, " Mom, are you going to die?" Choking back tears, a very firm NO came out of my mouth. I had to show them I was strong. I had to find it in me to hold back the tears and get my children through this. That, right there, that very moment, was the hardest thing I had to do since burying my father. We hugged them, Bob was crying, promising that I was going to be ok. We quieted them down but I know their silent thought were full of worry. I kept everything normal. That is one thing about children, they keep things going, whether you want to or not!

The first thing I did the following morning was to place a call to the schools. I wanted their teachers to know what was happening and I told them I wanted to be made aware of any behavioral changes. I wanted to be on top of it all. My kids needed to be normal and I would cover all bases to be sure that happened.

Biopsy day. Walking back into the imaging center again, I was brought into a room. A long table with holes in the upper part. As you lay face down, your breast that will be biopsied drops through the hole. After numbing the area, they go in with a very small needle. They aim for the center of the tumor to get the best result and cut a piece out. While this is happening, you can actually watch it on the monitor. It looks like the huge pieces are being taken out but it reality, they are microscopic. Truly amazing is the science of it all. It would take about 3 days for the biopsy results to come back. So we were scheduled for the following week again to see Dr. Logan. But, I had the promise of his office that if they received the results prior to my appointment, they would call.

Thank God because day 3 was Friday. The thought of this hanging over my head all weekend was not something I wanted to do.

As promised, they called. I was home a lot with nonnie. Thankfully she was sleeping. Yes, it was cancer. Just as they thought. I asked to speak to Dr. Logan. Was it possible? Yes. He would call me at the end of the day. I put the phone down. I have cancer. I said it to myself. I said it out loud. I screamed a silent scream. My knees hit the floor. How could this be happening. This is too surreal. I have cancer? I took my rosaries and threw them across the room directly at the 2 foot Blessed Mother statue sitting on the top of my armoire. " I started screaming," ARE YOU KIDDING ME????? YOU TOOK MY FATHER FROM ME AND NOW YOU ARE GOING TO TAKE ME FROM MY KIDS????" Those first days were tough. I hated God.

We went back the following week to see Dr. Logan, this gentle giant, who I felt so comfortable with. Our appointment was late in the afternoon and this doctor never rushed you. We were scheduled specifically for this reason. He had the heart to understand that people needed time to digest it all, not a quick in and out. God Bless him. He was an amazing doctor. You need that, that type of doctor. You need to feel it deep inside that you have the right one because you need to have total faith in your doctor. He took his time going over everything with us. They had found evidence of evasive cancer, although this wasn't an aggressive cancer. He talked about what was next. He wanted to do a lumpectomy. That's where we would start. My head was spinning. I swear, he must of talked for 10 straight minutes and then I said to him, " Ok, can you repeat all that because all I heard was blah, blah, blah. " It is so hard to take it all in. You cannot digest it all at once. But the one thing I did hear loud and clear was when he started talking about marriage. He was very clear as he said that he has seen marriages become stronger during this and he has seen marriages fall apart. Bob, who was holding my hand during all of this, just gripped it tighter. It was him telling me he would never let go. The doctor went on to say that with surgeries some men just can't handle the changes in a women. I can't remember his specific words, although I know he was referring to disfigurement after surgeries. Something else I had to worry about. The kids now knew. Nonnie knew. She was so sad. I would find her in her room saying rosaries all the time. Can I have anymore to handle??? The older two wanted to know everything. Zach and Regina were just too young to understand. I tried to make it as a casual thing. You know, no big deal. Our oldest, who was always an introverted child started crying, along with Ali, who inherited my emotional side. This was gut wrenching. I'm hurting these kids. That isn't what a mom is supposed to do. I hugged them all and promised that I would be alright. My God, I needed to get thru this. I had to get a hold of myself and find it within me to cope. I was so damn scared. I had to handle it all. I know Bob was there for me but he was so busy with the restaurants. I wondered at times how we would get through it all.

Having to deal with this all thru December meant that nothing was going to happen until January. It was hell. I am not a patience person. I had a lumpectomy and node biopsy scheduled for mid January. They have to set markers in your breast prior to surgery. This was the worst experience EVER! Using the mammography machine as a guide and sticking what looks to be like acupuncture needle in my breast to mark clearly were the doctor was to biopsy. They couldn't get it right. And if anyone has spent any amount of time getting a mammogram, you know how painful it could be. I was in that position for several minutes at a time. I was in tears. This 20 minute procedure ended up taking over an hour and a half. The operation, thankfully, went smoothly.

Back to Dr. Logan's office the following week. Good news, bad news. My entire body deflated. "What?" We didn't get clean enough margins." With a lumpectomy, the main purpose is to remove the cancer and take enough clean tissue out to make sure nothing is left behind. My problem was that the cancer was located very close to the epidermis, the top layer of skin. He wasn't happy with the margins. He also decided on taking out another area, a very small area, one that would have been watched on a mammogram closely. Thank God he did, there was my evasive cancer. That one area, left alone, would have hit my nodes. But thankfully, my nodes were clean. No cancer had advanced that far. Given this situation, Dr. Logan, was willing to try again with another lumpectomy, although he wasn't convinced he was able to get those margins. He wanted me to opt for a mastectomy. My cancer wasn't aggressive but it had probably been in me for a good 5 year period he thought. 5 years??? It was unthinkable. I mean we get colds or the flu and what happens? We are knocked down, sicker than a dog, feel like we are going to die and all this time I had a cancer that COULD actually kill me, in me. So I had a choice to make. Another lumpectomy? Try for those clean margins? Mastectomy? My head was spinning. Will that be it? No, depending on what I chose, my treatment would be different. Treatment? What treatment?? That dreaded word. CHEMOTHERAPY. He had said if I opted for the lumpectomy, and it worked, I would need chemotherapy and then radiation treatments. If I chose a mastectomy, then no radiation and just chemotherapy. This could not be happening to me. What the hell do I do? How do I make a decision? I know nothing about cancer. Living in a small city, hearing time after time to get a second opinion, and Dr. Logan, being confident in his ability, encouraged us to get one. We opted for Memorial Sloan Kettering in New York City. 4 hours away from us. With the appointment made, my choice of doctors for a second opinion was the department head, or the surgeon who has done more node biopsies than anyone in the country or the doctor who actually did the first node biopsy. Wow! Is there a bad choice? We opted for choice number 2. Driving out to Albany to catch the Amtrak train into New York was so stressful. Our train left at 10 am. We had left our house early enough. Albany was only 90 miles away. Our appointment was at 3 pm. Upstate NY is no stranger to snow storms. My area averaging around 90-100 inches a season. Obviously, Albany, 1 ½ hours away, isn't used to snow. A few inches set the traffic to a stand still. We missed the train by minutes due to traffic and had to catch a later train. Arriving in NYC late, Sloan Kettering was so accommodating. Knowing we were under the gun to catch the last train back to Albany, I was so stressed from all day, I felt like I was a New Yorker! I could yell and scream on the street and no one would even care. And trust me, I did.

It was well worth the stress. The doctors there looked over all my charts, knew my doctor at home by name and held him in great regard. I asked if they saw or would do anything different than Utica did. They said no. Big relief! The only thing they disagreed about was that they thought I should try another lumpectomy. Why go through all that if it wasn't necessary? Now what? It would have been so easy if both said the same thing. I came home. My brain was overloaded. I had to make a choice, although he didn't rush me. I think I put the rush on myself. I just wanted this out of now! The weekend was upon us and I was so stressed. I kept changing my mind. Bob didn't know what to tell me. He just said he'd back me on whatever decision I made. Boy, that's a big help! I remember just sobbing, alone in our bedroom, I had to cry there. The kids, nonnie, Bob, I couldn't let everyone see me like this, although I knew Bob knew that I was in a bad place. That day, I walked into his office, which was right off our bedroom. Bob had a big recliner in the corner. I grabbed an afghan that my grandmother had crocheted years before, I wrapped myself up in it, curled in a ball. Not an easy position for me because my back was not in good shape. I just sat and cried, alone in the dark. The house was never so quiet. Bob didn't know what to do with me, the kids left me alone as did nonnie. It was then, right there that my faith came through. As the minutes turned to hours, there was a point when I just closed my eyes, I felt so defeated, I just started talking to God. " Please help me. God, I give this to you because I don't know what to do. Please help me figure it out." I sat there, alone for nearly 8 hours, not once leaving that chair or changing positions. But by nighttime, when I finally emerged from the office, I knew what I had to do. It all came to me. Unquestionably, I knew. I walked out to find Bob. I'm going to have a mastectomy. My head was clear. It was amazing. I was going to beat this. I knew it. I had found the strength I needed. I knew that not only was this a physical fight, but a mental battle too. Body and soul had to work together, whatever the stage was.

I don't think Bob noticed the change in me immediately, except for the fact that I wanted this done yesterday! Another appointment was upon us and now I had to make decisions regarding reconstructive surgeries. Options? Implants? Tram flap? " What the hell is that??" I asked. Simply put, in laymen's terms it was using your own body to reconstruct the breast. I didn't have a comfortable feeling with the implants. I learned to trust my instincts, so he continued with the tram flam explanation. First and foremost with this surgery, which was quite extensive, you needed to have extra meat around the middle! After 4 kids and my thyroid meds not working right, I had more than enough! What the procedure actually consists of the breast surgeon completing the mastectomy and then the cosmetic surgeon opening the abdomen side to side and removing the stomach muscle on the opposite side of the mastectomy, taking not only the muscle but the blood supply as well. They actually slide it up under the skin, and attach it to your collar bone. It was an 8 hour surgery, my body was going to look like a road map, but, I was going to get a tummy tuck from all this! HELL YEAH!!!! I decided I wanted this. Believe it or not, making that decision was easier than anything. I was scheduled for mid February. I now had my plan. Once this surgery was over I needed 5 weeks to heal and I would start my chemotherapy treatments at the end of March. Next stop, the oncologist.

There were a few options in Utica and I decided to go with the recommendation of my breast surgeon. I chose Dr. Jonas, female and I think a bit younger than I was. She was originally from the area but spent time at another hospital outside the state and for whatever reason, Returned home. I liked her. She was aggressive and straight to the point, could have used a bit more attention in the bed side manner department but I could live without it if necessary. I was to undergo 4 rounds of chemo, each 3 weeks apart. At this time, our area underwent this huge expansion of a REGIONAL CANCER CENTER. My girlfriend Debbie, who had gone through this 5 years ago, her mother was an instrumental part of this entire center. My treatment would take place in this state of the art facility. All I wanted was my life back. It was the end of January 2005. I promised myself that cancer would only have me for 6 months. Then my life was my own. Screw you cancer, you picked the wrong bitch!

I had enough. I was not in a good place before the cancer came. I hate that out of control feeling. I wasn't a control freak, but nothing seemed to be working for me. Dieting, exercising. I couldn't drop a pound. Every endocrinologist I saw told me my thyroid was fine. I knew it wasn't, now cancer. Enough! It was time to work on me. I started exercising again, slowly because of my back. I started eating better. I got more sleep than ever. I promised myself that from now on if I was tired, I went to bed. I didn't care if it was 7pm, if company was there, nothing. The kids were old enough, nonnie was always looked after, thankfully she was still so self sufficient. No pipes were unscrewed or feces on any walls. Short term memory loss. That was it. She was remarkable.

The night before surgery came ,I said my prayers, talked to my father, my grandparents. I had angels looking out for me. Usually before all surgeries, I was so nervous. I slept like a baby. Bob couldn't get over the fact that I wasn't nervous. I looked at him and told him, " I'm fine, I'll be fine. Don't worry about me. "

I awoke ready and anxious for surgery. And it went perfectly. Normal hospital stays for this operation was 3-5 days. I told all my doctors that I was not staying for 5 days. No way. Bob and 4 kids, 13 and under alone in my house for 5 days? Are you kidding me? Did they have any idea what kind of a mess I'd be facing? Me and my Obsessive Compulsive Disorder? I'm not a nut but I do like things in there place. Bob had a habit of using every table like his end tables. He would just put things down. My doctors kind of fluffed me off and said we'll see. They did not realize who they were dealing with. My tolerance for pain was very high, living with back pain and sciatica for years now. I was no princess. They would soon learn. But I also had come to realize that I needed to take it easy. I learned to ask for help. My core friends and my niece were there. Without question. As much as I wasn't a princess, I also wasn't superwoman. I had to give myself time to recover.

I don't remember anything before being sent to my room. It was so hot. OMG! And it had to be. I had to lay flat all that day through night because of the surgery. The blood supply HAD to take. I had to stay warm. So the room was set for high heat. I also had those compression stockings on my legs AND this contraption on top of me that looked like a pool float. It was heated. It was imperative that this heat stay on me all night. So far, this was the worse thing I went through. Thank God for that morphine pump! I was so out of it. I also had a room mate, an older woman who called for the nurses all night. I felt sorry for myself but I felt sorry for her too. As much as she irritated me, the heat had to irritate her. They honestly should have given me my own room.

By the next morning I was wide awake, begging the nurses to get the catheter out. My back had reached the end. I could not lay down anymore. The pain was excruciating! Finally they did. They helped me up. I was determined to get up, go to the bathroom and show these doctors I could go home. The worse part of it was the drains. Ugh! The drains! One on each hip and one on my mastectomy site. They were to stay there for the next few weeks or until I drained less than 30 oz in a 24 hour period. Every position I tried to sit in was uncomfortable. Having 3 cesarean sections, the pain was similar to that. But when the doctors walked in and saw me sitting on the side of the bed doing a crossword puzzle, I shocked the hell out of them. They couldn't believe I was moving around. I told them that I wasn't a princess. If you don't have back pain then it's hard to understand that you absolutely cannot lay down like you are expected to. They knew I was serious about going home and said if I continued like this I could go home the next day! Thank God, because within a hour or so Bob walked in with all 4 kids. He was carrying Zach. Zach had no shoes on! " Why doesn't Zach have shoes on?" Shaking his head, Bob says, " Well I told the kids to get ready and get in the car because we were coming to see you. Zach, jumped in the car without shoes and Regina was playing dress up and had her plastic heels on." I couldn't even laugh, it hurt too bad! See, this is why I needed to get home! I could only imagine bob walking down the hall with Zach, who wasn't a lightweight, huffing and puffing and Regina, clip clopping down the hall in her princess shoes! Oh my God, what did my house look like????

I did go home the next day, and surprisingly enough the house was in good shape! I honestly couldn't do much for the first month. I couldn't bend at all because I had to let that blood supply build and get strong. They explained it like cutting a hose off mid stream when bending it. If the blood flow wasn't strong and constant, the tram flap would fail and then it was a mess to correct. I heeded that warning. I was good. The drains were another story. Every visit to the doctors I bitched. They were stead fast. I had to hit that 30 oz and under mark in 24 hours. It took 3 full weeks. Definitely the hardest part. But everyday I felt stronger and stronger. I couldn't wait for chemotherapy to start so it could end.

Chapter 4

March 2005. The drains were out. It was the longest 3 weeks of my life. I hated every minute of it. Looking back, that was the worst part. I keep saying that, don't I? No showers. Just sponge baths for 3 weeks. I felt disgusting. Long tubes that I had to pin to my t shirts. They would catch on my kitchen cupboard handles. It didn't hurt, but it was a very weird sensation. After the second week of this, the drainage slowed down a bit. But the rule was, I had to drain less than 30 oz in a twenty four hour period. I would go 18 -20 hours and boom, it was like someone squeezed me! FRUSTRATION WAS MOUNTING! When I finally had them removed the bandages were also removed. I was afraid. Did I want to look at myself in the mirror? No, not really. But I did. I cried. Skin from my abdomen was sewn into the mastectomy site. I looked like a patchwork quilt. Red, swollen and uneven, stitches gone. My belly was still swollen with what looked like train tracks all across my waist. This is what the doctor was talking about. This is what men can't handle. Hell, I cried looking at myself. My first thought was Bob was never going to see me naked again. I didn't want to see his face when he looked at me. Would he be disgusted? I knew if this was happening to him that it wouldn't matter to me. My love for him was so deep that nothing would change it. I knew how much he loved me, but would I look disgusting to him? I was never sorry for doing it. This entire situation, so surreal. It was hard to believe all this was happening to me. It took a long time to get used to seeing myself, the new me! But, the cancer was gone, they were sure. They biopsied every inch of the breast that is removed. They got it all. No other tumors were found in my breast. I was on my way to a prognosis of 97% clean!

I don't remember how long it was before he walked into the bathroom and saw me naked. I flinched. I was embarrassed and grabbed a towel. He looked at me and said that nothing would change. He loved me. I was alive. That was all that mattered. I know he meant it. Bob was not a good liar. It was easy to want to believe that but in my head the proof would be his reaction to me when he saw it for the first time. I dropped the towel and searched his face for his disgust. It wasn't there. He looked amazed actually. I remember this so clearly because he moved closer to me and touched the scars and asked me how I felt. He wasn't disgusted at all. If it was at all possible, I loved him more that day. I was one lucky woman.

We all have periods in our life when either good or bad is prominent. For some reason, the old saying " When it rains, it pours" really is true. But I believe our true character comes out during the worst times in our lives. It's easy to be happy when everything is sunshine and roses, but life isn't fair. Something I have told my kids over and over again. I'm the old school parent that teaches my kids, not everyone gets a trophy. When you compete, compete to win. During the first few months of my cancer diagnosis, and I believe this is true for anyone with an illness, you do a lot of reflecting. Your life really does flash before your eyes and you wonder how much life you really took for granted. We all do at some points in time. But now, with reality hitting you directly in the eyes, you are faced with an unknown future. So what do you do? How do you deal with it? What made me a fighter? Was it my hot headed Italian bloodline? Was it because I was an athlete and competed to win? Was it my faith? Well, in my situation all 3 contributed. I remember going through the divorce with my first husband, in a sense, many people who go through the trauma of a divorce consider it like a death. A series of emotions. I felt that too. But what really got me over the hump was simple. I got angry. That's how you beat the mental aspect of cancer. GET ANGRY. I had pity parties, all by myself, and you need them. But once my tears stopped, I got angry. Damn it, I want to live! You have to get up and fight! It is much to easy to lay down and die. And that is honestly true with any illness, not just cancer, I knew people that went into a emotional downward spiral. Remembering that day in neonatal ICU, talking to God, Remembering that day in my husband's office, asking God to lift this burden. Remembering how strong I felt after a conversation. That was real. It did happen. My faith exploded! I talked to God all day. Sometimes they were actual prayers, sometimes novenas, but a lot of the times it was me talking to God like he was next to me. He carried me. Footprints. I remembered the writing, " FOOTPRINTS"

" One night a man dreamed he was walking along the beach with The Lord. Across the sky flashed scenes from his life. For each scene he noticed two sets of footprints in the sand: his, and The Lord's. When the last scene flashed before him he looked back at the footprints and noticed something. " Lord, during the most troublesome times in my life there is only one set of footprints. I don't understand why, when I needed you most, you would leave me." The Lord replied," My precious child, during your times of trials and suffering, when you only see one set of footprints, it was then that I carried you."

That writing was always around me. You can find it in at least 3 places in my house. I always loved it. But it really never held any true meaning for me until I realized the power of prayer. He did carry me. I was so strong inside. I got up everyday, did my hair, my makeup and lived life. I had been through so much, even with the dysfunction of my family. That was a continuing issue. I hated it. I didn't want my kids growing up in a family where you never know who was going to throw the next knife at you. I spent the better part of 30 years in a war with one, two or all three of my sisters, my mother, my brother, all to forgive and forget until it happened again. It was insane. I couldn't deal with it anymore. Christmas, my absolute favorite time of year started to become burdensome. Who wasn't talking to who. Every year for several years I would hear someone say, and yes, I said it too, "It's Christmas, can't we just have a good night?" Never happened. I remember one Christmas Eve. It was the last year that I spoke to my mother, actually. We had just moved in to our house the year before. Bob, doing very well as company operator of a local WENDYS franchise, had received a $10,000 bonus a week or so before. This was the year. I told everyone Christmas was on us. We paid for " The Feast of the Seven Fishes" the traditional Italian Christmas. We invited everyone over. And it actually was a good night! But then, my mother, in her brilliant way, caught Bob alone as she was readying herself to leave. Knowing the history, this was bad. But she was sneaky. She commented on what a nice night it was. Then somehow, And she did this brilliantly, she turned the conversation around to his parents. Early on in our marriage, Bob's mother and I clashed. That's all the ammo my mother needed. When she had someone's weak spot, she knew how to use it. Playing on his emotions, she said how horrible it was that so much time was lost with his parents and how sad she was for him that he didn't have them to celebrate with....she liked going for the jugular...and that it was a shame how I lied to him about the house. Then she stopped....wait for it. Well, naturally, Bob was going to question that. And he did." What house, what are you talking about?" A few years back, my sister, Corinne, was arrested on drug charges. My mother, refusing to put her house up, again, had asked me. I, in turn, asked Bob and he answered with a resounding "NO." Not that I could blame him, after all, this is all he had seen of my family. But, knowing that she wasn't going anywhere, I did the wrong thing, and did it behind his back. Now this had happened at least 5 years before. Why now? What purpose could it serve. That was done and over, we sold that house. Why did she do that? Turmoil. She didn't want me happy. Bob was successful. We had a beautiful home, healthy kids, financially stable and a strong marriage. A parent's wish for any child? Not in my dysfunctional upbringing. So all my family had left. The kids were settling down and Bob and I would start putting out Santa's presents and crash. Morning would come very early with Santa's inpending arrival. Bob was quiet. Too quiet. " What's wrong?" I asked him. He sat down, serious as could be, and me not having any idea what the hell was going on. I was just so happy to have gotten through a Christmas Eve and everyone was still speaking! I was happy! Why is he bringing down the house???? He said to me, " have you ever lied to me about anything with the house?" I looked at him, where was this coming from? I answered honestly, " I put our old house up for bail for Corinne even though you said no. It was the wrong thing to do and I did it anyway. I'm sorry, but where did this come from?" " YOUR MOTHER!" I think my face fell. I know my jaw dropped. " What do you mean, my mother?" He explained as he was walking her out that she had just mentioned it and when he acted confused, she apologized that she said anything because she thought he knew. There is was. The innocent act. She played that well, she had it down pat. That was it, he was pissed. Our near perfect Christmas Eve was destroyed. Gone. We got into the biggest fight of our marriage. I lied to him. He hated liars. I can't believe she did this. By the time she got home, a 15 minute drive, she had just about destroyed our marriage. We weren't speaking. I put the toys out myself, tears streaming down my face. I called her. " What the hell did you do?" Full of innocence," Lorrie, I don't know what you are talking about!" ARE YOU KIDDING ME???? I wanted to lunge at her through the phone! " Do you realize the fight you caused? Do you realize he isn't speaking to me? Do you realize my marriage is on the line!" I was so pissed she didn't have a chance to respond. I was done. No more. Bob ended up sleeping downstairs in his mancave and I went to bed crying. Christmas was ruined. Christmas morning the kids woke up and Bob was smiling and laughing with them but not a word to me. It went on for 3 days before he would talk. One thing was for sure. My mother wasn't welcome here again. I know all families have issues and my friends were closer to me than anyone. Family, then, I realized, doesn't have to be blood. I thought about it logically. If I just knew these people and they weren't related to me, knowing what I know, would I want to be friends with them??? No, I wouldn't! So why, why, did I feel forced to deal with the same things over and over. Flash forward... I had cancer. I needed peace. I had a husband and children to care for, my grandmother to take care of, why did I need the negative energy around me now??? I didn't. Then it hit me. THE SERENITY PRAYER. I had this in my house too. My God, my answers were in front of me all this time and I didn't get it until now!

" God grant me the Serenity to accept the things I cannot change, the Courage to change the things I can, and the Wisdom to know the difference."

That was it. I had all the answers in life in front of me all this time and it took an illness to bring it all to me. THERE WAS MY SILVER LINING! Cancer didn't defeat me! Cancer made me stronger. I had the will, I had the power all this time. With God's graces, I took total control of myself.

I made a decision that no negativity was going to intrude in my world. In order to become well, in part, I had to follow that Serenity Prayer. I was now going to have the peace, the serenity I wanted and needed, not only for me, but my family, because I now could accept the fact that I could not change my family. I could only change my reaction to my family. I now had that courage to tell everyone that I am not willing to live with this behavior anymore. It wasn't a judgement against them, it was me deciding how I was going to allow myself to be treated. I had the wisdom to know the difference. This was an amazing moment for me. God gives us this power! All you need to do is ask for it! The secret is that you control your behavior and don't allow anyone to control you! Of course, the battle would still continue, every few months something would start. I blocked her phone number. So instead of calling and starting fights, she would email things, horrible things to me. We kept changing emails. One day, my brother stopped over to see my grandmother and he brought her a bunch of magazines. Nonnie loved looking through those supermarket rag magazines. He handed it to me and I put it down, busy with something else. A few days later when I realized I never took them out, I pulled them out of the bag, only to find a folder in the middle of these magazines. Confused, I opened it, there it was, the negativity, my mother had emptied out all of the things I had made as a child, in school and put them in this folder. Here I am, going through cancer, and she is doing this to me. I knew I had made the right decision. I would have only one other time that I was forced to see or talk to her. When my grandmother died. I told her in no certain terms, I wanted no relationship, what I am doing is teaching my children a lesson. Sometimes we are forced into a situation that is more important than the person. What I did was for my grandmother, no one else. The last conversation that I would have with my mother until the one on her death bed went something like this…" You beat cancer because I prayed for you." I returned with, " No, I beat cancer because I got away from you." During this time was the death of my mother in my eyes. The mother I grew up with, the mother I adored, was gone from my life. Like a cancer. I had to cut her out of my life.

Meeting with Dr. Jonas, my oncologist, after all the surgeries were said and done, getting the thumbs up (I was a fast healer I was told), to go ahead with the chemotherapy . I wasn't looking forward to it, but the sooner I started, the sooner I finished, and then I take my life back. That's all this was about. Taking control. We talked about the side effects. All I cared about was my hair. " Within 2 weeks of your first round of chemotherapy , you will lose your hair." This is where the bed side manner could have been better. She said it so casually, I'm sure she said it a thousand times before, but now she was saying it to me. " My hair? My hair? I'm going to lose my hair? "My eighties hair. My long, curly, big 80's hair was going to fall out. "I'm going to be bald?" Oh my God. I cried. Here comes another pity party. " Why is this all happening to me? Why do I need chemotherapy ? It's all gone! Can't I skip the chemotherapy ?" Well to be honest, I did have the choice to skip it. But no one recommended it. Not Dr. Logan, the breast surgeon, not Memorial Sloan Kettering, not Dr. Jonas. It was a logical decision, I was

42. This was not an aggressive cancer but, I was only 42. I have 4 children. If I was 70, they wouldn't have put me through it. But my prognosis following the mastectomy- tram flap, chemo and 5 years of tamoxifen, an anti estrogen drug given to women who still had their periods, would render me 97% clean! Not remission, CLEAN! I had to. This was cancer. I had to fight it as aggressively as I possibly could. I just looked to the heavens and cried. I closed my eyes and cried. Help me God, I need to get through this.

My first chemo was in the 3rd week of March. I was told that I was going to be gone most of the day. Everything I did had to be scheduled around the kids, Bob's hours and my grandmother. At that point I was speaking to only one of my sisters, Jody, and she was able to come and sit with nonnie. I would leave in the morning around 9. The kids were in school. My core group of friends were right there with me. Picking me up and driving me home. It took time to check in the first time and until you do, they don't have your chemo ready. Like a prescription, me being checked in was like having the prescription made. I walked into the REGIONAL CANCER CENTER, it was a beautiful facility. Going into the infusion unit, cheerful faces met me at the door. I decided on Tuesdays for the simple fact that was the day Bob stayed in Syracuse. It was the easiest day of the week and Thursday would be my " bad day". As I learned walking in, Mondays and Thursdays were the busiest days. I picked a good day. They had open rooms with several very comfortable looking recliners, and they had semi private rooms. With all my friends I chose that. It was maybe a 10x10 area, a few chairs for others, an overstuffed recliner for the patient and a built in wall unit complete with stereo and tv. I looked like I was having a party. I had a room full. Lisa, Gina, Gina's mom, Terri stopped in and a few others. All were welcomed. Volunteers came and asked if anyone was hungry or thirsty. It was actually a very pleasant place to be except for the circumstances that put me there. The first time took the longest. They hooked me up to the IV. Me, never afraid of needles saw this huge needle coming at me. Serious stuff coming through that IV. I was started off with saline and an anti nausea drug. Once that was started the nurse came into the room with what was the first of 2 chemo drugs. It was bright red and she hooked it up to the IV. This was referred to as a " push" IV. It took about 10 minutes with her sitting there with the syringe and putting it through my system. When she was done, I immediately had to go to the bathroom. Really bad. Having to maneuver around with the IV hooked up I almost didn't make it. I peed all red! . I got scared for a minute before realizing I peed out all she put in me. Holy shit, it went through my system that fast??? I went back and sat. Thank God for my friends, they made it a party. I started to feel woozy and nauseous and I suddenly became very sun sensitive. Needing to close the curtains, to get through the day, not realizing I was having a reaction to the anti- nausea drug, I finished the treatment, all in all taking about 5-6 hours that day. I went home and was told to take it easy. Thursday now was supposed to be my bad day and I just wanted to get myself organized so I could have Thursday free. I decided to go grocery shopping Wednesday night. Up until that point I felt fine. I bought my wig a few weeks before. Synthetic, not real, because I couldn't afford the $1500 it would have cost to get a wig to be my color and length. The one I bought was beautiful. Bob came with me, and naturally he thought I should try a few different ones on. He picked out a blond wig. Really? I have dark brown eyes and hair and he wanted me to try a blond one on. Only Bob! I looked horrible! I'll stick with the same color thankyouverymuch! You absolutely couldn't tell it wasn't my hair. Bob nicknamed it " Roxy" my alter ego. His sense of humor sometimes could just lighten the entire mood! So as I was walking through Walmart, just about ready for the checkout line, it hit me. Hard. I felt like I got hit by a Mack truck. I got so weak. I was fatigued. Holy God, it took forever to get through the line. I called Bob on the way home. " Oh God , Bob, it just hit me." I got home and immediately went to bed. They gave me an anti nausea drug, the same as the IV drip to counter any nausea. I slept thru the night. When I woke, I felt like I had the worst flu. That's what it feels like. I had stomach cramps that wouldn't let you sleep. Curled up in a ball on the couch with absolutely no strength at all. Holding the phone was an effort. I soon realized that the cramping was being caused by the anti nausea drug! Once I stopped that, I was able to sleep, nausea was one thing, stomach cramping was another. I decided after that to use marijuana instead. By Friday afternoon I was on the upswing. Still a bit tired, but by nighttime I was pretty much myself again. The nurses in the infusion unit were very good with suggestions on how to counter some of the after effects. It was important to drink a lot of fluids to get the chemo out of your system. They showed me how to make a mouth rinse so I could avoid mouth sores and the metallic taste that I would get. But the one thing they couldn't prevent was the hair loss. And I was only days away from this happening. The first week went by and I felt fine. I honestly believed that maybe they were wrong and I wasn't going to lose my hair! I was so worried about my kids and how they would react. They would cry. I know how scared they were. I had to just keep it casual. The way I reacted to it was the way they would. If I freaked out it would be over, I couldn't do that to them. A very close friend to both of us was Tracy. Married to Bob's best friend's the 4 of us were very close. As a matter of fact, both Tracy and I gave birth to our children, during the same months. With Danielle and Ali having the same birthdate! Tracy was a licensed hairdresser and told me whenever I was ready to shave my head, let her know. She would be there absolutely anytime I called. As the end of the first week approached, heading towards that second Tuesday, my head began to feel strange. If the wind blew, there was an odd sensation on my head. Hypersensitive, I guess would describe it. It didn't hurt, but it actually felt like I could feel every hair on my head. I kind of tugged at a few hairs and they came out. Well, I didn't do that again! It scared me straight. That Tuesday night, I went in to take a shower and wash my hair. It was then that it hit the fan. Every time I put my hands in my hair, handfuls would come out. It got all knotty and I was just trying to get the shampoo out and get out of there. I was panicking. Our Ali was in my husband's office, on the other side of the bathroom wall thank God, because now I had a reason to try to remain calm. I remember my heart pounding out of my chest. Trying to keep it together. I got out of the shower. Looking at me, nothing looked different. I had so much hair that right then it wasn't noticeable. I put it up in an scrungee and walked down to the family room. Bob didn't miss a trick. He asked me what took so long and if I was ok. I sat next to him and told him that I lost a ton of hair. He couldn't tell. "Feel it." I told him. He touched my head and was able to really feel my scalp. " Are you ok? Are you going to call Tracy?" I didn't know what I was going to do. I was in denial. I wore a baseball hat for the next few days. Knowing that I had to make that call, because I couldn't wear this hat forever.

It was Saturday morning and I finally called Tracy. She answered the phone." Hi Trace, um, I guess it's time." I called Bob to let him know. Very quietly he asked if I was ok, and if I wanted him to come home. I told him I was and no, stay at work. I called my sister too, and asked her to take the kids for a few hours. She lived up north of me and loved to hike. I told her what was up and I thought it would be better if the kids weren't here. She came and got them and although the kids didn't know, they knew something was up.

Tracy came, as promised, about an hour or so later. God love her soul, she walked in with a box of Godiva chocolates and 2 bottles of champagne! " We are doing this the right way!" We opened the chocolates and drank the champagne. Bob would call periodically, "Did you do it yet?" "Nope, we just started in on bottle one and the chocolates." After an hour or so, feeling no pain and finally accepting the inevitable, I said let's do it. I sat down and very professionally she began to shave my head. Ending with putting in the number "48" in the back of my head for my favorite NASCAR driver, Jimmie Johnson in the LOWES 48! I was ok! The worst that I worried about was ok! I called Bob back and told him her better find me a Jimmie Johnson hat! " You did it? Are you ok?" I answered, " Yes, I'm fine and by the way, we need more alcohol!" Little did I know he already left work in search of my hat. Stopping by the liquor store and on his way home he saw a friend's car, Regina's Godfather, Dave. Living out of the area, he was home unexpectedly due to his mom being Ill. Bob called him to tell him what was going on and to invite him over. Dave had made the promise that if I had to shave my head, he would too. He told Bob that he was tied up and would try. An hour later, he shows up with champagne and says to Tracy, I need the 3 for Dale Earnhardt in the back of his head! My sister came back with the kids. And they knew. They came to me and cried. I hugged them all and told them it was ok. My hair would grow back. They took my wig off, tried it on and rubbed my head. They would be ok. It was all going to be ok. " This too shall pass" Donny, Tracy's husband walked in, along with others, and it turned into a party. It was all ok. We laughed, we hugged each other. The day I was dreading the most, the day Bob was dreading the most, turned into a party, a celebration. Cancer wasn't going to win the battle. I was. And I was ready to take on whatever needed to be done to get my life back.

Believe it or not the time in between each chemo went by quickly. I got myself on a good schedule. Eating good foods, exercising, and I made sure, every night I was showered, undressed and watching tv in bed by 6 pm. I promised myself that I had to give my body a chance to heal and become stronger. For the first time I'm my life I told myself that you have to be a princess and so I was. For a little while anyway. You have to shut down. Everyone around you needs to understand that you have to shut down. With the exception of my hair loss, you wouldn't have known my condition. I didn't want to be called sick. I wasn't a victim. And I refused to look like one. My wig was so perfect that when people saw me out, they never looked at me twice. Although it helped me tremendously to talk about it. Bob was the opposite. He internalized everything! We used to get into fights because if something was wrong at work, he would never say anything to me. I used to take it personally, although I know he didn't mean it like that. Over the years he's gotten better but at this point, he was struggling to deal with this. My strength helped him more than I realized. I would get calls at home from his friends saying that they heard I had breast cancer and why the hell didn't he say anything? He saw talking about it as a weakness I think. That's a big issue. Cancer just doesn't effect the patient. It becomes a family issue. Friends and family are on hand to help the patient and naturally the kids. The kids are always the first thought after the patient. But what about the spouse? It's not done on purpose, but it does happen. The spouse or partner of the patient needs someone to lean on. Bob was able to lean on me. His friends were willing and able but he couldn't. Bob was a strong man, someone I could always lean on. But he was never the type of guy that needed to talk to anyone. But, thankfully the stronger I became, he was able to gain more strength. The more I said " I have cancer", out loud, the more real it became and the more real it became, the more determined I was to get my life back. I guess maybe it was like AA. To defeat it, you must admit it. So I told everyone. Pretty soon I was getting phone calls from friends who had friends who had just received the news that they were diagnosed with cancer. " Could you talk to them?" Absolutely! I was all about paying it forward. I got on the phone immediately, talking through what I went through. I gave my phone number out. Whatever they needed. It happened just recently. This year, 2015. I had my mammogram mid January, as I sat and waited, the stress is still there. I say my silent prayers, now, my mammograms are only on my right side. As I was sitting there, waiting to be called in, a woman sitting on another couch, head in her hand. I could Feel her tension. I hesitated. I knew this was more than just a mammogram. She was waiting to see if she was going to hear that LIFE CHANGING WORD….CANCER. I walked over to her, I put my hand on her arm and quietly, I apologized for

Intruding. I asked her if she was ok. She told me that she was being checked every 6 months and she couldn't handle all this. I told her that she could. I told her to just breathe. I told her I understood. I told her where I was with cancer and where I am now. I gave her the best advice I could. I told her that I would say a prayer and if she needed to get a medical oncologist, please leave the area, she laughed and said, everyone tells me that. She was called in just then. I said a little prayer. I'll probably never see her again. But I am here for a reason. Only God knows the plan, but I'm beginning to think that it has something to do with me paying this forward. I felt, deep inside, there was a purpose for all of this. I felt it. I was given this insurmountable amount of strength. Was God preparing me for something? I wish I could see the big picture. Faith…."FAITH IS BELIEVING IN SOMETHING THAT COMMON SENSE TELLS YOU NOT TO." I had faith. I had to be patient.

Prior to each chemotherapy, I would have blood work done and a doctor visit to Dr. Jonas. It's very important that your blood levels stay up. It it imperative that chemotherapy patients eat iron rich foods. Healthy foods. You need to keep your body strong. Now that I had one down and 3 to go, I had a few things to discuss with her. My brain started working. I was going to counter every side effect that was going to hit me. First of all I told her that the anti nausea meds didn't work, they made me sicker and I was going to get marijuana. The second thing was would getting in a steam room help open my pores and flush out the chemo? Dr. Jonas told me that a lot of her patients used pot. While she couldn't recommend it, she heard it did help and she couldn't stop me. I just wanted her to know for the sake of knowing. As for the steam, she said to try it, it wouldn't hurt, just be careful not to dehydrate myself. Off to my second round of chemo. My posse of friends came, it was a bit shorter this time, but not really by that much. They had to change the anti nausea drug to something else because that what was making me woozy the first time. Same advice came from the nurses. First and foremost. Flush the chemo out. Drink as much water as possible. Well I was lucky enough to have in my house an actual steam shower. The previous owners put one in. It was a regular shower but I had the steam system, within minutes the shower would fill up with moist heat. You had to be careful, you could dehydrate very quickly. The longest time recommended was 20 minutes. Less with a heart condition. I figured I'd start with 10 minutes and see how it felt. I came home and immediately went in. I was very tired when I came out so I laid down for a while. The following night, I was expecting the symptoms to start again. They didn't. Thursday, my bad day, was still bad, but not as bad. I had my unnamed source find me pot. When the nausea would start, I would go hide from all the kids and take a few hits, and it was gone. I was able to sleep. That's what you really need. By Friday again I felt good. Actually, this chemo treatment was better than the first, did I stumble onto something here?

I thought after round three, maybe I can get in for a bit longer. Two down, two to go. My count down now was in 3 week intervals. By the end of May, I'd be done with all this.

I was preparing for my 3rd round of chemo when I got a call from my friend, Debbie. Bad news. Her breast cancer returned. Unbelievable! A reoccurance and now she was to go through a mastectomy and chemo too. Here we are, good friends, going through it together. Our doctors were the same as well as the radiologists. They knew we were good friends and didn't hesitate to tell us both how similar our MRI's were. Debbie's also was referred to as " twigs and branches" so similar, in fact, that our X-rays were nearly the same, except for mine was left side, hers was right. I was excited by the fact that I had discovered this steam after treatment. I could help her. I never got sores in my mouth, I never had that metallic taste either. The only thing I developed during chemo was high blood pressure. Wonderful. Cancer and HBP! My 40's started off really great. I can't wait til 50, I used to think! My 3rd round of chemo came and once again I got into the steam immediately. Then again, later that night. Thursday came and I felt better than the second chemo! I would have to lay down still but the nausea was less. Friday morning I felt so good! Screw you chemo! I found a way to beat you too! Once in a while I would get a little stomach flip but all it took was one hit and it was gone! Medical marijuana! I was ready to testify before congress! But, only in cases like mine. Cancer. Not the way the some states have passed it. Anyone who knows the side effects of pot knows that you get hungry. Well, I never did drugs really, so one hit would get me stoned. Before this I would sleep, now this one day,I went over the top, just a bit. Feeling good, I decided to cook. Italian greens, sauce, meatballs. I had mopines thrown over both my shoulders, all the stove burners going when Bob walked in…." WHAT

THE HELL ARE YOU DOING??" I was laughing at how stoned I got off that hit and I decided to cook, EVERYTHING! Big mistake, by the time I got done cleaning the kitchen I was exhausted! Lesson learned! But it was funnier than hell!

Debbie went through her mastectomy and started chemotherapy. I wanted her to start with the steam. She did once. Then didn't again. Oh she was so stubborn! But, I knew I had stumbled upon something because she had the exact chemo I did and had the metallic taste in her mouth and the sores. I had none of it. I was heading into treatment 4. I was soon done! It was May and we were facing the inevitable, our 15 year old shepherd was going to have to be put down. On top of everything else. Ugh! But it was time. Actually it should have been done before this. We were keeping Brandy alive for us. He was in pain. We brought him up to the humane society. As we walked up to the door, they let a beautiful full blooded shepherd out at the same time. The dog ran up to the fence line. Our Brandy and this dog touched noses. It was fate! I said to Bob " Brandy said take care of my family!" Nonnie loved german shepherds wanted to take him home right away. She wouldn't stop talking about it. We had a golden retriever at home, Bob always wanted one. Sami. All Bob's dogs had to have rock and roll names. Sami, for Sammy Hagar. Brandy, when we adopted him, already had his name and we didn't change it. The following day we brought our Sami up there. Poor thing was so sad, she was seriously depressed. She was only 6 weeks when we brought her home and she loved Brandy. We decided to take this shepherd home. Nonnie insisted on paying the adoption fees. He was named Shep. We didn't like that name. He was about 2 ½ years old. Brought back twice to the pound because he was too aggressive. No he wasn't, he was just a german shepherd. You have to love and understand the breed. Highly intelligent, great family pets, and will guard there territory without question. Once you have the love of these animals, it is forever. You belong to them, they don't belong to you. They are high strung and high energy. With a huge backyard and a lot of love, we renamed him Zeppelyn, and he was the greatest dog we ever owned.

At the end of May every year was the start of SARANAC THURSDAYS. The Saranac brewery would open up their lot and there was a party every week. Every Thursday through summer Bars along the streets would all be open. Thousands of people would head down there. Summer was finally here and I refused to miss the opening night. My last chemo was a real celebration! My infusion room was once again loaded with friends! This was it. I walked out of there and into the elevator. It happened without warning. I hit the ground, crying. I was so happy, so relieved. I think it was just a stress relief. I walked out of there and home to the steam. I hit it 3 times this time. When I got home, a few hours later and the next morning. I really wanted to get to saranac the next day so I was taking it very easy and hoping that the extra steam worked. Thursday morning. I felt tired, a bit nauseous, but not bad. Saranac didn't start til 6 pm. It was so hot that day. No way I was not going to wear my wig. I made it! I actually went. I didn't stay out as long as I would like to but I made it. I promised myself that I was going to do it and I did. It felt good! May 31st, 2005. I was clean! But nobody warned me about what would happen next.

Chapter 5

It felt so good to be done with it all. The last phase of my treatment started immediately. I was to go on tamoxifen for the next 5 years. This was an anti estrogen drug given to women that were still menstruating. I thought about choices. Do I have a hysterectomy now. Tamoxifen increases the risk of uterine cancer. It's all about the weights. Does the good it does outweigh the bad it could cause??? My gynocologist was the same through the years and he knew me and my history well. " Why put your body through any more?" He didn't feel I needed a hysterectomy. I was stage one. Now I'm clean. Cancer never hit my nodes, or was found anywhere else in the breast. He was very thorough and promised to do biopsies every other year. I felt as though I was in good hands.

A month so so had passed and I'm seeing myself gain all this weight, 15 lbs to be exact. Side effects of tamoxifen. Why couldn't one of these side effects be weight loss? Other than that I can't really say I had any other symptoms. Then the paranoia hit. Out of no where. Every time I had a pain, a what if went through my head. Breast cancer goes to lung cancer or ovarian cancer or brain cancer or bone cancer. I had a bad back and always had pain. What if this was the bone cancer, what if everyone missed it. What if? What if ? It was horrible. I was making Bob crazy! He was constantly telling me to stop. I couldn't help it. I was becoming compulsive about it. During a regular check up with my primary, I mentioned to him that I had some anxiety over this. Without even asking, he starts writing a script for anti anxiety drugs, another one for depression. "No, wait. I'm not depressed. I don't want those." That wasn't what I wanted. All those damn pills do is mask the issue. I know what the issue was. I just didn't expect it. He couldn't understand why. I told him mentally that I was very strong. And more over no one told me this would happen. I asked him for a prescription for Valium. 5 mgs. He hesitated. Here he is ready for the Zoloft and other meds and I just wanted him to understand that I had no intention of taking the Valium. I wasn't a pill taker. I just needed them there so if I did decide they were there. It was like a security blanket. Finally he gave in. One prescription, no refills. 30 pills, one per day. Well they stayed there for years, I never did end up taking any of them.

This anxiety went on for about 6 months before, once again, my anger took over. I had to yell at myself! I was eating right, exercising, taking my medicine, getting my check ups. It was in God's hands. I couldn't do anymore to prevent it. When I finally got that through my head, the anxiety went away. I had mammograms every 6 months. Every 6 months the anxiety was incredible. I would only have the right side checked since the mastectomy. They were incredibly conscientious with these mammograms. I was asked if I felt anything, I had to endure additional pictures. I remember one 6 months after my treatments and I picked up the phone in the room where the mammograms took place and called Bob crying. It was horrible. And there is nothing you can do to change that. Everyone with a history has the radiologist read the mammogram before you leave. The others, with no history will receive a letter in the mail a few days later. After 2 years it went back to yearly. I was checked every year by both the breast surgeon and the oncologist, never fully understanding why all the oncologist did was a physical exam. I finally asked " Why isn't there any blood work done?" The response was " The protocol for follow up to stage one does not see the need for bloodwork. " Boy, do they need to change that protocol! And I think that will become my new mission. To change that protocol. It needs to be changed.

It was September 2005. Our oldest started high school. Ali was in 7th grade, Regina 3rd and Zach was in 1st. All the kids were in school this one morning when nonnie gets up and is talking funny. Her mouth, all twisted, I couldn't understand her. She didn't know my name. Oh no, did she have a stroke? I called the visiting nurses who prompted me to call the paramedics. They came immediately, evaluated her, by this time she was a bit better. She refused to go to the hospital but promised to let me take her to the doctor. Well she really had no intention but told the paramedics she would so they would leave. I had to practically drag her to the doctor. Once there, his concerns were serious. She needed to be hospitalized and tested. By now she was acting pretty much normal. But she wouldn't say my name. I knew she recognized me but I know she didn't recall my name. The one mistake I had made when I took nonnie in was never changing the power of attorney. My mother held it, being the only child. I just hoped that my grandmother would die peacefully in her sleep. After all she was 94. I wasn't in this situation for a power play. I was taking care of her. No one was going to take her from me? Right? Wrong! Upon her entry to the hospital, because my mother held the POA (power of attorney) and because she was the daughter, all decisions were up to her. I met with the social worker, begged her to help me. I told her the story. I really don't think she believed me. Who would? (If we auditioned for a reality show they would turn us down because nothing could happen like my family in real life!)They were going to place my grandmother in a nursing home for a few weeks for an evaluation. My mother pounced. The year my grandmother stayed with me, her income was solely social security. The elder group that I had her enrolled in took $300 a month and that covered the visiting nurses, 4x a month, car rides to and from doctors appointments, any equipment needed in the house to aid her with bathing, like the tub chairs, etc and the day care program she went to every morning. $500 a month I put into an irrevocable trust at the funeral home. Knowing that every penny she had was gone, thanks to my mother, she wasn't going to have a welfare funeral as one of my sisters had suggested. In one year I had nearly $6000 saved, that no one could touch, even her. My mother had her removed from the hospital, my sister took her. Yes, the same one that put her in the nursing home. That was the last time we saw her. We could have no contact with her. My kids cried. How do you make children understand behavior that I, as an adult, did not understand? Money. It was all about her money. I found out in April, 2006, she was in a nursing home again. By the time I saw her it was the end. She was lying in a recliner, in the hallway of the nursing home, unresponsive. I couldn't let the kids see her like this. This never should have happened. I don't even know how long she had been there. Did anyone visit her?? She died 2 days after I saw her. We were heart broken.

It was October, 2005. My life was once again my own. All the kids were in school and it was just over a month after nonnie was taken from us. A part time position opened up at our kid's elementary school. I took it! After cancer, after losing nonnie, I needed something.

How I loved this job. The kids. I ended up being the recess monitor most of the time but had the chance time to time to be in the classroom. I was in the school with Zach and Regina, how I loved all these kids. Especially the kindergarteners. They were so little. Every year there was one or two that would just cling to me. I would hug them all. I always hoped that the people who had my position when my kids were little cared for them the way I took care of these kids. Regina wasn't too happy, it wasn't cool to have mom there. Bob would laugh at me because I would come home with story after story, this 2 ½ hour a day job would fully consume my life! It's been over 10 years since I started. The faculty and staff have become family to me. My children were Blessed enough to have these amazing people in their lives. I have never in my life held more respect for a group of people. They are going to have to throw me out, because I'll never leave!

After nonnie's death in April of 2006, my relationship with my family was minimal. I kept my promise keeping to the SERENITY PRAYER. The troubles in my family were there still, ongoing. Drug problems that were never to get fixed, so sad really. To see the potential each of my family members had and the fact they they really didn't excell at anything they were good at was very sad. Wasted potential. I heard that in a movie once. It's true. How sad. It's not that they tried and gave up, they never tried. It was months later, after my grandmother's death that I heard from Jody, the only sister I I talked to. She was in contact with our mother. Not really sure who else. Seriously, it could and would change monthly at times. Huge blow outs, horribly mean things said, then nothing. Until something happened, and everyone forgave. Or did they? I don't think so. I think things were built up inside and never forgotten until the next time the rage started. But honestly. Some of the things said, you don't say to people you love, ever! I wasn't innocent in this. Trust me, out of my mouth came some vile things. All the more reason to get away. But once in a while I got sucked back in. So she calls me and asks," do you think that you could help mom out on the funeral costs for nonnie? She has a balance of $2000. "WHAT? ARE YOU SERIOUS? YOU ARE ASKING ME FOR MONEY?" I went off the wall. I mean I had nonnie with me for one full year and managed to put nearly $6000 thousand dollars in her trust. The funeral home knew and appreciated what I did. My father and the funeral director's father were close growing up. There were no secrets, the director knew exactly what was going on. My mother pulled her out of the hospital, and had access to her social security for 7 months prior to her death. They could have put money in just like I did and would have had her funeral paid for, instead, they spent it. And now they were coming to me. Bull. Nope. Not one dime. I couldn't believe the nerve. The next call I received was from my brother, Labor Day weekend, mom doesn't have the money for her medicine. If you can give me the $150, I'll give it back to you in a few days. Yeah, right....I told him," call the prescriptions in and then tell me what you need and I'll write a check out to the pharmacy." I got hung up on. Well, that wasn't the end of it. I started getting phone calls from Jody , screaming at me, calling me all names because I wouldn't help my mother. There was no talking to her, she was partying and completely off the wall. I kept trying to reason with her. She wasn't listening. All he had to do was call in the prescriptions, give me the amount and I would write a check out. The fact that I couldn't get it through their heads told me my instincts were right. He wanted drug money. So I hung up on her. I kept hanging up, she kept calling. My kids were all upset, I was starting to get that uneasy feeling in the pit of my stomach, I was so over this. I don't need this stress. Name calling. Then the final blow..... The phone rings again, Bob just happens to walk in from work, no idea what has been happening. I planned on letting it ring. Enough. He answered it, but before he could even say hello, my sister started screaming, thinking it was me," I'm going to tell Bob you are cheating on him, I hope your cancer comes back!!!" BOOM. He lost it. Can you imagine telling someone that you wish cancer back on them? The worst part was that she was also a breast cancer survivor. Having a very aggressive form, after I went through mine. One full year of chemo she went through, and she was wishing mine on me? That was it. He told her in no uncertain terms, never to call this house again. There would never be anymore ties again. Ever.

With stress like this is was no wonder why my blood pressure was high! I ended up in my doctor's office one day, feeling dizzy and very light headed at school. I stopped at the school nurse's office for her to check my blood pressure. It was sky high. She sent me immediately to my doctor who ran an EKG on me and said everything looked fine. Fine? Really? He sent me home. Time for a new doctor. I found a heart doctor who would also serve as my primary care. I was glad because bob's father had a bypass several years earlier and while he was in excellent health, I felt better that Bob was looked at more carefully. I met with this new doctor, Dr. Martin, he was one of my closest friend's doctor and she loved him. Very thorough, I felt much better in his hands. Something was up but he wasn't sure. Stress test. Really? Well I can't really remember if it was a pass or fail because the results were mixed. My heart wall became stronger as I walked but my palpatations increased. Next stop, heart catheterization. It was December 2007. Three years earlier I found out about cancer. I had clean mammograms on my right side now for the last 2 years. Six months apart. Now my heart. Really?? So I've had hypothyroidism, cancer, high blood pressure, palpatations, now a catheterization. I'm 45 with all these health issues. What else can I go through? It was so hard to stay positive. Tears flowed. Prayers. It seemed endless, one thing ended and something else was starting. No one else I knew close to me had any issues. Not that I wished anything on anyone, but I was in a full blown pity party. Enough was enough.

Thankfully, the test went off perfectly. My heart and arteries were like a 20 year old. No one could explain the palpatations. All he could say is " Lorrie, it just may be the way you are wired!" There was nothing wrong. I was placed on beta blockers to control the palpatations.. So I was now on thyroid meds, HBP meds, cancer meds and beta blockers. I was spinning out of control again. Something had to give. I wasn't looking forward to getting older. All I could think was if I'm like this now, what am I going to be like at 50? The answer was still a few years away!

A few years pass, nothing medically happened during this period of time with the exception of my ongoing thyroid condition. My mammograms were good. Then I get a letter in the mail. My endocrinologist was leaving the area. Since I only saw her once a year and my appointment wasn't due for 6 months I put it aside. No one was helping me anyway. I was frustrated. I was so overweight and tired and my hair was like straw. My skin would welt up if I scratched myself. I always felt bloated. It was right around Christmas time, why, always around Christmas, right before the schools went on Christmas break at I was in a classroom and I found myself light headed and dizzy again. I was getting some severe hot flashes. I had to sit. It passed relatively quickly and I walked out of the room as the teacher walked in. This had happened to me a few times before and all I could think of was my blood sugar had dropped. Walking into the office, one of the other aides I worked with was there. She knew the signs because her son was a diabetic. This couldn't be happening. Not something else! Christmas break came and like everyone else, I was on Facebook. I decided that this was the year, I'm taking back my life! Once again! I was going to cut out sugars and fats and I happened to mention the incidents that occurred. A friend of mine immediately inboxed me. " It's the thyroid medicine. You have to get off the SYNTHROID. It's killing you" " What are you talking about?" I wrote back to her. I picked up the phone and called her. This was way too much to type. She explained to me. She was a sales rep for a drug company and was also a thyroid patient. She told me I needed to get off of the meds and get on the real thyroid medicine. The original one used prior to the synthetic, SYNTHROID, was around. She told me to go by the book, " STOP THE THYROID MADNESS" I went out and bought it. It was written by lay people who, like me and so many others, were treated for years with SYNTHROID and never felt good. The book took you through their battles, their stories. The more I read, the madder I became. Here it was, written, everything I argued about for years. These people were saying the same damn things. Fatigue, weight gain, issues with skin, hair and nails, anxiety. It went on and on. There were symptoms listed that I had that I never realized were from the thyroid! In a nutshell, the thyroid controls the body. Or meaning if the thyroid isn't functioning correctly, it will start to effect other body functions . Vitamin levels drop. Adrenal glands become fatigued. It's all a chain reaction. But the thing that got to me was when I started reading that when the thyroid is off, your vitamin D levels drop, putting you at risk for....BREAST CANCER. When your thyroid isn't working properly, heart functions are effected....HIGH BLOOD PRESSURE and PALPATATIONS. It starts affecting your sugar levels. There it was. Could I prove all this medically??? I don't know. That really didn't matter. All I knew was that I felt and looked like hell for years and everything that was wrong with me was because of my thyroid! I was livid! I needed my doctor's reports! This was perfect, now that she was leaving, I could call and ask them to send me everything because I haven't found a doctor yet. I did. I couldn't believe what was in these reports. It was like I was reading someone else's report. This couldn't be me. I actually went back to the first pages of my yearly reports to make sure it was me. She never mentioned the inability to lose weight, that I was fatigued, nothing. Instead she wrote that my weight that I complained about starting way back in 2002, was because I had stopped smoking. She wrote that at one point I told her I had lost 30 pounds and I gained it right back. She never mentioned my thyroid antibodies. She was lucky she was out of town. I started to have less and less respect for doctors. It was becoming clear that I had to become my own advocate. I realized that it was up to me to change doctors when they refuse to listen to my symptoms. I kept reading STOP THE THYROID MADNESS. There was a lot to take in. For example, our adrenal glands. If you read the insert that comes with the SYNTHROID prescription. It clearly states that the adrenal glands should be checked prior to this medicine being prescribed. No one checked my glands. It went on and on. I contacted my friend again. I had to find a doctor to treat me with this new protocol that the book talked about. It would take me over 3 years to find one.

She gave me a list of things I had to do. Have blood work. Everything checked. All vitamin levels, my thyroid antibody levels, thyroid levels. I had to order online an adrenal test. A spit test. To check your adrenal levels 4 times during that test period day. I was going to have to do this all by myself because there was no one in this area willing to treat me. Even my primary doctor. Although he did agree on running all the tests for me. When I approached him initially, he agreed that the thyroid does effect heart functions. Why would he have questioned my endocrinologist? She was sending reports that my thyroid levels were fine. Well they weren't. I asked Dr. Martin if this could be the cause of my palpatations? " Yes" . There it was. I had suffered for so many years and now I had the answers.

I got my results to find out that my levels were way down. Vitamins B, C,D, my iron levels, magnesium, my cholesterol levels were bad, well over 200, how? I had been eating fresh fruits and vegetables. I didn't fry anything. I didn't understand! and the worst part, my thyroid antibodies were way off. Normal levels on both tests were in the range of 0-40. I was 692. And I was told there was nothing wrong. When I saw these results I decided I would follow this protocol and treat myself until I could find someone. The first thing I did was to start taking vitamins. In order for the medicine to work properly, everything had to be in order. I started treating my adrenal glands with hydrocortisone cream, 4 times a day I would rub it on my stomach. I had to start taking my temperature, 4 times a day. The temperature is important because I came to find out that when your adrenals are compromised, your body temperature is below 98.6. Mine was 98.2. Once your adrenal glands come up to level, your temperature will increase and if you can have your temperature stabilized with in .10 for 3 days straight, your levels are back up. I know this all sounds crazy, but it worked. I started this new protocol in February, remaining on the SYNTHROID. My base line bloodwork was done in January. By April, I asked my doctor to run the same tests. All my levels were good. I knew my adrenals were good I finally had the 3 days straight of constant temperature. I kept on eating all fresh fruits and vegetables. I learned that with hypothyroidism, specifically Hashimotos Thyroidosis, my diagnosis, we have a gluten intolerance. Not celiac's disease but an intolerance. That's were all the bloating came from and that intolerance causes the antibodies to rise, putting us at a higher risk for lymphomas. I stayed away from all white starches. I drank 60 oz of water daily. I started taking cytomel. No doctor would prescribe it so I would order it from Mexico. It was an American company that I ordered from, so I wasn't worried. Cytomel is a t-3 treatment. Simply put, in laymen's terms, when your thyroid is functioning properly, when your level of T-3, the active part of the thyroid gets low, then the T-4, the inactive part of the thyroid converts to T-3 and boosts your energy. That doesn't happen when you have hypothyroidism. Basically what happens when you continue to take SYNTHROID which is only a T-4 treatment, it pools in your bloodstream, creating a "plugged drain"type of issue. And that is when other problems are created. You become what is called " reverse T-3". Once I stopped taking the SYNTHROID and started taking the cytomel, very slowly, I saw huge changes. It didn't happen over night but by July, I cut my antibody levels in half, my cholesterol levels dropped drastically and by the end of the year, I dropped 30 lbs. I had never felt better in my life. My hair was gorgeous. My skin was soft, not scaly, my nails grew and I didn't have to nap every afternoon because the fatigue was gone! Everyone commented on my appearance. Now, if I could just find a doctor! I didn't like doing this on my own but I was determined to stay on this path until one came along.

If there was one thing I had learned through all of this, cancer and my thyroid issues, was how much strength I really had inside of me. I don't think I was special in any way. I believe we all have it in us. My strength came from prayer. I knew it did, because I felt it right away. It was a deep, inner peace. It was a feeling. I learned to listen to myself. During the time when I brought nonnie home, the first few weeks were hell dealing with my mother. I remember having this nauseous feeling inside, a shaky feeling, I knew my body was breaking down. I remember thinking, I need to get away from everyone or I'm going to get sick. 3 months later is when my diagnosis came. I learned that the shaky feeling was my adrenal glands. They were so fatigued. And that isn't an unusual feeling. The majority of the country I guarantee have fatigued adrenals. Whether or not your thyroid is functioning properly. It's the stresses in our lives that cause it.

So how do we alleviate the stresses in our lives? Unfortunately we can't get rid of all of them. But removing the negative people from our lives is the first big step. Growing up it was embarrassing, I thought, that we were the only family with issues. The older I got, the more I realized that every family has issues. May be not to the extent of mine, but they exist in all families. " We can pick our friends, but not our families" how true is that? But, like I touched on in one of the earlier chapters, why do we have to associate with them if we really cannot have a healthy relationship? Trying to fix other people doesn't work. I had to get that thru my brain. Repeatedly.

The holidays! God how I love the Christmas season! Growing up, when my father was still alive, he loved Christmas! He was an incredible cook. All the men in his family were. He loved nothing more than cooking. The issues were still there with my older sisters but I was young and while I could feel the tension, it didn't seem to be so bad. It was, really, but some of the stuff I didn't understand until I got older, so honestly, I wasn't effected by it all then. But after my father died, the family really seemed to fall apart. Strange, isn't it? Usually it's the mother's death that causes families to tear apart. Truthfully, it was my mother's controlling that caused all the issues. She played us all like puppets at times. My father was really the only one that could control her.

It was hard for Bob to understand the dynamics of all this. He, after all, grew up as an only child. But when we met, there wasn't any peace in my family at all and he had a very hard time dealing with this. My mother had made it quite clear to me that she really didn't care for Bob. Why? Because she could not control him. He was a man that held his ground with his opinions. Worked his way up to a position, company operator of the WENDYS franchise, made a very good living and supported his family. My mother loved to be in control. She spent 20 years on the local school board and helped a lot of people get jobs. My mother did a lot of good for children in the district. But only people who knew her intimately knew the other side. But here was Bob, needing no help from her at all. Little did I know that behind my back my ex husband was in contact with her and every year since our divorce, she did his taxes. I couldn't believe it. Knowing what he had done to me, she let him in her house? The house I grew up in? That told me a lot. She would have rather seen me with him than Bob. That wasn't my opinion. She actually told me that. My ex was controllable, having gotten him a job. He needed her to get him that job. He would be grateful, thankful. My mother was all about who needed her. She liked to be looked up to. Bob didn't react to her like that. She was my mother, he respected her as my mother, but never as a person, looking from an outsider's perspective, he saw her angle, but never needed her and therefore he was expendable. So as our family grew, and we moved out of the starter home and into our new house, I was so excited. I will never forget bringing my mother to this house prior to closing. It was just the 2 of us. This house. A dreamhouse. Something I never would have thought possible. But there was a problem. The house was bigger than my mother's. The competition she felt. Not me. But her. I remember walking through this house, room by room. Wanting her to be proud of me. I married a good man. He supported me and the kids. We had a good marriage. I wished every day my father could have met him. I know he would have respected him. And I said just that to her. " Mom, I think dad would be proud of me. Look at all Bob has done for me. I never thought I would have a house like this." Her silence was deafening. Not one word. No words meant more than a thousand words. She was telling me I was wrong. Her silence, actually was her telling me that my father wasn't proud, he wouldn't be proud. I was so hurt. Why did she want me to fail? What have I ever done? Like a fool I still thought at times there was a chance of having family holidays together. I would have Christmas here. But it never worked out, why? BECAUSE PEOPLE ARE WHAT THEY ARE AND JUST BECAUSE ITS CHRISTMAS TIME YOU CAN'T EXPECT PEOPLE TO CHANGE! It was like getting hit over the head with a boulder! No more. And so our holidays became just us. Bob's parents spent half the year in Florida, leaving in October and returning in May. Our kids were sad about not seeing my family, not understanding why. But it was the healthy thing to do. Eventually they would see it clearly. I refused to keep this cycle of dysfunction going.

It would be very easy for me to have a "poor me" attitude. And I can't say that having that thought run through my mind never happened. It did. But that is dangerous. "Bad things happen to good people all the time." But we have to keep living. We have to believe that all things happen for a reason. I'm not writing this to give anyone faith. I cannot give you that. But I can give you hope. Hope to believe in a higher power. Hope to understand that God has a plan for us and we can't see the big picture. I can't explain to you why it seems like there are some people that just seem to glide through life effortlessly. We all know someone like that. We all wish our lives were that perfect. But in reality, no one's life is like that. One thing I would keep telling myself during my life trials was that there was always someone worse off than me. Thinking about it that way keeps you humble. Keeps you from having that "poor me" attitude too often. We are all entitled to pity parties. But We have to be willing to change things. Change is hard. Deciding to exorcize my family from my life, my mother especially, was very difficult. It was like a death. But things were there, in my face. Things Bob saw for years and I was unwilling to accept it. But now I had. Over 5 years would pass after my grandmother died before I would see her again. And it was on her death bed.

Chapter 6

Christmas time, 2011. Again, Christmas, again, issues. Always, Christmas time. It had been over 5 years now since my grandmother's death. I spoke to no one in my family except my niece. Since she was little, I took care of her so much, like she was my own. But, she remained loyal to her mother and so our relationship was as close as it could be. She had her own family now, married for several years and 3 beautiful children. My nephew, her brother, I had stopped talking to also. I didn't even have a reason. . A relationship casualty, unfortunately. My brother, whom I had not seen or heard from in months called me. The issues with my brother all stemmed from his addictions. I would have done anything to help him. All in all he was a good guy. He had a heart. He started on the wrong path after my father died and instead of getting him help, my mother tried to hide it. She was his biggest problem. An enabler. I wanted to help him. I wanted an invervention. She wouldn't allow it. My mother would tell my brother all the time I was jealous of him. When I tried to defend myself against these attacks and say, " what the hell am I jealous of?" She would turn it around as though my comment was to mean I am better than he is. I couldn't win, He believed her, hell, we all believed things that she said at certain points of our lives. Unfortunately, his lifestyle wasn't conducive with mine and raising my kids. I didn't want them around that. But now with my mother severely ill and in a nursing home with COPD, emphysema, and I heard through the grape vine, breast cancer. How interesting. First me, then my sister and now her? During the 90's she would complain of soreness under her left breast. She wouldn't go to the doctor. She had become ill after my father died when she went on to get her insurance license. Working for an insurance company in a new building, internal areas of the building still being built. Air ducts and air conditioning units releasing chemical smells and no outside ventilation coming in. She developed sick building syndrome. As she aged, continued smoking, her health deteriorated rapidly through the years. My brother, always close to her, insisting now, that this is it. She's dying. Whether she was or wasn't, it didn't matter. I had no desire to see her. I had mourned my loss of my mother already. Bob questioned me. " Lor, you know I don't care for your mother, but are you sure? I mean you know she isn't well. I just don't want you to regret not seeing her." But, I was sure. I told my brother I had no intentions of visiting her. That was it. And I wouldn't hear from him again until New Years Eve day. He called, and my girls, Ali and Regina were in the room. Again, he told me, this is it. Seriously, it's over. Once again, it told him that I wouldn't go. But my girls heard and as I hung up the phone they said they had wanted to go. Now what? Tell them no? Ali's relationship with my mother had really ended when she was little. Regina's memories were from pictures and stories told. The last birthday I remember my mother being at was when Regina turned 2. Maybe it was a bit later than that but, Regina didn't have any personal memories. My girls insisted. Ali was 17, Regina was 14. They were old enough to understand everything and by this point had started asking questions. I was always honest with them. Well, since they wanted to go, I thought to ask the boys. Our oldest was 19 and closest to my mother when he was little. As he grew up, I knew he was angry with all that happened. . Right after my treatments ended, she took me to court for the grandparents right to see the grandchildren. Here we go again. We had to have a court appointed attorney speak to my kids about her, get their opinions and question them on how I spoke about my mother. My kids handled it well, both stating that her name never came up. We never talked about her. They both said, separately, during their interviews, that they didn't want to see her. The only time conversations were held was when and if the kids asked questions. But now, we were forced into court. It had been all of 5 years since my mother had any contact with any of them. We appeared before the judge. I was angry, but respectful. I knew my mother couldn't and wouldn't contain herself. My oldest sister was there with her. Quietly, I turned to Bob and said," don't speak unless spoken to. They will bury themselves. The judge is going to get very angry, very quickly." And he did. They were yelling out, throwing questions at him. I had to control myself not to smirk because they were showing their contempt of court. As a ruling, the judge sided with us. We were a family unit, and we had the right to decide who our children had contact with. Thank you! But on this New Year's Eve day, the boys said no. They had no desire to go. Zach was born in the midst of everything so had no relationship at all with her. I left it at that. I wasn't forcing anyone. I was the only one being forced. But my kids, who always came first, had to have closure if this was it. I wasn't going to let a death happen and not give them the chance to do what they deemed necessary. I called my brother back to tell him we were going. He was speaking to Jody, who had wished my cancer back on me, I had no intention of seeing her. I wanted to be sure if I was going, no one else was. I would have about an hour up there. More than enough time. He said as they were headed up he would call and let me know. That was fine. I wanted no more confrontations. I have had enough for one life time.

We went up to the nursing home. The same one I took nonnie out of. Still angry at them for never persecuting my sister for the theft of nonnie's money. I walked into her room, or I thought I was her room. Only one person in the room, I had to look at her a few times. I was shocked! Honestly, not thinking about what to expect when I saw her I was taken aback. This was an old woman. I mean a really old woman! Doing the math quickly in my head I realized that she was 81. It didn't even look like her at first. I found myself looking for distinguishing marks to identify her. This was my mother? She always had a birthmark on the top of her forehead on the right side. Right next to her hairline. That's how I knew it was her. I was so horrified that when my girls walked over to the side she was laying on they gasped way out loud. They started crying. I walked them over to the other side of the bed and hugged them. I told them not to cry. It was alright. Just stay here for a few minutes until you can calm down. She did very much so look like she was on her death bed. And while I was honestly emotionless over seeing her. I was compassionate enough not wanting her to get anxious. I wasn't even sure she was conscience. Her eyes closed, breathing was very labored. While my girls were closest to the door, I walked over the side of the bed my mother was facing. Her eyes opened. She looked at me. " Hi mom, it's me, Lorrie" not sure if she could see well, I knew she was having trouble seeing. Her eyes widened. It was like she saw a ghost. She began shaking her head, side to side, like she was saying no. Her hands were mangled together, and in-between her hands was her rosary. With the shock of seeing me, she dropped them. I kneeled down to her bedside, they fell very close to her bed and with her oxygen tank there I had to reach almost underneath her. I picked them up and gently wrapped them around her fingers. Violently, again, she was shaking her head. I stood up and ignored it all. Calling over to the girls. I told my mother that Regina and Ali were here to see her. They walked over, crying gently, much better composed than they were a few minutes prior. " Hi nonnie" they both said. I don't remember if they touched her. I do remember them telling her that they loved her. They were visibly getting upset again so I told them it was alright and go stand on the other side again. It was obvious that my mother wasn't able to talk and knowing her, that had to be extremely frustrating in her overly verbal world. There wasn't much I had to say, but I felt it was necessary since I was standing there. It's not like I had ever thought about this minute. I was unprepared. The room felt a little cool and the mother in me did something just instinctively. I reached out and attempted to cover my mother's shoulder up with the blanket. Noticing how frail she had become, she must have been cold. I was not prepared for the response. Upon me touching her, with all the strength she had in her body, with her mouth closed, clenched teeth came the loudest NOOOO! I took a step back, thinking are you kidding me? So the shaking of her head back and forth and now this. It was apparent. She had not forgiven me! She had always seen me as the problem. I didn't come there for an apology, nor was I looking for one. But this, this I did not expect. It was unbelievable to me. This woman, on her death bed, still having this much negative emotion. How could it be possible, that this Christian woman, up to this minute, still hasn't looked back upon her life and chose to be humble, be sorry, ask God to forgive her, be aware that the afterlife was on her door step. Would God take her to Heaven? To be honest, I was worried for her. I just kneeled down in front of her, put my hand on her frail arm and said," Mom, let the past go. Let it go. Dad is coming to get you. Go see dad. " There was no I love you, nothing. Because I didn't feel it. We left shortly after. There was no reason to stay any longer. The girls said their goodbyes and we left.

My phone rang at 1:26 that morning. We had a small New Years Eve party with a few friends and we were cleaning up. My brother, " She's dying. They called me to get up there." Thankfully I was stone cold sober, not having to worried about getting pulled over, I jumped in the car. I was there in less than 10 minutes. With the exception of the aide sitting by her side, who was reading a story from the bible, I was the only one there. She was gone. I missed her passing by just a few minutes. How horrible, I thought, she died with a stranger. A few minutes later my sister, Corinne walked in. I walked away from her body, letting my sister near to say her goodbyes. Hearing her cry, I found myself totally emotionless. Was I that cold? I didn't think I was a cold person. Here was the moment Bob worried about. Did I regret it? No. I didn't. I felt I did what I had to do and I was glad that I brought the girls up. Next my brother and sister, Billy and Jody came storming in one after the other. Obviously they came together, drunk, stoned, one of them, not sure which. I just walked outside the room, overhearing Corinne quite loudly question the head nurse why the hell wasn't anyone called??? The charge nurse calmly informed her that she started calling my brother, who was the only contact listed, at around midnight. He never called anyone. Unable to handle this, he binged while she died alone. I knew this was going to haunt him forever. I couldn't deal with this scene anymore. 4 out of 5 of us up there. Me not speaking to anyone. Jody and Billy high. Corinne yelling at nurses. What the hell, even death has to be dysfunctional? I got in the elevator to go downstairs to call Bob. As he answered, Billy comes flying out of the elevator, hysterical, running out the door, proceeding to throw up. Wonderful, this is getting better by the minute. I finished my phone call. Went back upstairs for a few minutes. The staff was giving us time to say goodbye and they would call the funeral home for them to transport the body. I left shortly after. Saying a prayer over my mother's dead body, wishing that I could feel some emotion.

We had been having New Years Eve's at our house since we remodeled Bob's mancave a few years after we moved in. It was the ultimate party room. Large screen tv, sound system, bar and pool table. This was strictly his room. I hardly ventured down there. Except for party nights. That was the best part of our marriage, while we needed each other, we didn't need to be in each other's faces all the time. We respected each other's need for space. There were the nights we watched tv together or there were the nights after a particularly stressful day that he would just go downstairs turn his music on, mute the tv and unwind. That was his stress relief. Lately, he was having more and more stresses when it came to running the franchise. A few years prior, one of his managers was moved up to a DM position as corporate wanted a DM for every 5 stores. Bob would oversee everything and Bob only answered to the owner. The owner, living only about an hour away from us was very ornery at times. Bob handled him well, respectful what he had built, and the knowledge he had and believed him when he said that this little company was " a family!" Through the years, Bob had felt bad that he wasn't around a lot. He was home every night but running one restaurant was hard enough. He managed 9! He was brilliant, in my view, with all he had accomplished. He loved numbers and put his heart and soul into this job. Working it like it was his own. Bob played fantasy sports for a period of years now and on the back of one of his magazines was an ad for something, I can't remember. But I remember the ad. " OBSESSED, DRIVEN, FANATICAL ...I laughed. That was exactly how he was. When he did something, he was all in. He was always a good husband and a good father. Old school values instilled in him, he took the job of supporting his family seriously. But lately, things had not been going that well. He had the feeling that his assistant was undermining him. Bucking for his position? The owner, very much like my mother in his own way, used to like to play both ends against the middle. Obviously having harmony wasn't a good thing. He thought if he could press a few buttons, he could get more out of both of them. Bob would get emails by mistake telling Bob's assistant to " Stick his chest out, don't be afraid to stand up to Bob" this had happened more than a few times but things were to get much worse. Every Tuesday, meetings were held at the office. This one particular day, Bob had caught a manager falsifying records. Not necessarily wanting to fire her but demoting her and having a manager over her, holding her accountable was his recommendation. He left the meeting, all parties agreeing only to get home 45 minutes later to receive a call from his assistant saying that this particular manager had put a complaint in against Bob. " Seriously?" He asked," we caught her lying, and now there's a complaint against me?" Well the complaint was that Bob was too hard on her. Company policy was that it had to be followed up on. His assistant, now was to run the investigation and Bob was not allowed in that store until it was over. Interesting, Bob just lost the store. During this investigation, other managers were asked about Bob. Well, here's another complaint. He's too hard on me. He expects too much. Then there were those that defended Bob. He's hard, but he's fair. You always know where he is coming from. He will back you if need be. But he has a job to do. So as it would turn out, this manager, female, in her complaint said that when she went through surgery for breast cancer, Bob refused to allow her the time off. Bob hearing this during a meeting regarding this investigation, jumped out of his seat," ARE YOU CRAZY? AFTER WHAT MY WIFE WENT THROUGH?" The powers that be informed him that they didn't believe that part of her complaint. So here they were, picking and choosing what to believe and what not to believe. The final outcome was to be a warning in Bob's file. After 18 years with this company, Bob now had a jacket. The country in turmoil, jobless rate rising, profits not what they used to be, Bob started to think that because he was the highest paid in the company, full benefit package, paid for, Obama care setting in, he had become a liability, not an asset. And if the assistant could take over, well, that is going to offset all costs. Could this be true? His assistant was good, as an assistant, but didn't have Bob's business sense or his personality with managers. Prior to the complaint, Bob had several people that had worked for him for years, and that, simply didn't happen in fast food. It was hard to believe after all that he had been through that this was happening. A few months later, the manager that had filed the complaint was caught falsifying records again and was fired and subsequently, the other manager from another restaurant who had backed up the claim was fired for stealing. But, Bob never got the store back and the complaint remained in his file. Not a good sign. He put it in the record the sequence of events to cover himself, incase anything happened. We now knew that Bob 's position was on the line.

Talk about stress. High paying job, living in a small city. No jobs around. Bob kept looking but wanted to push this as long as he could. But the stress was starting to mount. Little by little, daily operations were taken away. He just had to deal with it, what else could he do?

The death of my mother was, I thought the beginning of the end of all the issues. She was the tie and now that she was gone, no one had to talk to anyone. But we had the wake and funeral to get through. My mother, once so good with money, ended up with nothing. The addiction that she tried to hide regarding my brother had cost her everything. Co dependency. Control. I was finally able to figure it out. He was the only one that could be controlled. If he got healthy, he may not need her anymore. So sad. It didn't have to be this way. My tears flowed now. I was just angry that it had to be this way. She was so unwilling to budge.

New Year's Day 2012, my mother's body was brought to the same funeral home our family had always used. This was where nonnie was taken and like I mentioned, the funeral director was a family friend and she knew the situation intimately. That evening, my niece, my nephew's wife called me. I hadn't spoke to her in years. She was just a causality of the situation. I had never spoken a harsh word to her or her to me. " It's Julia. I think it's time that this family talked again." I agreed. I haven't seen their children since the oldest was born, now there were 2 more. Along with my niece, and her children, I missed these kids. We all went up, them living in the house I grew up in. My brother wouldn't go, Eunice, my oldest sister, who spent the early 70's in a drug induced haze, was back into that and no where to be found and Jody, the one who wished my cancer back was a no. Good. I didn't want to see her. I could never forgive that. It was a good thing. I was glad she called. I was glad some of the family could heal. Maybe now that mom was gone we really could heal. Some of us anyway.

The financial situation was bleak. No insurance. Unbelievable. My mother was always insurance heavy! Left with nothing. She told a cousin of hers once, and it was relayed to me, shortly after this that she had every intention of controlling her kids from the grave. Eerie thought, isn't it? I knew that we couldn't let my brother go into the funeral parlor and make arrangements. He would have no concept of money, not caring and there were 5 children that this was supposedly financially responsible for. I'm sitting there, knowing in my head, that I was the only financially responsible out of the 5. This was not going to fall on my family. My mother was a public figure. We knew her turn out was going to be big. Wakes and funerals had changed tremendously since my father had died. His was 3 days, no way can we do anything like that or did any of us want that. We decided on one day, three hours of viewing and a short viewing period the next morning prior to the funeral. It was me and my brother finalizing everything. I was worried about any cards coming in that would be pocketed. I was worried if any cards came to the apartment they were living in they would never make it to the funeral home. I kept the cost down as much as I could, still rounding out to under 10 grand. I knew cards where going to the apartment. People told me. My brother would take off, couldn't find him. A girl I knew at a check cashing place admitted to cashing checks for him, made out to my mother. All for the expenses. I called a few people, asking, it was so embarrassing, if they had sent checks to the apartment. Yes, they did. Yes. They were cashed. SON OF A BITCH. HE WAS CASHING THE CHECKS AND GETTING HIGH. AND JODY

WAS WITH HIM. I couldn't believe it. I shut my mouth, talked to the funeral director to let her know what was happening. She sat everyone down after the funeral. Armed with the information I had given her, she spoke like she knew nothing. This balance needs to be paid. Oh yes! Everyone agreed, everyone promised. All I know is as of today, I am still the only one making payments, monthly. So much for promises....guess who is being controlled by the grave?

2012 wasn't a very good year. A month later, my cousin had passed away. Younger than me with a long term illness. She was a sweetheart. There was a time when I was close to her. But growing up, we still ran into each other, and her greeting was always the same arms open wide, " Hiya cuz!" Life just wasn't fair. It also wasn't a good year for a lot of people we knew. So many deaths that year. It was like the new normal. Since we were starting to get older, a lot of our friends' parents were passing. It wasn't a good thought, thinking we were next to be " on deck."

Bob and I had a good friend. He and Bob went back light years before me. Bob stood up in his wedding. When Bob and I got together his boys were little. He and his wife would come over to our house often, they were good people. Then he found out, after years of being treated for a illness, wasn't what he had, instead, it was an autoimmune disease that would attack his vital organs. A true familyman. He and his wife had their own business. They were couriers. Those boys traveled with them every day before school age. He taught them hunting and fishing and he loved those Yankees! How the years seem to fly by. All of a sudden, we are middle aged and he is in need of transplants. Not one, but 5. He put it off and put it off, making sure his boys got through college. Even at the expense of his life. Sick as he was, there was always a smile on his face. As the new year came, so did the phone call. The unfortunate news for one family was the saving grace for him. They had found the transplants. Traveling immediately to NYC, this was the first transplant of it's kind. He would be a test, they could and would learn so much from him. He was a lot like Bob and never would discuss it. But during the Christmas season of 2011, he would give Bob the best present ever. With his wife's hours, they had their Thanksgiving and Christmas on different days. So, those days were left open. He spent them with us. His last Christmas season on this earth and he chose Bob to spend it with. . He did live through the surgery. His road to recovery was long. He was bed ridden and extremely weak, he would text Bob and reveal nothing except for silly things. That was just his way. Then walking into a store, I ran into his wife. She had incredible news! He was thought to be coming home the following week. He was making good progress! Unable to walk, bedridden since the middle of January, it was now April. That was the least of their worries! He made it! Then the surprising phone call. Complications set in. He died of congestive heart failure. We lost him. Bob was inconsolable. My heart was broken. Not him. Bob went into a funk for a few days. Dreading, absolutely dreading this wake. What a year. Enough already. I remember Bob telling me of a few serious conversations they had. He didn't regret that he put himself behind his boys. He had lived his life, his boys had yet to. He felt that was his place. Knowing he knew that, as we walked to the casket. Bob, holding my hand as tight as possible, I looked at him, I loved him as much as Bob did. I cried. But my tears turned happy for him. There he was, with a smirk on his face. There was no way any funeral director could have molded his face the way it was. It was him! I half expected him to sit up and scream, " BOB-BAYYYY" because that was exactly the look he had on his face. Bob saw it too. But he was too heart broken to feel anything but pain. But I could accept his death now. I took it as a sign, he was happy, he was home.

Chapter 7

December 2012. Here we go! I'm not kidding, don't you see a pattern here? We are invited over to Sam's house, Bob's boss for a Christmas gathering. I honestly didn't want to go. It was a small group, just the people from the office and their spouses. I have a very difficult time being in a closed environment with the enemy. I don't have a natural filter. I'm not a politically correct person. Usually saying exactly what I mean has a habit of coming out of my mouth. But I had to go, knowing full well that Bob's assistant, Phil, who now was acting, with Sam's blessing, as his boss, was going to be there. This was dangerous. I thought we were going to have a scene like the movie, "THE GODFATHER". No, not the horses head, but a scene at the table with Phil sitting at the right hand of the father. I ended up laughing out loud, Bob being the only one to get the joke because I ended up sitting at Sam's right side. But, I have to admit, Sam, once out of the restaurants, was a very charming host, and his wife, Jane, extremely pleasant and an excellent cook. But the most enjoyment of the evening was watching Phil jump every time Sam opened his mouth. Literally, Sam would ask for something and it was like Phil had a spring in his ass, that's how fast he would jump. I knew Bob never jumped. Bob was a secure man. He knew his job. He would stand toe to toe with Sam and be honest. And Sam, we thought, had always appreciated that. That's what bothered Bob most of all during this. Respect. Or the lack of it. It was obvious that for some reason at this point, Sam needed, wanted a lapdog. Well, Bob wasn't it. Phil was. I thought Sam was smarter than that.

The kids were growing up. Our oldest, now 20, took a year off after high school worked full time at WENDYS. He wasn't sure what he wanted to do and we reluctantly agreed. He was always a good kid, we tried to teach him the important things. He had a good head on his shoulders and we taught him well. Save half your paycheck. We helped him build his credit. He understood that things he did now, could and would affect his life later. He had started dating one of his co workers, Cora and he seemed really happy. She was a year younger, but graduated high school early. She had a path to follow and was on a direct line to her future. Her parents were both doctors and she was following suit. We thought that she was good for him. I vowed as my kids were born that I wasn't going to allow anything like I grew up to happen to them. The kids were all close growing up but as they got older, the sibling rivalry took hold. Nothing serious, until they were in high school together. High school had changed since I went. One thing about this generation that I noticed was that the kids didn't have the loyalty towards each other. It was very cutthroat. High school could be tough enough but when today's friend was constantly turning into tomorrow's enemy, boy oh boy, I was glad I didn't grow up during this time. Girls, though, were always the toughest. They would turn on you in a minute. There were a few times word got back to me that Ali was having trouble in school. Name calling and all that. She could take care of herself, no doubt, but what bothered me was that her big brother wasn't there sticking up for her. I called him on it. My rule was if someone says something about your family, you defend them! With all I went through with my family I wanted all our kids to value and love each other. When I would hear them yelling at each other, I would remind them that Bob and I weren't going to be here forever but the four of you need to be there for each other. If there was anything I wanted, it was for them not to grow up like I did. Regina and Zach were close too. 14 months apart. Twins the hard way I was told. The memories of those two will always make me smile. They were inseparable. They would hold hands and drink bottles watching BARNEY and TELETUBBIES! As they grew, Ali and Regina became closer and the boys too. Zach at one point was just so in awe of his big brother that he would walk around calling him big brother. I loved that! Relationships between all of them were changing, that's life. Zach's big brother had finally decided on ophthalmology. He and Cora Were talking about a future and her plan was to take over one of her parent's offices. Working together as a team.

Ali, now out of school, started out locally at a community college. She was talking elementary education. She was allowed to come to school with me and shadow the teachers she grew up with. I thought it was a great career choice for her. She was excellent with kids. Regina was now a freshman, and Zach was in 7th grade. It was good to see Ali with a plan. She was a handful during those high school years. There were days that I thought we'd never make it through. But I always told Bob that she had a conscience. That was the difference. She'd come through alright if we lived through it!

It was New Year's Day, 2013, We had our usual small gathering on New Years Eve and like always we started taking down all the Christmas decorations. I loved Christmas and the run up to it, but once the holidays were over, I was ready for it to all come down. I always hated New Years Eve out because no matter what, something happens, usually a fight, whether you were looking for it or not. I really wanted Ali to stay home. She was our handful. I told her that her boyfriend, Stephen, could sleep over on the couch, I actually told all the kids that. Typical mother hen, I liked my kids home! But no, she swore up and down she was to stay at her friend's house. That her mother was letting her have a party and everyone was sleeping over. I believed her. MISTAKE. Shortly after 12 noon on New Years Day, I get a phone call from Ali. "Um, mom, Stephen's parents are on their way over to talk to you." Oh no….. " Where are you Ali????" "Um, I'm with them, we'll be there in a few minutes." I call Bob out to the kitchen and relay the message. It doesn't sound good. Is this the way 2013 is going to start???

Ali walked in, head down, Stephen followed, head down, his parents right behind. They all looked absolutely exhausted. We waited a beat, Shelly, Stephen's mom spoke. " The kids were involved in a fight last night." She said, almost expressionless. I could feel my temperature rising. She freaking lied to me. Shelly continued to tell us the story about how they went out to a party, a lot of people they didn't know, and Ali, had a smart mouth. Stephen, sensing trouble, tried to get out of there and they were jumped on the way out. Calling his sister to pick them up, he protected Ali until his parents and sister got there. But then it got worse, Stephen's dad, was knocked over the head, out cold and a vicious beating to him and Stephen began. Stephen, throwing Ali in the car, Stephen's sister ended up with a broken nose, his mom had all defensive wounds on her hands but the emotional trauma she would suffer was worse. Thankfully able to get away and driving to the police station, it would take all night and when they came to our house, they had just got done giving their witness statements. I was ready to kill Ali. She caused this. And I let her know it. She knew who the boys were, and they were arrested. Trial ahead. But these boys were gang related. We pulled Ali out of college, knowing they all went there and not willing to have her jumped again. 2013 was starting out just great!

New Year's Day fell on a Tuesday that year and Bob had taken vacation time and was due to go back that following Monday. That Sunday, the last day of his vacation, he wasn't feeling that well. He felt bloated and uncomfortable. There was just no relieving it. At first, I thought it was a stomach virus, but there was no diarrhea or vomiting. I really had started to worry about him. Physically, I could see this job was taking a toll on him. Not only physically, but mentally as well. He never smiled or laughed anymore. He was becoming more and more withdrawn. I hated what Sam was doing to him. At one point, probably a year or so before, I had actually emailed a letter to Sam, without Bob knowing, because he would have killed me, and I asked him to sit down with Bob and Phil. I told him how much respect Bob held for him. I reminded him of how loyal Bob was all these years, giving up family time for the "FAMILY" as Sam liked to call it. I reminded him of all Bob had done. I didn't hear back for several weeks, as he apologized and said that my email was in his junk mail. He never sat down with him. Ever. That told me a lot. As the day turned into night, the bloating had become more uncomfortable. It was obviously something more. He went to bed very early that night because it got to the point that sitting up was impossible. I was starting to think appendix. I never went through that myself or our kids, but after 4 kids, I also thought that moms have as much knowledge as a RN! When I touched his right side, he flinched. Not good. I wanted him to go to urgent care. No way. He was stubborn. I told him that if he woke up like this that he was going, no matter what. He didn't argue. The next morning, we were at urgent care, thankfully, it didn't get much worse, but it was still as bad. Testing took a few hours but it was conclusive, Bob needed an emergency appendectomy. I rushed him over to the hospital and they took him in immediately. What a wonderful way to start the new year! Strike 2 in one week, at least my mammogram came back normal...strike 3 in a week would have been to hard to take!

We had to call the office now, Bob with all this was going to be put out of work a minimum of 6 weeks, maybe 8. I was glad he had to take that much time off, at least now maybe he could reduce some of his stress level. It didn't really. Bob was always too much of a thinker, and I knew where his mind was. 3 years left to pay on our house. He just wanted to make it through that. Then he could go and find something for less money. Bob earned a very good income, but he didn't think he could or would match it.

He went back to work after 8 weeks. Just around the beginning of March. I could see him clenching his jaws as he was getting ready. Just the thought of it all was killing him. I was on the edge, I was so ready to jump down someone's throat. But time has a way if making everything happen and I knew I would get my chance with Phil. Maybe even Sam. Ali, was also working at WENDYS part time, not really liking it and in a bit of a funk with all that was going on. She started rethinking elementary education. So she starting working in the mall at a very popular childrens store. Like mother, like daughter. Bob had called me one afternoon after I got out of work and needed me to pick something up at Best Buy that he had purchased. I needed to get the receipt so I had to stop by the restaurant he was at. By this point, I had my own little Sam boycott going on. There were times when Bob would bring dinner home but most of the time we paid like every other customer. It was important to Bob to set that example to all his employees. He was an honest man. He had met me out in the parking lot this day, unbeknownst to me that Fabulous Phil, as I now had dubbed him, was in the restaurant, and me, with my filterless mouth, Bob worried, that I would let loose. But I wouldn't do that inside of the restaurant, ever, I wouldn't make it worse for him. So as I was getting ready to leave, here comes fabulous Phil right towards us, as we were literally standing on the side of his car. I didn't realize it. He was parked right next to Bob. He was never very brave and I knew I could break him very easlly, but I just ignored him....until he actually had the nerve to sheepishly wave and attempt to say hi! ARE YOU KIDDING ME???? This was bad, my blood pressure rising, I could feel the "F" bombs on the tip of my tongue. I put my hand up and cut him off, " DON'T YOU DARE SAY ANYTHING TO ME YOU PIECE OF *#^£!!!" I took the receipt from Bob's hand and walked around him to my car. It was then, right then and there, as I grabbed my door hand to close the car door, did that little devil that sits on your shoulder came out and whispered.....” You're walking away? This is the opportunity you have been waiting for!!!” The poor angel on the other shoulder didn't stand a chance, I was out of that car like white on rice and had my finger in his face. Calling him every name I could think of and a few I made up, I told him exactly what I thought of him. I told him that this entire situation was personal to me. He ate at our house on several occasions, holidays, he broke bread with my family, I sent him home with medicines, care packages of food, you sit at my table and you stab my husband in the back? I was livid. He looked like he was going to cry. He ran to his car but there was no stopping me now that I started. I had waited 3 years for this moment. Bob, off to the side, I think was actually enjoying Fabulous Phil's red face...every once in a while I would hear, half heartedly,” ok, Lor, that's enough” but I kept going, pushing myself In-between the car door as he was attempted to get in the car and drive away, I called him a little girl he started screaming he was going to call the cops. Laughing, I thought, ok, that's enough. As soon as I started back towards my car he started calling me some nasty names, so I turned around and went back over and started in on him again. “ COWARD, YOU DON'T HAVE THE BALLS TO SAY ANYTHING TO MY FACE, GO ON YOU LITTLE GIRL! GO CRY!” Now I know I may have sounded a bit like a bully but I've got to tell you, that was the best stress relief I had in a long time! He backed out of his parking spot, squealing his tires, almost taking out a car in the drive thru. I knew, Bob was going to have to answer to this. No way fabulous Phil was going to not call Sam.

And the call came. Bob summoned to the office the next day. I felt bad after the fact but Bob went in and defended me. Being smart, Bob had started taping the conversations he had with Sam. This started the year before when Bob called him on an email that was sent mistakenly to Bob. In this email, Bob was referred to as the “ OLD MAN” I wanted to go after Sam, legally. Bob didn't. Bob wasn't that kind of man. Bob walked out of that meeting the previous year with a $5000 raise. Blood money. Sam was scared, he didn't like confrontation. This meeting resulted in me being banned from the restaurants. It was laughable, I boycotted myself a long time ago.

A few weeks had gone by, 3rd week of March and Bob comes home early for a Saturday. He looked completely defeated. “ I was escorted off the restaurant premises today and I am on a weeks paid suspension!" I couldn't believe what I was hearing. Bob, having a hard time staffing a managerial team in one of the stores, had been stuck in this location. He was trying to get the staff up to the company's expectations. Food was disappearing, the restaurant wasn't in great shape. The hourly kids just wanted to do what they wanted to do. One girl out on lunch had punched in 15 minutes later than her break and then went back out to continue her previous conversation, he had then noticed that the pants she had on had writing on the back side of them. He told her that she wasn't following the proper dress code and she needed to change. She walked out. Quit. Done. A few hours later, Phil walks in and tells him this girl filed a complaint against Bob and he was going to be investigated again and this girl was given her job back. It was obvious that he was not wanted. This was unbelievable. He was out again. A week went by before he was contacted again and asked to meet at the office. I had started researching EEOC, wanting to file a complaint for not only a hostile work environment but age discrimination. Bob, at this point had nearly 3 hours of taped conversations where Sam clearly refers to Bob's age as an issue. But Bob didn't want to. He had enough. He just wanted out. He signed a waiver that he wouldn't sue and accepted a 19 week severance package. He was done. All of a sudden, our life, our future, our retirement. All in jeopardy. 20 years in this "so called family". Gone. It felt like my dysfunctional family again.

The first few weeks were very traumatic for him. He didn't know what to do with himself. After 20 years with the same schedule and all of a sudden you have nothing to do. He had a hard time. He always worked. He always supported us. He took that seriously. He was from another generation. He needed a few weeks just to unwind, it was over, but his mind wouldn't relax and it needed to. We had another chapter to open. A few years back, a family owned banquet facility was quietly looking for a new owner. In his family for over 60 years, it was time to let go. Bob and Peter went back and forth for a few months back then, but Peter pulled out, his kids wanting to give it a try. 3 years later, I catch him jogging around our block, I told him the situation, excitedly, he told me to have Bob call him. May be this was it.

We had never been in this situation before. A complete unknown. I would walk around the house like always, talking to God like HE was in the room. I know this was a Blessing in disguise, I would have buried Bob. There was no doubt of that. I prayed that we would find the right path. Things happen for a reason, I BELIEVE that. The year before, Bob's parents, getting older, had sold their condo in Florida and were looking into a senior living complex. It was the crème de la crème. But they had to sell their home, right down the street from us. My father in law, God love his soul, is the slowest moving man you will ever meet. I mean when it comes to decision making. You cannot make him budge before he is ready. He will hold out on all decisions until his terms are met. He was the only man I have ever met that could list, sell and get cash for his condo, all in one week. Some people just have it! This senior living complex was so eager to get my inlaws to commit that they actually rented them an apartment for a few months to help them make up his mind. We were left with the clean out of their house. This was great stress relief for Bob. Normally he would never have had the time to spend with his parents and help them out. He was beginning to relax a bit. He lost some weight, the bloat was gone from his face, and most importantly, he was smiling. The house that my inlaws had lived in was an average size ranch. About 1500 square feet, double lot, very well kept, although it needed some updating. But it was a solid structure, well built and I told them that we'd get it painted and that I knew a lot of realtors. My father in law hesitated, he didn't want to have to pay a realtor if it wasn't necessary. He did have a point. Our neighborhood was a well kept, beautiful homes, quiet and the elementary school literally 3 minutes away. Perfect starter home or for a small family. Houses moved fast here. I put pictures up on Facebook after we had painted it, and it sold! I sold their house in a month and got their price! It was bittersweet, the house Bob grew up in, the kids would miss running down the street to see grandma and grandpa. But, my mother in laws health was starting to fail. Dementia. This was a safe place. Restaurant, deli, gym, hairdresser, game room. The apartment was gorgeous with a full kitchen. They didn't ever have to leave unless they had to go grocery shopping.

The job prospects were bleak. On line applications. Every morning, that's what he did. Who wants a 53 year old man? We kept moving forward with the negotiations on the banquet facility. Big money. Bob's parents had already decided that if that is what he wanted to do. They were prepared to back him. His dream. He always wanted his own restaurant. This place needed some updating. New life. It did well enough but in our eyes it could be doing so much better. It's the difference between people being hungry and those that have enough and are content. Bob was hungry. I was all in. He knew this business. He knew numbers. He would sit with our accountant and go over numbers for hours. I would cry if someone made me do that. 3rd grade math is my limit. I hate math! I used to send the kids teachers notes that if the math homework wasn't completed due to the kids not understanding, bob didn't get home early enough to help them. It was a mental block. I couldn't see it. And me trying to explain was worse. It was better to leave it alone!

For 3 months we went back and forth. A beautiful, newly remodeled apartment was upstairs of the banquet venue that Peter and his wife lived in, just shy of 3000 sq ft. Same size as our house, not including the bedroom and mancave downstairs. If this went through, we would have to sell our house. Not right away but within a few years. My heart sank. I loved my house. Bob loved this house. The kids loved this house. The blood, sweat and tears we put into this house was too much to let go. I was sick at the thought of looking out the window and seeing an air conditioning unit. I looked out my kitchen windows into my fenced in yard to see our dogs running around. Our pool, the flowers, our fire pit. Did we want to leave all this? I didn't want to. It was something that we would have to do in the course of a few years. But I was getting desperate. Zeppelyn, our 11 year old German shepherd couldn't make it up the stairs" we also had a younger shepherd, Asta, that we bought after our golden retriever died the previous year from bladder cancer at 8 years old. Damn cancer, even our pets! Poor Sami, she was such a sweet dog, we cried for a year! I didn't want to leave this house. I told him we were going to have to put in an elevator in because his parents weren't going to be able to make it upstairs either! There was so much to this and as the days went on, we started thinking maybe it isn't our path. Bob started to get an uncomfortable feeling. " We are putting all our eggs in one basket, I think Peter is having second thoughts and we are running out of time with the severance package. We better start looking for a back up." He was right. Panic started to set in. What the hell were we going to do??

Bob found an alternate location. Not for banquets but a small restaurant. He checked out the area, traffic patterns, traffic counts. Businesses and residential properties. In a 5 mile radius, this restaurant had 100,000 homes around. Businesses. Competition. Pizzerias, bars, doctors offices, a hairdresser in the same complex. He loved it. It was formally a well known pizzeria that had closed under some financial issue, leaving the owner in arrears for several thousand dollars. Bob wanted me to look at it. He kept saying that we need to have a plan B. We need to jump at it. By this time, it looked more and more like the banquet facility wasn't going to work out. Peter was stringing us along. We put a end date on it. He didn't meet the date. We decided we needed to move on. I can't begin to tell you the amount of praying I did. To God, to my father. We needed a clear plan. In this economy, we were ready to open up our own restaurant. No name recognition, nothing. We were definitely living on a prayer!

We walked into PLAN B with the realtor. I know me. Instantly, my gut was going to tell me good or bad. I love potential. I'm talking decorating. I could care less about the kitchen. That was Bob's expertise. The first minutes walking through that door was going to tell me a lot. Bob liked the kitchen. It was good size. Filthy, but good size. It was a pizzeria and the dining room looked like a pizzeria. a lot of work was going to have to go into this. There was an upstairs. It was filthy and full of junk. But it was a good sized room followed by 2 more back rooms with dirt and junk and grease. Potential! I had a great feeling. " small banquet room." I said to Bob. " Parties" there aren't a lot of venues for small gatherings. He didn't see it. " No, more dining spaces". He thought. No, no way. Guess who won that argument?

The owner was a bit hesitant with us. Yes, Bob had 30+ years in the restaurant industry but he had never done anything remotely like this. He suggested that we reopen as the former pizzeria, using that name. Naturally, we would have to get permission if we decided to do that. But that wasn't even a consideration. If we did this, we did it on our own. We went home and thought about it. Sundays during the summers was the best day. If it was sunny, our friends and our kids would be poolside. Barbecues every Sunday, sometimes fires on Saturday nights. We enjoyed the hell out of our backyard. We would sit there and brainstorm. What would we serve? Italian! Naturally. One of our closest friends, John, nicknamed several years ago, Sticky, had a son who loved to cook. Brian was very talented, one year in culinary school before circumstances didn't allow him to continue, but a very good palate, he would bring samples of things he cooked every time he was came over.He had been jockeying for this job for years and didn't know it. My recipes, Brian's recipes. We would go round and round. Finally settling for Italian American cuisine. Home style. Nothing fancy. Things you would make at home. Comfort foods, soups, salads, meatballs, lasagna, chicken parmesan . Hamburgers, wraps. Lunch and dinner menus. We signed the 5 year long lease in August 2013. Planning on opening in October. There was a ton of work to do. Bob's parents, gifting us a considerable sum to start out.

It would all have to be repainted. Up and down. We needed furniture, booths, flooring, counters, lighting. Bob brought our power washer and gunned down the kitchen. 2 months of work. I loved potential. I had it sitting in front of me. I couldn't screw up. I thought about options. Colors. What I loved. Earth tones. Warm colors. Debbie, our accountant, and also one of my core group of friends that went through breast cancer, twice, had given me valances that she loved the colors of. She remodeled her kitchen and didn't want to throw them out. Browns, plums, greens. This would be my pallet. Slowly it came together. But we didn't have a name. Floating in the pool, alone one day. Thinking, just thinking names. Then it hit me. PAPA JOES. Plural, not possessive. My father was papa Joe. Bob had told me that growing up, because his parents were older, all his friends would call him papa Joe! A tribute to our fathers. An Italian restaurant. Italian heritage. Bob's name didn't resemble anything close to Italian but actually, his grandparents were here from Italian one generation before mine. His grandfather's name, Anthony Marchese, was changed as he came to America to open a meat market in the heart of utica's Italian district. Bleecker St. Changing the name to Markason to Americanize the the business in this country. An Italian restaurant. Comfort foods. Italian hertitage. Family. We settled on PAPA JOES. Now, on to finalizing the menu.

Bob and Brian brainstormed. Brian had a lot of ideas. He was good. He was going to be our secret weapon! No one knew him. Long hours, so much work, so much potential. So much hope. I remember driving into

Walmart one morning, talking to my father. I found myself doing that a lot lately. Driving in, talking out loud to myself, I remember exactly what I said to him, "Dad, help. Please help." I almost got into a car accident as I hit the brakes hard. I heard, clear as day, "You will have everything you have ever wanted." I started to cry, right there, right in the car. I heard it like he was sitting next to me. It was real. We were on the right path. I couldn't even call that a message. It was a direct quote! It was amazing to me how often my father could punch his way back in this world to help me. I couldn't wait to tell Bob.

Through the years I had told him about visits or voices or smells that I had happened to me. In our earlier years, telling him about these things, I know he thought I was nuts. When we first started dating, he took me to meet his grandmother, she was so cute, I don't think she was 5 ft tall and as we walked into her home, she grabbed him and hugged him, it was the sweetest thing, it made me smile through my laughter that when she hugged him, she didn't reach his chest. The next time I saw her was at her wake. Bob and I were engaged by that point, and he was crushed. He loved her so. All she wanted to do was live til 90. She died at 89. One night, after we were married, in our first home, I was in a sleep- like state. It's very hard to describe. But I remember opening my eyes and at the bottom of our bed, I see a woman. White hair, white flowing, what I thought to be a dress, she looked very tall because she was above the bed. I wasn't afraid. She wasn't looking at me. She was looking at Bob. She wasn't smiling but I knew instinctively it wasn't bad. Not evil. Then she was gone. The next morning, I told him that a woman was at the bottom of our bed. He gave me a face, the face that said, yeah, right. I didn't know who it was until a few days later as I was dusting, I walked by a picture of her and stopped. It was his grandmother. Honestly, he didn't believe me. It's so frustrating when things like this happen because I know I'm not nuts! It happened again, with my father on his birthday, the year our first was born. I remember being, again, in a dream- like state, my eyes, opened and I'm watching, looking up, a hand with the finger pointed, reaching toward another hand, a bit lower, but the hands were coming towards each other. I knew it was my father reaching toward me, when the fingers touched, our room exploded in light, like lightening, a flash and at that moment, I started with contractions. But then they stopped. I couldn't get that picture of the fingers coming towards each other out of my head. It was familiar, tho I couldn't place it. Months later, I was at the CATHOLIC BOOKSTORE, and as I walked in, there it was, my "dream" it was called "THE CREATION" I never saw that picture before. I couldn't believe it. That picture now sits in my living room.

We got it all done. It was time to open. We were nervous as all hell but absolutely believed we were doing the right thing. We planned a friends and family night a few days before our actual opening. To get the bugs out. Inviting 50 of our closest friends and family. From 5-7 that night, they came in, ordered and ate.

It was a disaster. We were devastated. Now what. This was harder than we imagined. We weren't ready. We wanted to delay the opening. . Panic set in. Ok, maybe a delay, get the bugs out. A bunch of my co workers at Harts Hill Elementary had planned to surprise us on our opening night. Bob wanted to delay 2 weeks. Brian wasn't sure. Once I heard people were planning on coming, I said to Bob, " no, we have to." And we did. The best thing we ever did was fail on that Monday night. We worked it all out and our opening night went smoothly. Our friends came out in force, to support us. We gained a lot of confidence during this time. Our banquet room upstairs was doing well. We booked several parties for Christmas. We were confident! Bring on 2014! We were ready!

We were exhausted. Bob was used to this pace. I wasn't. Everything hurt. Reality was setting in. This is now our life? We have no life? There was no time for anything. Christmas was coming, forget our usual party. I started to cry. I hated Sam. This was Bob's dream. But even his dream took a toll on him.

Blessings. Friends. We had them both. Surprising us, one Saturday night, one week before Christmas, the weekend that we would have had our Christmas party, my girlfriend Gina, I thought, was hosting a party in our room. Gina always had things going on and so I questioned nothing she asked for. We were that tired. At one point, Gina called me upstairs, actually she needed both Bob and I. We stopped what we were doing, walked up the stairs and the blindside. Over 40 of the people we knew and loved surprised us. They were sneaking up that back staircase. We never had a clue! They brought the party to us. Both

Bob and I cried. How do you thank people who think of you that much? What words to you say to express your gratitude? All that we went through this year, from Bob's emergency surgery, to Ali's fight, to the job loss. It was a 13 year! Bring on 2014, we were so ready for a new start and a new beginning.

Chapter 8

2014. New year. New beginning. After the beatings we took in 2013, we were so ready for a new year! We made it through the first few months of Papa Joes. We were exhausted. Mentally and physically. We had learned so much during this time. We had a real rhythm going. We had come so far from our friends and family night. But, we knew we had so much more to learn and that our struggle to make this work was well ahead of us. We were all in. Bob was just incredible. The hours upon hours that he put in, and continued to put in is a testament to just how important this was. His dream. That was the thing. If hard work does really make dreams come true then we had nothing to worry about, Bob was/ is the hardest working man I know. We had so many good people working for us, everyone cared. Everyone wanted this to work. It had to work. His parents had put their lifesaving on the line for us. I can't tell you how many prayers I said. The general consensus with restaurants was that we had to hang in there for a year minimum. And now, the dead of winter. These months were going to be long, and rough.

About mid January, I had started having issues with my left arm. That was the side of my mastectomy. My hand was tingly, my elbow had a dead nerve pain. My shoulder hurt. My arm started swelling. Lymphedema? Now? Lymphedema is a condition that occurs after nodes are removed from the armpit, which mine were during the node biopsy done when I had the lumpectomy done in 2005. Swelling can happen because your lymphatic system isn't working properly with fluid drainage. I never had this issue before, well, very minor issues but nothing like this. I once made the mistake of not paying attention to a nurse taking my blood pressure. They did it on the mastectomy side, which is a no- no. Boy oh boy was that painful. The pressure in my arm, under my arm, it was horrible. It felt like I had a baseball stuck in my armpit. It took a few days to start to feel better. But this was so much worse. I wrapped it in a ace bandage, I never had the Lymphedema sleeve. I never needed it. I contacted Dr. Jonas, and not even realizing it, I had missed last year's appointment. With all Bob went through, I forgot and the office never called. I made an appointment and had to beg her to give me a prescription for lymphatic massage prior to my appointment ….this would be the first of many battles!

I started to see a therapist for the lymphatic massage in late January. It seemed to make some difference, but it would not go away. I had exercises to do and I did them faithfully. My body always responded well to exercise, it wasn't working. My appointment with Dr. Jonas would be 3 weeks later. Hoping to get this under control by then but my arm wasn't cooperating. By the time I went to the oncology office, there really wasn't much change. Some days were worse that others. The constant nagging ache in my arm was making me crazy. It was like toothache. It was a dead pain. My arm just felt heavy. I didn't see my doctor, just a nurse practitioner. She was new in the office and honestly, I don't even remember her name. She totally ignored my symptoms. Not questioning at all, why, after 9 years I am having these problems. This starts after the surgeries. That should have been a flag right there. But here I am, not seeing the doctor, AGAIN. That always got to me. I am paying for a DOCTOR visit, not a nurse. No offense to nurses at all. But charge a different rate! I just never thought it was fair. She did a physical check, no bloodwork, again, I asked why. "Protocol for stage one, doesn't call for it." That didn't make sense either. But, this was my 9th year after cancer. My mammogram on my right side was normal the previous month and I was given the " ALL CLEAR", silent prayers being said as I walked out, thank you, thank you, sweet Jesus!

By this time we were well into February. The weather was brutally cold. I think we had a span of 20+ straight days of air temp under 20 degrees. Coldest weather in years. Naturally, we are going to have to fight everything to make this restaurant work! There were days that our high was -1. It was horrible. We were struggling big time in the restaurant, anxious for the LENTEN season to arrive. We were planning having fish fries at the restaurant, hoping to catapult us into bigger sales. My arm was worse. The swelling was spreading. My back, my side, I was in so much pain. I started gaining weight. I was down 30 lbs now from the start of changing over my thyroid meds. In that sense I was feeling great. Now I'm watching the fluid build up take over. It was now March and with March came my yearly Pap smear. I get on the scale and I am 18 lbs up from last year. I can't understand it. Was my thyroid off again? What the hell is going on? I was feeling fatigued. Something was up. A random hand to my neck and I feel a bump. A little one, but a bump. Oh no. It can't be. Maybe the lymphatic massage has something to do with this? Complete denial. So much so that towards the end of the month as I go to see my primary care for a check up, I don't tell them, I could not put a voice to these words. . But, now I'm up 20 lbs. My heart rate has dropped and my pressure is high. Shit, what the hell is going on. The nurse practitioner is questioning my weight gain. She wants to put me on another blood pressure pill! Oh no. Not going to happen! This doesn't make sense to me! What is causing my heart rate to drop? My HBP meds always worked unless the pain I was in was severe. I argued that I didn't want another pill. She gave me 2 weeks to try to get things under control and if I didn't then she was going to prescribe something else. 2 weeks go by and there is no change. Except that I'm up a few more pounds. I finally told her." I feel a lump in my neck." I said it so quietly, it was like I was trying to make light of it all. She felt it. Naturally, with my history, she sent me for a CT scan the next morning. I knew under my arm, the sight of the lumpectomy and node biopsy, that I had scar tissue there. I was pretty good at convincing myself that it was just all inflamed and Once I started wearing my new lymphatic sleeve it would all rectify itself. Lisa, the nurse practitioner, sent me home with another prescription. I argued but she gave it to me anyway. But the thought that kept on nagging me was why is my heart rate dropping and my blood pressure medicine not working? There had to be a correlation here. But like most offices, they are quick to write a prescription instead of looking into the issue. I took the pill when I got home, as instructed, and later that night I took a shower. As I stepped out of the shower, looking in the mirror, I noticed that my groin area was swollen. I looked like I had a protective cup on. When I touched below my belly button, it jiggled. OH MY GOD! I started screaming to Bob. He came running down the hall. He didn't know what to say but something was definitely wrong. Could it be those pills? I frantically pulled the insert out of the garbage. "This drug may cause ankle or leg swelling." Well my legs and ankles were fine, but my trunk, my body was starting to become disfigured. I called the doctors number. The answering service was reached. I needed the doctor to call me. Unfortunately, my doctor wasn't on call this night. Still, I had to talk to someone. I had the answer service call the on call doctor return my call. . He did, relatively quickly, and in as much detail as I could provide, he didn't have an answer, except that he didn't believe the medicine could do that. I hung up the phone, completely frustrated and adamant about never taking this medicine again. There was nothing I could do except wait until morning to call my doctor.

I called the next morning, after my CT scan was done. They didn't believe it was the pill. I refused to take it anymore. I couldn't figure out what was wrong and nobody seems really concerned. All I could do now was wait for the scan results. Maybe that would tell me something. After all, the swelling in my arm has now turned into the swelling in the trunk of my body. I was retaining all this fluid. Then it hit me. Fluid retention! Lower heart rate, high blood pressure. Oh my God, this is like congestive heart failure! But I wasn't having any issues with breathing. But this fluid, building up was obviously affecting my heart. Do I have to be my own doctor? No one could figure this out? From December 2013 thru March of 2014 I had gained nearly 20 lbs and no one found this serious?

I finally get a call from Dr. Martin's office. It's Lisa, Dr. Martin's nurse practitioner. We have the CT results and I'm sending them to Dr. Jonas. "Ok, what is going on?" " Well you probably should contact the office and talk to her. "There is obviously something going on. There is a mass under your arm. Oh boy, this isn't good. Trying to remain calm. I'm at school, on the playground, trying for the sake of 45 children to remain calm. I call Dr. Jonas's office. Voicemail. Naturally, that's all I ever get. Message left," it's Lorrie Markason, can you please call me back regarding my scan. All day goes by, nothing. Nervous as a cat, I drive over to the restaurant. I text a friend who does billing in my oncologist's office and explain the situation. The nurse practitioner is the one who calls back I'm told. Julie. She promises to have Julie call me. And she does, while I'm still at the restaurant. Julie, sounding aggravated for being bothered, isn't interested in what I have to say. Instead, insisting that I accept an appointment for the 3rd week of May. Nearly 3 weeks away. " This is the first available appointment, Dr. Jonas has reviewed your CT scan and she wants to see you on May 23rd, she is going to schedule a biopsy and she will see you after that. We should be able to schedule you by that time." ARE YOU CRAZY?" I ask her, not exactly in my inside voice. I insist on an appointment immediately, having a hard time trying to understand why as a patient of 9 years, never calling with any issues, is being given a runaround. I insisted. I wanted a biopsy immediately. Then Julie has the nerve to say, "Look, I'm not going round and round with you anymore!" Breathe....I'm trying to breathe... I tell her, " I'll call Sloan- Kettering and get an appointment faster, so you better tell Dr. Jonas I want to speak to her now!" I get hung up on. Yes. I GOT HUNG UP ON. Minutes later, to my surprise, Dr. Jonas calls. " Lorrie, it's Dr. Jonas, what is the problem?" She couldn't have sounded more put out if she tried. I couldn't believe I was being spoken to this way. "The problem?" Trying like hell to stay calm, "The problem is that something is going on with me and I want an appointment to see you and I'm being told that I have to wait for 3 weeks and that you don't wish to see me before a biopsy and Julie wasn't sure how fast she could get it scheduled. This is bullshit, I want to be evaluated by you. I don't call every time I have a bruise. Now I want to be seen!" " Well," she says, I'm booked solid today and tomorrow but I can see you Monday. Will that work?" " Yes, that will work!" I tell her. Then she says something so odd, that I had to stop and think about it. " Lorrie," she says," I looked at your CT scans and I'm underwhelmed." UNDERWHELMED. Hmmmm, I don't think I ever heard that phrase before. UNDERWHELMED.....the opposite of OVERWHELMED??

Totally panicked. I wished Dr. Logan was around. He had retired a few years earlier. If I had access to him, he would have taken me in immediately. But in his place was another doctor, Dr. Chase that I had seen once before. He was seeing Dr. Logan's patients and I had an appointment with him a few years back just to establish myself with him. He seemed like a decent man. It was Thursday, heading into the weekend, Dr. Jonas was trying to get me a biopsy as soon as possible. Later that day I received a call from Dr. Chase's office, he could schedule me in June for a biopsy. " JUNE?" I fired back, "It's the end of April and you want me to wait until June?" This was unbelievable! There was no way I was going to settle for this. Dr. Chase had another surgeon in his office. I asked if he would be willing to do the biopsy? The nurse actually said to me, "Well, since you are Dr. Chase's patient, the other doctor won't do it. They don't like to step on each other's toes." I was silent. I was just not told this. I felt like I was in a LIFETIME MOVIE OF THE WEEK. This couldn't be happening. "He doesn't want to step on his toes? Seriously, that is what you are telling me? I may have cancer and a doctor will not help because he doesn't want to step on his associate's toes???" I hung up. It wasn't worth it. I didn't want that level of doctor to look after me anyway. I got home that night, so frustrated with this entire process. I decided right then and there that I was going to be a biopsy whore. I was going to call Memorial Sloan Kettering in New York, Strong Memorial in Rochester, and I was looking into Syracuse offices. I was going to go to the first place who could schedule this. I didn't care. I wanted it done....yesterday. Thankfully, Dr. Jonas came through this time and was able to get me a biopsy scheduled for the end of the following week.

I got myself through the weekend, not an easy task, just trying to remain calm. I kept repeating the word, UNDERWHELMED, to myself. Maybe it is just a mass of scar tissue. May be the lymphatic massage pushed it through. It was possible. I ran through every scenario in my head. It couldn't be cancer, they got it all. It never hit my nodes. My protocol, mastectomy, chemotherapy and 5 years of tamoxifen, an anti estrogen drug was the most aggressive treatment recommended. Please, God please. Monday finally came. The restaurant is closed Monday and Bob comes with me. In part so I don't find out who Julie is and grab her by the throat for talking to me like that. Dr. Jonas walks in. I immediately had told her what happened during the phone conversation with Julie. She defended her! She actually fluffed it off as though I was overly sensitive. She asked me to take her back to when everything had started. Then she did a physical exam on me. She steps back, " I'm very concerned." "WHAT? You are very concerned?" What happened to underwhelmed????" She wanted blood work, immediately. It was obvious that she was backpeddling and Bob and I were trying to stay calm. " I had to fight for this appointment, you tell me you were UNDERWHELMED, and now you are very concerned??" My world exploded. I felt like took a bullet.

I went for my bloodwork immediately leaving her office. There was a draw station a door down. Her offices were right across from the infusion unit. A few years earlier she had combined her practice with 2 others, her former partner had retired. Looking at the door of the infusion unit. I just said to myself. Not again. This was all so surreal. I asked Dr. Jonas if she would call me and she promised she would, if she had the results. My blood work was done before noon and the phlebotomist had said that this blood work would come back before day's end and it is emailed directly to her. I should have known better. Nothing that afternoon. This was the mindboggling part of this office that lacked so much compassion. You know walking in there, that your visit is related to cancer. Period. Waiting for results is the most mentally exhausting, nerve wracking time of your life. You just want answers. Why they just don't hire a liaison to make the calls and take messages. People dealing with illnesses, waiting for answers, shouldn't have to be stressed further. I realize some doctor's offices are better than others. Dr. Logan's office always called and if they didn't, I could call, speak to a person, not a machine, and get my information. I gave it to 4pm before I called. Answering machine! UGH! I texted my friend again, asking if she could please relay this message. I know I was putting her on the spot, but I was desperate. She texted back that Dr. Jonas left early. I couldn't believe it. Could Julie give me the results? No, only Dr. Jonas had access to the emails. I would have to wait until Tuesday.

Tuesday morning, first thing, I call, and naturally, again, I am forced to leave a message. Now the message is to Julie's voicemail and her message is that she will return this call within a 24 hour period. BULL. It was now Tuesday, midday. Enough. I called again and pretended I was going to make an appointment. Sometimes that kicked you to their front desk, sometimes it was another voicemail. I got lucky. I asked for Dr. Jonas to call me immediately with the results. I would have rather done this in person but I knew that it would have taken forever. The receptionist promised to get the message to her and NOT Julie. It is probably fair to say that I was yelling by this time.

It's so difficult, probably the most difficult time when you don't know what you are facing. Your head is spinning. I knew in my heart that it had to be cancer. A reoccurance? My biggest fear was a lymphoma. With my thyroid, my diagnosis was Hashimotos Thyroidosis. I went all those years on that SYNTHROID which did nothing for me and having my thyroid antibodies off the charts for so long but me at a higher risk of lymphoma. Patience is not one of my virtues. I don't think I am above anyone but I expect a certain amount of respect as a patient and I was angry that I had now waited a good 24 hours for a result from blood work that I was told would take less than 3 hours for the results to be sent directly to Dr. Jonas computer.

Finally, her call comes. Unfortunately, I was on the playground with about 50 kids. I backed off a few feet away from the kids so I could hear. She was quick and to the point. " I would rather have done this in person." It's positive." Confused, I asked, "positive that it's negative for cancer?" "No, positive for cancer. Your cancer is back." My knees buckled. I hit the ground. " WHAT? HOW? WHY? YOU TOLD ME I WAS CLEAN, YOU TOLD ME I WAS 97% CLEAN! WHY DIDN'T YOU DO ANY BLOOD WORK ON ME ?? " The kids were starting to look at me. She wanted off the phone, " I'm setting you up immediately for a pet scan. Julie will call you with the date and time and we will meet after." Wow! We have come along way from underwhelmed, I thought. I hung up the find that a few of the little girls came up and said, "Mrs. Markason, are you ok? " I had to compose myself but my partner, the other aide, knew something was up. He gave me a look like "Are you ok?" I just shook my head no. We lined the kids up and some other kids starting asking. I spent a lot of time with these kids. They always saw me happy and hugging them, they never saw me like this. I told them " Kids, I'm ok. My dogs got sick and I'm just worried. But they'll be ok." I smiled a fake smile. Thank God kids are so innocent and they accepted this excuse from me. We walked them down, actually he took them down, I stopped mid way in the hall and walked into the office. The secretary and the principal standing there, seeing the tears streaming down my face. I couldn't talk. " WHAT'S WRONG????? LORRIE WHAT HAPPENED??" I felt like someone punched me in the stomach. I felt like I took a bullet. I said it so quietly. " My cancer is back." Gasps came out of both their mouths. " I have to go home. " I was devastated. They were so good to me. They didn't want me to drive home. They wanted me to call Bob. They wanted to take me home. I told them I was ok to drive home. It was literally a 3 minute drive. I got very claustrophobic just then. I just needed to leave.

Now I have to tell everyone. Again.

I walked into my house. Bob was out running errands but was due to return shortly. Regina and Zach were due home in about an hour from high school. Ali was working at the mall and not due home until 9:30.

Our oldest was another story. That is why you never hear me refer to him by name. The sweet girl that he started dating turned into a nightmare. They had gotten engaged the year before. We were happy about it although we were hoping they would wait to get married. This was his first girlfriend and he was head over heals. Her controlling side was becoming more and more evident. Slowly we had begun to see a change in him. The previous year I got into a fight with him because on Father's Day, he chose to spend the day with Cora's family. I texted him and asked if he had called his father to wish him Happy Father's Day. No, he hadn't, and until late in the evening, he wouldn't make that call. I was furious. And I let him know. I told him if he had that must disrepect for his own father, a father that was there all his life, he should find his own place to live. He left, staying at Cora's house. He came back after a few weeks, but there was a clear line in the sand. This introverted, nice guy, was gone. In his place was an arrogant, rude and disrespectful young man. We couldn't do or say anything right. He was turning into Cora. A pattern was developing. All holidays, he would go to her house first and then grace us, late in the evening. All the while Cora would sit at the dining room table with her coat on. It spoke volumes. Self righteous. I knew this type. Nose in the air, believing that they are above others. I had a cousin like that. They just outgrow people. Suddenly, we weren't good enough. Especially me. I had the strong personality. Not that Bob didn't. But it was me, as mom, naturally that had a lot of influence on him during those formative years. Two strong women in his life wouldn't do. So I became the enemy. So much that when he traveled to Buffalo for college, he changed his address without telling us and when I asked why, he said he was staying there and not coming home. I felt horrible. If he wanted to stay, that's fine, but why the deception? Cora. It was simple. She needed us, me, away from him. Suddenly it was a full blown issue. And it's been over a year now, that we haven't heard from or talked to him. On the eve of my pet scan results, I texted him and told him that tomorrow I would find out about my cancer. His last words to me were goodbye. It was happening again. The dysfunction I did not want was back. He wouldn't take calls from his brother or sisters. They were heartbroken and angry. They were all old enough and saw what was going on. They had lost a brother and Bob and I, a son. I made the sign of the cross on him. We didn't cause it. Keeping my promise to my SERENITY PRAYER, I couldn't change it, I accepted it. I knew, that someday, she would outgrow him, if he didn't continue on to be a doctor it would be a matter of time before she outgrew him too. Until that time I wanted nothing to do with him if he was with her. I had to accept this now. I had to. Because I knew if grandchildren were born, she would never allow me to see them. Bob had faith he would come around, I did too, but I knew our wait would be long. He destroyed what I had worked for since he was born. It was unforgivable.

I sat in my house alone. Waiting for Bob to get home. I was hoping he got home before Zach and Regina. I had to tell him first. I knew I was going to break down. I couldn't do that in front of the kids. How was this happening again? I just couldn't understand. I was clean. Damn it CLEAN! They told me that! 97% is a guarantee? Isn't it? Meteorologists don't give us 97%. But I had it. Bob walked in. He saw my face. He put his bags down and said, "What?" Tears welled up I my eyes and with nothing but defeat in my body, I answered him, " My cancer is back." I saw his face fall. I saw the defeat in his eyes. He came towards me and hugged me. Tight. I just fell into his arms and cried. I had no strength to hug him back. I felt like I just didn't have it in me to go through all this again.

Zach and Regina walked in. I tried to hide my face as they said hi to me. I knew I needed to talk to them. I didn't want it out there yet. I had some friends asking on facebook and I didn't want Ali to learn about it that way. We called the kids back into the family room. Their smiling faces went blank as they looked at both Bob and I. "What's wrong!" Regina said it first. Oh Lord, how do I tell these kids, especially Regina, who's friend's mother had just died less than a month ago when her cancer returned. Regina was by her friend's side all during this. A few times she came and cried to me. "What if it happens again to you mom?" And here I am, I have to tell her it did. Shit! My hesitation was enough for both of them to realize it was bad enough that I couldn't say it. " My cancer came back." An immediate burst of tears from both of them. I grabbed them and hugged them. Bob cried, I cried. I told them I would be ok. They couldn't understand how. I couldn't explain it, I didn't understand either. I told them everything I knew. They saw the condition of my arm. I had just about lost usage. It was getting to the point that I couldn't hold a pen. Nothing. Total use of my left arm and hand were gone.

I asked them both not to say anything to anyone until Ali came home. I did not want her to hear about it on facebook. I called her boyfriend and told him, I wanted him to know so she didn't go anywhere after work. I needed her to come home. With each admittance to my kids, I felt so awful. Moms aren't supposed to hurt their children and here I was, breaking the most brutal news to them. So when Ali walked in, Zach and Regina came out from their rooms, immediately Ali knew something was wrong. I just wish there was an easier way to say it. But there wasn't. Ali started crying and I grabbed her and hugged her. Regina and Zach started crying. I held them all. Bob had no words. What could you say? Each time I told those kids, it was like taking a bullet.

They wanted to know the details, in which I had none. Until the PET SCAN was done and the biopsy results came in, I had no details. I went on Facebook and told my friends what had happened. To my surprise, prayers, words of encouragement were everywhere. I just sat alone that night, needing to find myself. Knowing how strong I was the first time. Knowing I wasn't even close to where I needed to be. I prayed for strength, for guidance. I asked once again for God to lift this burden. What a year. Our restaurant, losing money every month and now me, with cancer. Again. Why, oh why all these trials? Now? Isn't there enough on our backs? I didn't even know what I was facing yet. I had never had a PET SCAN before. You are injected with a small amount of radioactive sugar. You need to lay down, with little to no movement for about an hour so it can circulate. The scan itself takes about 30 minutes. In my case, with cancer, the radioactive sugar will light up where the cancer is found.

One of my oldest friends, Bernadette, moved out of state several years ago. Her husband was hired as a play by play announcer for a pro hockey team. Thankfully she was only about 4 ½ hours from me. She didn't get home as often as when her kids were little but we were still in touch. She immediately sent me a novena to Padre Pio. I read it everyday. I said my rosaries. I prayed to my father. I was so scared. I could feel several nodes in my neck now. One especially, that was the size of a grape. I had to take hold. I had to BELIEVE. My prayers had been answered before. I prayed for the Grace of God. How life had changed for us. In a matter of 2 years, our retirement, our security, our future, my wellness, everything was up in the air. It had all snowballed! The stress level in our house was incredible. Every aspect of our lives were in question. Everything had been quiet with my family. Only in contact with Corinne and that had started the night my nephew's wife called when my mother had died. We weren't close by any means. I had tried a few holidays to get everyone together, but it seemed like there were always excuses so I stopped trying. Ali and Regina had become close with my niece and her kids. That was fine with me. My troubles with family were my own. My girls were old enough to make up their own minds. As a matter of fact, Bob and I were disgusted because as I assumed, the bill for my mother's funeral was on us. My brother made a few payments on it but that was it. I never could understand how they could walk into the funeral home for other wakes knowing a balance was due, knowing they haven't paid. Not us. We pay our debts. But I did make it clear that I was 1/5 of the bill and when I reached the $2500 point, I was done. I went as far as giving the funeral home phone numbers, or the most current ones if I knew them. I didn't care. I was sick and tired of others getting away with everything!

Once again, we were in waiting mode. PET SCAN results were to be read to me the following week, along with the biopsy results. I had serious doubts now about staying with Dr. Jonas. I couldn't handle the constant pressure and aggravation that came with every phone call. It wasn't necessary and it wasn't right. We were all cancer patients and deserved some respect as well as some dignity. I went ahead and called New York City's Memorial Sloan-Kettering. I had one of the most respected CANCER hospitals in the country only 4 hours away. I had to get them involved. I could not believe the simplicity of it all. I called the number for new patients, seeing that it had been over 9 years now since my first visit. The website was very easy to navigate through. Starting with what type of cancer, Dr. Jonas was sure it was a reoccurance of my breast cancer even though no results came in yet, so I started with that. To my surprise, a person answered. Wow! Then I was asked for the location I preferred, I wanted Manhattan. They asked me a few questions regarding my history and told me that I needed to have my biopsy results sent. They would hold a date for me but until I got my biopsy result to confirm it was cancer they would not commit the date. I couldn't believe how easy it was to do all this. It took less than 10 minutes.

And so my appointment with Dr. Jonas finally came. All my questions I hoped to have answered. Sitting in the office, waiting for her to walk in, Bob and I sat there in silence. Each deep in our own thoughts. Saying silent prayers. Every once in a while, we would catch each other's eye, we knew each other too well. Words weren't necessary. I just couldn't grasp this. It was surreal. Bloodwork, it all came down to bloodwork. I was so angry at myself for not insisting on it yearly. And to think that I was here 2 months ago and was told everything was fine. Answers. I wanted answers.

In my head, I tried to figure out where I could be in regards to staging. Not that I knew a lot about cancer, because I didn't. I knew chances were it was in my nodes. For me to have swelling in the trunk of my body I figured stage 3. Stage 3 was survivable. I prayed I was 3. I also knew that breast cancer could and did travel to the bones, to the lungs and to the brain. All I knew was the pain I had was excruciating. It felt like someone would stick a knife in my left shoulder blade directly to my heart. I literally would stop what I was doing and grab my chest and moan. It was that bad. And living with back pain for so many years had made my pain tolerance very high. This was a pain like I never knew before. And I knew this wasn't good.

Dr. Jonas walked in smiling. I took that as a good sign. " Hi, Lorrie." She nodded to Bob. She got right to the point. " This is a reoccurance of your breast cancer." I sighed relief. I was worried with my thyroid antibodies being so high that this was a lymphoma. It wasn't. We won one battle.

Then my world exploded.

" But it is all through your lymphatic system on your left side. It's on your chest wall, under your arm, on the lung, not in. It is in several nodes under your left arm and several on left side of your neck. It crossed over to the nodes under your right arm."

I couldn't speak. Bob couldn't speak. With all the strength in my body I asked, " Where am I? What stage?" She spoke directly at me, emotionless, like she was telling me what time it was.

" Stage 4"

It was like I took a bullet. I know my mouth opened, but no words came out. I didn't even look at Bob. This wasn't happening. This can't be real. I'm going to die. Everything was swirling in my head. I wasn't going to grow old with Bob. I wouldn't see my kids grow up and get married. I'd never see my grandchildren. My house I loved so much. Everything. I was going to die. And that's all I could ask. It was a whisper, "Am I going to die?" Her response? "Lorrie, we are all going to die." What? What did she just say to me? I was just given a stage 4 diagnosis and she is being flippant with me? Finding my voice, I said to her," you know what I mean."
Bob up to this point has not said a word. I don't think he could speak. He finally addressed her as to the treatment. I asked if anything surgically could be removed. "No." Another bullet. I just started to cry. I was totally defeated. If I could have curled up in a ball I would have. She looked at me and said," Lorrie, you are a treatable 4". I didn't understand. Stage 4 was/ is stage 4. You hear that and you are ready to call the funeral home. What was she saying? Treatable? The treatment that she wanted to start me on was an Aromatase inhibitor. NO CHEMOTHERAPY! This was a drug that had been around now for about 10 years. So it was around just as I was finishing up my treatments in 2005. It could only be used with post menopausal women and what it did was block the estrogen that would come into my body. Since my cancer was referred to as her2 Positive the estrogen was feeding the cancer. Dr. Jonas's method of attack was to throw me into immediate medical menopause and start me on this drug. In a nutshell, once I was in menopause, I could start this drug and it would block the estrogen made in my body and ultimately "starve" the cancer. Since my cancer was caused by the estrogen, blocking it would stop the cancer from growing and God willing shrink it.

It was a lot to take in. Dr. Jonas wanted me to start immediately. I was somewhat hesitant because I wanted Memorial Sloan-Kettering's imput. If I started this prior to seeing them, they would not stop this treatment for a few months. They would give it a chance to work. I NEEDED to speak to them first. So I told Dr. Jonas the truth, "I have lost faith in you. Sloan-Kettering wanted to see my biopsy results to be sure it's cancer. I need the biopsy to be sent to them, immediately. Once I speak with them, I will have a decision made." I asked Dr. Jonas if she was willing to work with another doctor. She replied," I have no problem working with New York, but I won't be dictated too." There it was, her high and mighty attitude. Nothing about what was in my best interest. Only about her. I wanted New York to be on point on this. Hard as it was being 4 hours away. I was not in a position to have mistakes made.

I wanted to start a treatment now, but I needed to know what the other opinion was going to be. Dr. Jonas's office faxed the report over to Sloan-Kettering and I was therefore confirmed with an appointment for early June.

I called Sloan-Kettering to follow up with my biopsy. I asked if it was possible for my doctor there to contact Dr. Jonas. I was due back in Dr. Jonas's office in a few days and I really didn't want to wait too long. My new doctor in New York, Dr. Camen, was at the top of her field. A Harvard graduate who specializes in women with metastatic breast cancer. I felt like I was in good hands. I returned to Dr. Jonas's office a few days later happy to learn that both doctors had spoken to each other and agreed on this course of treatment. I would be following up with Dr. Camen about 17 days after my treatment. So that day I walked out of Dr. Jonas's office with my first shot of LUPRON. That drug would immediately put me into a medical menopause and the following day I would begin on AROMASIN.

I remember clearly how bad I felt physically that day I left Dr. Jonas's office. I had lost nearly all use of my left arm. I was left handed and could barely write. The pain in my back, shoulders right thru to my heart was brutally bad. I couldn't sleep at night because I had to keep my arm and shoulder at the same level. I had gained over 20 lbs with all the fluid. Dr. Jonas said if this drug was going to work I would feel it within 6 weeks. It would be at that point that I would have blood work done again. If this didn't work, there were other drugs available. But she was very optimistic with this one.

Cancer. Round 2. I wasn't anywhere mentally that I needed to be. Yet.

Chapter 9

Since I had found out the cancer had returned, I was well aware of what this could and would do to me not only physically, but mentally too. Physically I had been in good shape, minus my back. I learned the value of eating well. Staying away from glutens, I felt better. The stomach bloat was gone. I wasn't a big sugar eater, rarely drank soda, so I was ahead of the game at this point. I drank a lot of water and green teas. I continued my vitamin regimen. I walked, a lot. I looked better than I had in years. Mentally, well, that's a totally different game. As with any illness, you need to understand that strong mental health is imperative. Some people feel the need for anti-anxiety medicine or antidepressants. I would not go that route. I don't like taking pills. I always knew my strong will, my determination, my anger and most of all my faith would come through. It was just going to take me a bit of time to pull it all together. My girlfriend Bernadette, Bernie, had sent me a novena to Padre Pio. I had started saying it before all the results started coming in. Every day, I prayed for strength. Everyday my mornings started with novenas and prayers. Every morning I would wake up, make the sign of the cross with Holy Oil and tell cancer TO GET THE FUCK OUT OF MY BODY. All my facebook friends were sending me words of encouragement. Cards and letters came almost every day. I had one girlfriend that I hadn't seen in years, that went through breast cancer a few years back, she sent me a card every month. I was put in prayer chains and my friend Gina put my name in for a Healing Mass. I had support from everywhere. It was incredible. My family at school was wonderful. They had taken up 2 separate donations for me. They gave me words of encouragement, prayers and just a supportive hand as I walked down the hall. Prayers, prayers and more prayers. I was starting to feel the strength. I felt an inner peace. I can't explain that feeling. I wish I could. It was a deep calmness. Inside of me. I knew God was with me. I asked God to carry me, every day. I couldn't take on this burden alone. My faith allowed me to be weak enough to ask for strength. The road ahead was long.

With the first round of CANCER in 2004-2005, the only side effect I wasn't able to counter was the hot flashes. Not fun. Losing my hair during that time turned out to be a Blessing. That Spring- Summer was very hot. I swore I would never take off my wig, in reality, I never wore it around the house and I ended up with the greatest tan on my head! Once chemotherapy was over it seemed as though my body temperature would react quicker to heat from then on, right up until this happened. It never went away. As soon as those beautiful 70 degree days hit, I was in a tank top and shorts until Fall. Now? WOW! The first month of the Lupron shot catapulted me into full menopause. It was unbearable and immediate! Add in the aromasin and the severe fatigue it caused. Then there was the weight gain. If dealing with cancer wasn't enough, now add in severe hot flashes and fatigue and weight. I had lost just about all the weight caused by the swelling from the cancer but now every week I could feel clothes getting tighter and tighter. I started taking the aromasin in the morning with my high blood pressure pills, this way I wouldn't forget. That didn't work, within 3 hours the fatigue would hit me so hard and I would go into school at 11:30. I had all I could do to get through the next few hours. And when I got home, I would hit the couch and sleep for 3 hours. One thing about me is that my mind is always working. How can I use this to my advantage? It didn't matter what time I took it, so I decided that I would move it to dinner time. Afraid to not have it in my system and make a jump from morning to the following night, So every day I took it 2 hours later until I got to 6 pm. My logic as by the time my fatigue set in, usually 3 hours later, I would just go to bed and wake up refreshed. And it worked. I slept hard. One thing that is imperative during illness is the ability to stop. Just stop. You have to understand that your body needs you to slow down. And everyone around you needs to understand that too. With the restaurant being opened I got away from eating as good as I was and I wasn't able to walk either, I was just too tired. All this had to change. I knew what was needed but right now, I had to let the medicine take hold. I figured all in good time. One battle at a time. I knew me. I would learn to counter every last side effect I had to deal with. That's the stubborn Italian in me. I would win the war, I may lose a few battles initially but I would win the war. And that is the attitude you need to have! It gets so frustrating at times watching your body go out of control. The SERENITY PRAYER. Once again. I learned to lean on it. Right now I couldn't change it. Eventually I would. I would take my life back.....AGAIN!

I had been on the medicine for about 13 days when I really started to feel like my range of motion in my arm was getting better. I didn't say anything to anyone at this point because I knew they would think I was crazy. But I felt it! I was on Hydrocodone for the pain and would take it less and less as the days went on. By the time I was on my way to New York, 17 days after treatment began I was sure it was getting better. I was regaining my arm movement.

With the restaurant being open for only 8 months, trying to save as much money as we could, Bob was working a ton of hours. He was torn. He wanted to go to New York with me but he needed to be at the restaurant. My friend Gina's brother, Joey, was like a brother to me. He was a policeman who used to travel to New York frequently and offered to drive me down along with Debbie. Debbie had been clear now since her last bout in 2005. She had enough of Dr. Jonas a long time ago and had been coming to Sloan-Kettering for yearly checkups now since then. She was a good friend and very smart, informed person. She would have more questions than I would, if I knew her at all.

Since the last time I was down to Memorial Sloan-Kettering in 2005, things had changed. They now had an entire building dedicated to the treatment of breast cancer. It was a a gorgeous building with a doorman and a huge marbled lobby. As you walked in you were greeted at a main desk. I had the "Toto, we aren't in Kansas anymore" look on my face. Debbie knew her way around since this was where she would come. Joey took up a place in the lobby, found a comfortable chair and told us to take our time. We took the elevator up to the second floor and once off the elevator it opened up to a huge room with a square section in the middle which housed all the receptionists. No waiting, just walk to a free one. Wow! What an environment! I checked in and was given paperwork to fill out. We chose a seat and we were immediately approached by a young girl who acted as a hostess would. She welcomed us and asked if we would like coffee or tea. I was blown away. Back home, I couldn't get a person to answer the phone and here, well, they are acting as though they are happy to see me. We arrived about 15 minutes before my actual appointment so you would understand the surprise I felt as the doctor's assistant called my name EXACTLY at 12:40. My appointment time. Debbie and I walked into one of the examination rooms. Collecting our thoughts. Debbie had an article talking about massage therapy for CANCER patients. Because my cancer was in my lymphatic system, I was afraid any form of massage would push it through my system further. I put the article in front of me so I didn't forget. I added a question mark. Just then Dr. Camen walked in. Before we even got a chance to say hi, she walked by me towards her chair, saw the note with the question mark and wrote YES :) . I couldn't believe it. She was on the ball. I was in incredible hands.

She introduced herself, as did Debbie and I. She asked me to tell her about myself. And I did. She was so "real" as I like to say. She spoke to me as a person. She told me that this is an incredible drug. She made me feel so comfortable that I told her that being on this pill for 17 days I feel a difference. "am I nuts?" I asked her. "No." She replied. "it's that powerful, it's completely possible." She went on to say that blood work would be necessary monthly and that my information, meaning how I felt was imperative. She talked about side effects, unfortunately, we have no choice but to weigh the good with the bad. She asked why I came out here. "second opinion?" I told her what I was going through and I really wanted her to be the lead. She agreed and said that she could treat me from a distance while bloodwork would be done up there. I told her that my doctor at home was willingly to work with her but didn't want to be dictated to. Dr. Camen smirked at me. This is when I knew I had found the right doctor. She looked directly into my eyes and said, "Well, you go tell Dr. Jonas that I'm not a dictator. I'm a pitbull. I'm not looking to make new friends. I leave no stone unturned." I laughed out loud! I loved her. She had my kind of mouth. And she backed up her words, right then and there. She took out my report from the biopsy. Just then her cell phone rang. She looked at it and asked us to excuse her for a second. She took the call in front of us. It was her husband. They had a baby at home with an ear infection and she spoke to him briefly. Once she hung up the phone, she let out a sigh and said, "You have 4 kids, how are you so organized?" I couldn't believe this doctor, who achieved so much, thought so much of a stay at home mom. She listened. She looked at me. She answered questions. My God, with this woman in my corner, no way anything was going to get by! She looked back at my report and a look of confusion went across her face. There was a inconclusive result on my biopsy that dealt with the HER2 diagnosis. There was supposed to be an addendum to this report and it wasn't there. This could be a determining factor in my treatment. She got up, walked out for a few minutes and walked back in. She had given her assistant instruct to get Dr. Jonas's office on the phone, she wanted the answer. "THE PITBULL." As she was waiting for that she said she wanted to examine me so she lead us to another room. Before she left she said to me," How have you been treated here?" I was confused, "Good, everyone has been very friendly, not like home." Then she said something that I had NEVER heard from any doctor, ever..." Everyone here always needs to treat patients like that. I want to know if you ever get any negativity from anyone, I take this very seriously." Then she walked out. Debbie and I just looked at each other. We laughed, not because it was funny but because this is what is available and I had never knew it.

Upon examining me, she was able to feel the neck nodes. Every thing else, chest nodes, underarm nodes, nothing was palpable. Just the thought of that sent chills down my spine. All I could think was thank God for the lymphatic massage, that just may have pushed it through to my neck. If I didn't have that, it would have been through my entire body before I knew it. It may have been to late.

I believe we all have Angels around us. One thing that happened to me before, and it happened again, was that a situation caused me to find this cancer. Both doctor agreed, nothing was palpable. Nothing. My angels made my arm swell, which lead me to the lymphatic massage, which opened up my lymphatic system and had all the swelling in my body appear. If this remained in my arm, I never would have known.

After the exam, I was informed that there wasn't any addendum. Dr. Camen wasn't happy. She wanted me to have another biopsy to answer the inconclusive findings. She said she would speak to Dr. Jonas. She wanted me to come back down to have the biopsy here. I was going to get a call from the office in a few days to set it up. Then she started to talk about genomic testing. The commercials are all over TV. It's the future of cancer treatment. I asked Dr. Jonas about this when we were discussing my treatment and she waved her hand and blew it off. " We don't need to do that." That was the one thing that really pissed me off about her. The arrogance! She didn't want to talk. She wanted you to accept what she said without question. Sorry. That was just not going to happen. Dr. Camen asked if I was interested. "Yes!" All I could think was 10 years ago my treatment wasn't offered to me, and look at it now. They have 10 years of positive results! All they needed from me was blood work. They were doing other research and again, all it required was bloodwork. My case was interesting to them. I had gone 9 years and it showed up again, why? If they could find things out using my blood, to advance the treatment of cancer and prevent this, absolutely! As Debbie and I left the exam room, Dr. Camen met us in the hall. With her was another doctor. She introduced her to us. I couldn't remember her name but she was a researcher from Italy who was going to take my blood sample as soon as it was drawn. Signing all papers to agree to release my blood samples. This was impressive. They worked in unison. Very precise. You couldn't walk out of there without feeling like you were in the best hands possible!

We went down to the lobby area again, Joey was comfortably napping in a chair. We woke him up and told him I was just about done. Just blood work now. I walked into the phlebotomist office. There were quite a few people in there. I thought to myself that I was going to be here for a while. Wrong! There wasn't 2 phlebotomists back there, but several. After about 10 minutes, my cell rang. It was Dr. Camen's office calling from upstairs. I had left paper work and they wanted me to get it. When I told them I was waiting for my blood to be drawn, she apologized that it was taking this long! I looked at Debbie, it was like it was a movie. I hung up the phone and the phone in the other room rang. The room was so crowded that I was standing in the door way so I could see into the other room. One of phlebotomists answered the phone and I heard her say, "Lorrie Markason? Yes, ok, right now." She hung up the phone and called me in. Damn! I was brought back and just then the doctor from Italy, the researcher walked into the curtained area. She had a black box with a lock on it. As soon as my blood was drawn she handed her the sample. She thanked me for my willingness to have my blood be used for research. I swear, I felt like I was in a movie. She whisked out of there in one direction and I went the other. We were done.

I now knew what I wanted from a doctor. Like anything else in life, why should I be treated disrespectfully while dealing with cancer when I would not allow myself to be treated like this in everyday life. Changes were going to be made. With Dr. Jonas or without her. Period.

We were almost at the end of the school year. Our pool was opened, flowers blooming. I love summer. Although I knew with everything I was going through it wasn't going to be an easy one. Bob was gone all day until 8 pm most nights at the restaurant. Talk about will and determination. He was going to see this through! We were strong for each other. That was the best thing about us. I knew what he had to do and he knew what I needed to do. He prayed more than ever. I knew he did. I know over the years he questioned his faith. When Regina was a baby and sick I knew he prayed. He just never talked about it. I would never push my faith on to anyone. My kids grew up knowing how I felt. As teenagers, remembering before my father died, I never really gave it much thought. That's normal, I think. It's not until you have skin in the game and nothing worldly to rely on that faith comes out. I knew Bob would emerge. And I never doubted my kids.

It was going to be a hard summer in addition to my health and the restaurant because we had put off the inevitable. Our Zeppelyn. Our older german shepherd. The one Nonnie had bought for me during my first go round of cancer needed to be put down. His legs were so bad, he couldn't walk. German Shepherds are notorious for hip dysplasia. He would have constant accidents in the house. I wanted to wait for summer so the kids didn't have the pressure of exams and the entire change of our lifestyle since we opened the restaurant. We had planned for early summer. Now my cancer had come back. I couldn't bring myself to put him down. Maybe one last summer. He loved summer. I would be in our backyard as much as possible and Zeppelyn and our other Shepherd, Asta would love to follow me around.

It was a Friday, June 20th. The last full week of school. Monday would be my last day, since it was the last full day of school. Tuesday and Wednesday would be half days. And I didn't work on the half days. As much as I looked forward to a few months off, I missed these kids a lot. I liked to make sure I wished them all well, hugged my little friends and to tell them to look for me in Walmart! Regina was all finished with finals and she liked to come back to school with me when she could. I was on my way to the drug store to pick up my first refill of aromasin. I told Regina I would be back in 10 minutes and to be ready. I drove down the hill, coming to a complete stop as the car, two cars in front of me was turning left. All of a sudden, BOOM. It took me a second to realize I was just rear-ended. I sat there, upon realizing it and said to myself, " Are you frigging kidding me?" I got out of my jeep, and the young girl jumped out of her car crying, " MRS. MARKASON, OH MY GOD! I'M SO SORRY!" Obviously this girl went to Harts Hill but I didn't recognize her. "Honey, who are you?" I recognized her name immediately and saw the front of her car, totaled. Her air bag didn't go off. I looked at the back of my jeep and there looked as though nothing was wrong. My bumper ended up being loose. Her car was totaled and my jeep's bumper was loose. I will never own a different truck as long as I live. She continued crying and I hugged her and asked if she was ok. Miraculously she was. She lived just around the block and just left her house. I told her to call her parents. The police must have been right there, somewhere, because he was there instantly and informed me that I was not at fault at all. He asked if I was ok. I thought so. I told him of a pre- existing back problem I had and I would call my doctor to have him check me out. I needed to go to work. By the time all the paper work was done I started to feel a dull throb in my lower back. It proceeded to feel like a vice grip pain. Oh no. I don't need this. I informed the police that I had changed my mind. I was going to go to urgent care. He asked if I needed an ambulance. I told him no. I called Regina and then school to let them know what happened. I called Bob. "WHAT???" Yup, my first accident since I started driving at 16. 2014 really sucked.

I drove myself to urgent care which wasn't very far, thank God because I knew that my injury was now exacerbated by the accident. I really didn't think I had that much impact. Looking at my car you wouldn't think much. Looking at her car? She was lucky. With the damage and no air bag, she could have been killed. They did the X-rays on back and neck. Asked if my neck hurt at all. It didn't. They gave me a shot of a muscle relaxer, I refused pain pills, telling them that I was in treatment for stage 4 breast cancer and had Hydrocodone at home. Her mouth fell open. "God bless you," she said. "You would never know." She told told me to follow up with my doctor the following week.

The next morning I couldn't move my neck. My collar bone hurt. The muscles in front and in back were so sore I felt as though something was stuck in the right side of my neck. Wonderful. Whiplash. I called my doctor on Monday morning and made an appointment. They took me in and diagnosed me with whiplash. She told me to continue on the medicine and I got a soft brace for my neck. I couldn't believe this. I really didn't need this on top of everything else. After all these months I was finally sleeping better because my arm range of motion was returning, not to mention the aromasin made me sleep hard. . And now the pain in my back and neck on top of my arm was making it more difficult. Here I am, the one person who hates taking pills was now on cancer meds, HBP meds, thyroid meds, pain pills, anti inflammatory meds and muscle relaxers. I remember at 42 thinking how would 50 be. Well, at 52, I wanted to cry.

Those first few weeks of the accident were brutal. I wasn't sleeping at all. I found myself napping constantly during the day, on my couch, which was firmer than the bed mattress. Actually, we were due to buy a new one but financially, forget it. There would be no big purchases for awhile. On top of that, our hot tub had broke down the Fall before this and we needed a new one. Forget that too. I missed that more than anything during the winter months. We would turn it off during the summer. Once the pool shut down, we would turn the hot tub on. When all the pain and stiffness with my back kicked in due to the weather change, the hot tub was my salvation.

It was now the very end of June. Time for me to go back in for blood work in Dr. Jonas's office. I was interested to hear what she had to say about this second biopsy. I was due to see Dr. Camen for a check up in October. I was scheduled for a biopsy down in New York mid July. Both doctors had told me not to get nervous if the tumor markers rise slightly or have no movement at all. Sometimes it took a 6 week period before that cancer would be done peaking and if the medicine was going to work. I was at the 4 week mark of starting the treatments. Back in the office of Dr. Jonas, I waited impatiently, anxious to see what these tumor markers were going to show. She came in and happily announced that one marker had indeed dropped while the other one rose ever so slightly. She was happy with this! I was happy with this. I had told her how my range of motion was slowing coming back and that I had gotten into a car accident. She couldn't believe my luck, or lack there of. I asked her what she had thought of a second biopsy. She shrugged it off and said it wasn't necessary, especially since the treatment was working. Why bother now? Both doctors had said that the inconclusiveness of the report could simply be because of lack of enough tissue sample or that the sample had died. Dr. Jonas's attitude was well if this stops working then we can do another biopsy at that point. Complete opposite of Dr. Camen. Dr. Camen was proactive and wanted answers before anything else changed. Dr. Jonas would rather wait until something negative happens and be reactive. No way. I wanted that biopsy. I had an athletes frame of mind, IT'S ALWAYS BETTER TO BE ON OFFENSE RATHER THAN DEFENSE. Why couldn't she see that?

Unfortunately, Sloan-Kettering had to postpone my biopsy. Scheduling conflict on their end. We could not agree on a new date that worked for us both so Dr. Camen agreed to let me have it here. She spoke with Dr. Jonas, explained to her as she did me, exactly what she wanted. It was simple. She wanted the biopsy samples immediately sent to her. She wanted Sloan to examine them. Dr. Camen told me that they run the samples through as series of tests. Over and above what they could do locally. Hell, you had to expect that. This is one of the top cancer research hospitals in the country.

I went into my second CT guided biopsy in weeks. The radiologist was aiming for the same node in my neck as last time. That big one. The one that was the size of a grape. As he had me in the scanner, he said to me," Wow! This is amazing! That node has shrunk at least 4 times the size it was a few weeks ago!" I felt like I had one the lottery! My prayers were working! The medicine was working! He would have all he could do to get a viable sample. Please God! Let him. Like Dr. Camen, I wanted answers.

The entire process took about 30 minutes. It was considered an outpatient procedure so I needed rides to and from the hospital. This is where my friends always shined. They insisted on driving me, insisted on sitting there until the procedure was done. I didn't even have to ask, they would call and say, " What do you need." What I lost in family, I gained in friends. They were my family. Bob was able to leave the restaurant and pick me up. Before I left, the radiologist I had reiterated that these samples were to be directly sent to Memorial Sloan-Kettering. He had no idea what I was referring to. The nurses said to me that the request for this biopsy had come from Dr. Jonas and they would have to check with her. I agreed with her that it came from Dr. Jonas and explained the situation. I went as far as giving them Dr. Camen's information and fax number. They said they would contact Dr. Jonas first. Knowing her attitude, I hoped that this would just be done correctly.

After a few days, I contacted Dr. Camen's office. Speaking with her assistant, I asked if the samples had gotten there. " No" I was told. The biopsy was done in Utica! I was so pissed! I knew that was going to happen. Her arrogance wouldn't allow another hospital to do it. There were lines being crossed here that were just unacceptable.

July brought me to my yearly check up with my thyroid. I now had to travel about an hour and a half away because the nurse practitioner that I was seeing now stopped coming to my area. Gina and her mom decided to come for the ride with me. We planned on stopping at the Auriesville Shrine. A beautiful catholic shrine that I had not been to since I was a child. I felt with all that was happening, there was some evil around me. I wanted to pray and purchase a medal of the Archangel St. Michael. St. Michael is the one you take into battle with you. Boy did I have a battle on my hands.

On our ride out, just as we were approaching the Shrine, Regina had called me. Ali just before that. It seems as though Jody and Billy had found out about my cancer, it was a matter of time, I knew it. Both girls were texted by my brother. It was a simple text. Nothing mean. He told them he loved me and wanted to be there for us. As wonderful as it sounded, the answer was a no. Up to this point, nothing had changed. Why would I open my home up to him when he has proven to me by his inaction that things have changed. I was at a crucial time in my life and I was completely unwilling to let this dysfunction back into my world. I took the cell number from my girls and texted him a simple message. YOU UPSET MY KIDS TODAY WITH YOUR TEXTS TO THEM. PLEASE DO NOT BOTHER THEM AGAIN. That was it. No response, which was fine. As long as he got the message. Jody, well, she was another issue. Regina called again. Jody had just called the house. Regina answered the phone and since it was so long since she had heard her voice, she thought it was Corinne, the only sister I was in contact with. We all sounded alike on the phone. It wasn't until a few minutes into the conversation she realized who she was speaking to. She was unnerved by the call. I told her not to answer the phone again and to give me the cell number she had called from. As I was in the Shrine, tears and frustration and that sick shaking feeling came back. I can't deal with this shit anymore. Why can't she leave me alone? The following is the exact text messages that went back and forth between me and her.

Me: u and Billy have upset my girls tremendously. Do not call them or my house again.

Jody: Die alone then. Stage 4 is not a joke. If you don't think the kids will need family when you are gone then you are sadly mistaken. Get humble in the face of death. Vanity has got u in this position. U will need strength not hate. Good luck.

Me: That is exactly why I don't want u around. Bother me again and I go to the police.

Jody: Die. Sucks to be the first one to go...ain't it. Wished it on mom...karma baby

I did not respond. Nothing changed, why would I let her in my world. She was delusional, probably high and I wasn't going to get into a pissing match. I walked over to the statue of the Blessed Mother. I crossed myself with Holy Water. I cried. I asked again for strength. Gina and her mother rubbed my back and told me not to cry. It was bad enough with everything we were dealing with. I had to stay strong. Not only for me, but for my family. They weren't going to beat me down. I knew I had felt evil trying to break me. It was then that I realized that God wasn't trying to break me. God was going to carry me through. EVERYTHING. The devil, negative people, one and the same. No one would would enter my world with negativity. I rid most of my family. I bought St. Michael for not only myself but my kids. I felt that inner peace again. I hadn't walked into a church, with the exception of a funeral, in several years, ever since the problem with Zach and his first communion. But my faith was deep. Nothing changed. Like always, I would become weepy as I knelt in front of the Lord in his House.

We continued on to the doctor's office from the shrine. I really liked this nurse practitioner. I felt comfortable with her and the fatigue and weight was gone, up and until everything started with the cancer. But I was glad that I had this appointment because with all the stress, I knew my adrenal glands were going to become fatigued. I just wanted to be sure my numbers were ok. They were. This was the first time she had seen me since my cancer diagnosis. I had to be careful with any supplements I was taking. Nothing, but nothing could interfere with the cancer meds. We left and headed home. Thank God, thyroid good. One thing I didn't have to worry about.

Since I moved my time for the medicine at 6 pm, I found myself in bed around 9-9:30. Unable to keep my eyes open, I would usually fall asleep watching tv in bed. It was now   mid July , my next blood work and lupron shot was coming up right at the end of the month. Bob was exhausted. Poor thing. He just kept going and going. But it was Saturday and we decided that Sundays and Mondays we would close the restaurant. Everything else was closed around there on Mondays. He looked forward to those 2 days. Pushing 60 hours a week, he needed 2 days to recover. Besides, working all those years in fast food never gave him 2 days off in a row. He enjoyed this. He would usually go down in his mancave and listen to music. That always relaxed him. This night, I kissed him goodnight in the family room and Asta followed me to bed.

Asta was my baby. I brought her home at 5 ½ weeks the first week after school ended in 2011. My first German Shepherd puppy. No papers. I really didn't want to spend $1000 on a dog. But it was obvious she was full breed. She was adorable. And fresh. Zeppelyn was such an alpha male that I couldn't have brought another full size dog in the house. My only chance was a puppy. A female. He looked at her like what the hell is this? We took pictures of them nose to nose. She clung to him, he growled at her. And that never changed. She was an emergency from the time we brought her home. Every month I ended up at the vet for something she did. I forgot what it was like having a puppy. She was into everything. My plants, socks, you name it. I once found her with a Doritos bag over her head. It was hysterical but she could have suffocated. She ate scissors, got shocked by an electrical cords as she ripped them out of the wall. She would attempt to eat bees only to find out she was allergic to bees and hence, another trip to the vet. We had her scheduled to be spayed and she got into mouse poison and had to be rushed up to the vet again, to be given vitamin K to help her clot again. We had to reschedule her for surgery.

But she was all mine. She followed me everywhere and had the greatest personality. She was a typical female shepherd. Loved her family and those close to us but didn't want anyone else around. The funniest thing she would do was if everyone was in the kitchen, she would jump up on the couch with her paws hanging over the back of the couch, listening with a tipped head, like she wanted to be a part of the conversation. If you yelled at her, she would run down the hall to Bob's office and hide under his desk. She would not come out until the person who yelled at her went down and said they were sorry. She was a trip. I couldn't make a move without her there. Unless I went to bed too late. Then she would walk down the hall, looking back at me like, the hell with you, I'm tired. And she would go.

So as I went to bed, she snuggled up against me. I awoke to her thrashing. I thought she had an itch and as I turned around to look at her, she was in a full seizure! Now at this point I was just awoke from a dead sleep and couldn't comprehend what was happening. I started screaming for Bob and he along with the kids came running down the hall. It wouldn't end. Her legs were thrashing, mouth foaming, defecating on my sheets. I was hysterical. Suddenly it stopped. We were all around her. She sat up in a daze. Eyes glazed and panting heavily. You could see that she wasn't aware. She growled at Bob who was closest to her and jumped off the bed. I called the vet, immediately. She, meanwhile ran into our jacuzzi room. Still foaming and showing her teeth, we shut the glass door, still able to see her. She was uncontrollable. Trying to go through the window. I finally got through to the vet. Unfortunately, the vet on call had just started with this veterinarian hospital. He had come from another animal hospital and I knew him. And I didn't care for him. But I had no choice. I had never witnessed anything like this in my life. He told us to leave her alone, make the room dark. It sounded like a grand Mal seizure based on the amount of time of the thrashing and the fact that she had defecated and was foaming. It could take her a while to come out of it but just leave her alone. I wanted to bring her up and he said no. I asked if he wanted to see her tomorrow and he said no. I got so angry, maybe unreasonably so, because I was offered no solutions. He said this just may be a one- time thing and see what happens. I got so aggravated I threw the phone at Bob. Bob was always more diplomatic than I was. I was not a politically correct person. I was about ready to let loose. Better Bob talk to him. This was the worst thing I had ever seen. My baby was just over 3. What the hell was happening this year!

She finally came out of it and was crying, she was licking me and you could tell she was scared. I was able to reach my friend Bernie. She had gone through this with her Irish Setters. They were prone to this. Shepherds weren't. I had shepherds all my life and this had never happened. She said to just watch. Sometimes it may be a break through seizure, meaning it may just be starting or it could be a fluke and never happen again. We watched her closely. I wouldn't leave her alone. For the next 2 weeks she was always in someone's sight.

Then it happened again. 2 weeks later. And it kept happening. We got her up to the vet, worried that damage was done. She became non-responsive and I was a total basket case. The vet here, now working with one I liked, couldn't do any more. We needed her to get to an emergency vet. She needed intravenous drugs. We couldn't afford this. We were looking at an additional $1300 in vet bills for the emergency service. I didn't care. I didn't. I couldn't handle this. The stress was overwhelming. The kids were hysterical. Bob and I picked her up and drove an hour to the emergency vets hospital. She had seizures on the way there. Now, she wasn't coming out of them. She remained in a catatonic state. This was bad. What If it was too late. Brain damaged. We got her there and the technicians and doctors came out to get her with a gurney. They pumped her with valium, they pumped her with phenobarbital, they pumped her with another anti seizure drug, they pumped her with some drug to stop any brain swelling. We had to leave her. There she was, in a little cage, unconscious. My heart hurt. If you don't own a pet then you will never understand the feeling. I wanted to crawl in that cage and lay down with her. I wanted her to know that mommy was there. My God. I had felt the same way when they took Regina from me as a baby. Bob had to drag me from that cage.

The plan was that they would monitor her for the next 24 hours. They were an emergency service so there were doctors and technicians there all night. That gave me great comfort. They promised if I called in the middle of the night, they would be there. I knew I would. If Asta went 24 hours without any seizures, she could come home. If not, we were going to have to put her down. This couldn't be happening. I was going to lose 2 dogs in a summer? Lord, have mercy on me. Why? Why? I honestly felt that there was something trying to break me. How much more could I take. How much more could my family take. We felt like we were war torn.

She made it! She had gone 24 hours and we could pick her up. I couldn't get there fast enough. Ali and Regina jumped in the car. We just weren't prepared for what we would see. I remembered the only other time Asta had spent the night away. It was after she was spayed. I was a nervous wreck, picking her up an hour before I was told to. When she saw me, I dropped to my knees and she would hug me. She was so sensitive. Everyone laughed when I would say that. We were put in an examination room. Waiting on first the veterinarian to explain her condition and then they would bring her to us. . The doctor came in and said that she had been stable all night. She was heavily medicated and they had put her on anti seizure meds. Actually our vet had started her on them, but they made some adjustments. They also said that they thought it was epilepsy but unless we took her for further testing they wouldn't know for sure. That was something we absolutely couldn't afford. I added a novena to St. Francis of Assisi to my morning prayers. He was the patron saint of animals. We needed all the help we could get. Finally, they brought her to us. She looked horrible. She was attempting to walk on her nails. It was as though she couldn't find the floor. The kids started crying. I had to hold back my tears. As she got closer the kids and I got on our knees to hug her. She was frightened. Her eyes were horribly dialated. She could barely see. She didn't know us. Holy Lord, would she come out of this? We were quiet on the 45 minute ride home. We got her in and made her comfortable on the new pillow we bought for her. It was like bringing a new puppy home.

She peed in the house, bumped into walls and cried. She ate some food and drank a lot of water. It was horrible to see her like that. I closed off the door going down the hall to the bedrooms and shut the sliding doors from the family room that would allow entry into the living room and dining room. I thought keeping her in one area would be best. She was unable to go down the stairs to go out. We lived in a ranch so it was one step down to the deck and one step down from the deck. Her paws would knuckle under. She was tripping. This was horrible. I called Bernie to ask about this. "Yes" she told me. This is all normal. Her brain has sustained some injury but give her a week or so and she should come back. Ugh, this was bad. She was so off balance that I was afraid she would fall in the pool. And she did, at 4 in the morning. I had to jump in and get her. From then on, we had her on her leash outside someone was out with her all the time. I decided to sleep in the family room with her until she got better. She was afraid of Zeppelyn and for the first time, he seemed like he missed her. Usually as she came near him, he raised his lip and I would yell at him to be nice to his sister. It was like having 2- two year olds.

I slept in the family room for the next 10 days. Not once thinking about myself or cancer. It wasn't until about the 7th day that we started to see bits of her personality coming back. Just those stupid little things she used to do now were the most important things. I missed her under my feet at the breakfast bar. I missed her crying as we came home. I missed her tilted head when I talked to her. It was like she knew what I was saying. But thankfully she did come back fully. She would be on medicine for the rest of her life. I used to tell her, Asta, it's me and you with medicine all our lives! But she was back to normal. Thank you, Jesus! But now we still had to make the decision to put Zeppelyn down. I couldn't. I just couldn't. We all knew it was coming. He would never make winter. The ice, the snow. I couldn't bring myself to make the appointment. Just too much stress in our lives, in every direction. Everywhere we turned. I had never had a year like this in my life.

We were struggling big time with the restaurant. We knew the first year was crucial. Our feedback was incredibly positive but it just wasn't generating enough money. We were losing money every month. My inlaws had put their saving on the line. My father in law the most conservative man you will ever meet, kept telling Bob to keep it up.

And he would have been the first one to say let it go. We advertised as much as we could, which was radio. We couldn't afford anything else. We brought food samples around to area businesses. Entered contests, sponsored teams. Direct mailings. We did everything. And it was all on Bob. He wanted me to worry about me. And he would take care of the rest. I felt so guilty at times. Damn this cancer! Every thing, our future, our retirement, the restaurant, my health, the accident and now the dog? Why all the trials. Why? Why? Why? What had we done wrong? I know the people who disliked us would call it karma. Was it? I didn't think so. We took care of our family. Bob worked his ass off for years for all we had. I was always referred to as " the material one" of the family. That made me laugh. Like it was a criminal act to have a nice home and possessions. We never took trips but put our money into the house and yard. Our backyard was my salvation. I didn't apologize for anything we had. We earned it. Nothing was given to us. I remember one argument with Jody. It was during that time that my brother asked for money for the prescriptions. She was screaming at me about being money hungry and materialistic, yet when she was broke, which was constantly, she knew where to come. Call me materialistic all you want, but the truth was they were hypocritical.

Asta had been ok for 2 weeks now. Still I wouldn't let her be alone in case something had happened. During the seizures, as they come out of the actual seizure, they go into a catatonic state. I was afraid she would attack Zeppelyn. Zeppelyn was a huge dog, around 110 lbs. Asta was around 70lbs. He could hurt her badly, but with his legs, I didn't want her to hurt him either. What a summer. Before I knew it another month had gone by and it was time for my blood work again. Realizing that I had heard nothing on the biopsy. I had completely forgotten about it.

Walking back into Dr. Jonas's office became more and more difficult after my experience in New York City. It would have been impossible for me to make that trip monthly. We couldn't afford it. I had started going for my blood work the day before my visit so when I went in, all results were there. It was easier than going just prior to the appointment. Waiting for that office to call me back was torture, so I did it my way. She walked in with great news! My tumor markers had fallen. Quite a bit actually. She was very excited that my treatments were working so well. I had stopped taking the Hydrocodone by this point. The exacerbating pain that I was once in was gone, I still had pain from my accident, but I had other pain medication now. I didn't want to remain on Hydrocodone more than I needed to.

I saw my numbers, they dropped 30%. Those tumor markers had taken a huge drop. If that happened again next month, I could very possibly be near remission numbers. The cancer wasn't growing, it was shrinking. My God. Thank you. I was healing. Before I had the chance to mention the biopsy, she had brought it up. I asked why it wasn't sent immediately to New York? She replied that they didn't think there was enough tissue to get a sample. My node was considerably smaller. She didn't let New York make the decision. She didn't allow the sample to be sent. Then she went on to say she thought it was foolish to have it done again. Once again, she was dictating all that was happening. I asked her if she was sending my blood work down to Dr. Camen. She said it should have been sent and she would check on it. There wasn't an ounce of me that believed her. If she gave word to her staff to send it, it would have been sent. Period.

August. Summer seemed like a complete bust. I didn't have the energy to do much. My neck was stiff and I started having issues with my hands. Numbness and tingling. I was dropping things and had trouble holding small object. Pens, for example, if I held it for too long, would cause my fingers to go numb. I started massage therapy for the car accident injuries. I specifically waited knowing the swelling caused by the accident would take time to heal and I didn't want to cause further injury. I had gone to a chiropractor years before and he caused me nothing but more pain. I went through physical therapy several years ago too. My experience with my back was the more people touched me, the worse I became. I knew all the exercises so I just stopped going. At this point I was really was sick of doctors and tests and scans. Enough. Really. This was now my life. I had come to realize it. I would live the rest of my life having doctors and tests and scans.

It just hit me. Honestly it should have been something that struck me immediately, but it didn't. All I could think of in the beginning was if I was going to die. I was stage 4. I would be stage 4 until I died. Whether it be from cancer or something else. It was so easy to get into a funk. A depression. I remember thinking at this point, my God, I wish I had my stage 1 diagnosis. That was easy compared to this road I was on. I was worried about so much. Even if I hit remission, I would always be considered stage 4. This is when it would be easy to curl up in a ball and give up. Yes it's cancer, but it's an illness, a manageable illness. I wasn't going to give up. I wanted to live. My will was too strong. I just got angry. I have to say that I hope no one after reading this believes that I was stronger than anyone else facing an illness. It's there. In everyone, deep inside. You cannot imagine the strength you have inside until you are forced to find it. Ask for it! It will come! I remember Bob telling me after my first pregnancy. I could laugh about his admissions of how weak he thought I was as the fetal monitor was in the wrong place! He never had to see a fight in me. So when I was first diagnosed back in 2004 – 2005, he was amazed at my ability to deal with it. But now what was getting to me was that I just didn't have the energy to get my body moving. Total frustration! And the weight gain continued. I had to be patient. Remission. That's first and foremost. Then a hysterectomy. Dr. Jonas wanted a partial hysterectomy. That was a battle she wasn't going to win. I knew once the surgery happened, I would gain more weight. Then I had to heal. I was months away from starting over. I started looking so forward to 2015. I knew it would be a better year. I had that deep peace inside. It didn't stop Bob from worrying. I was a huge worrywart. And I wasn't worrying. Why? Faith. "FAITH IS BELIEVING WHEN COMMON SENSE TELLS YOU NOT TO." That came from one of my favorite movies. The original " MIRACLE ON 34th STREET. It meant more to me than Believing in Santa. I love that word. BELIEVE.

I remember the first time I had seen the movie, POLAR EXPRESS. The book is very old and I had never known about it. I'm a Christmas nut, how did that slip by me??? The first- grade teachers would surprise the kids with a Polar Express day. They would dress in their pajamas that day for school and wear tickets around their necks. I was so excited for them! How I loved Christmas! I would put up 12 trees through my house. Living room, family room, dining room, bedrooms, mancave. Santa would wave to you as you came into our house. I start on Halloween, putting up my Angel tree. That would take about 3 days. I would not be done until the week before Thanksgiving. Just in time to bake pies. Bob always required pies. Homemade. I spoiled him rotten. The Angel tree started this the year Regina was born and had her healing. I found an ornament, actually it was a wind chime, but it was small. It was a mother holding a baby up close to her face and it reads," Dear Lord, thank you for my little Angel." I cried when I saw it. Every year, it is the first ornament that is put on the tree, and Regina puts it on. One thing about Bob, he likes his TV's. We had surround sound in the family room, long before it became a common thing. By the way, we had it in the backyard too. We had just bought, the year before he lost his job, a new TV, a new blu Ray player and a copy of THE POLAR EXPRESS. BELIEVE, the theme of the movie. I knew Macy's had this theme. But I wasn't a Macy's shopper, really. This hit me. That word. It's more than Santa. It's faith. That word, upon seeing it at Christmas would choke me up. I would get weepy. Same as every time I walked into a church and kneeled.

There was a meaning here. I knew that this particular word would become very important to me, but I had no idea why. It became my Christmas theme. That would be come my mantra.

The one single word that would defeat cancer.

Chapter 10

I couldn't wait for the end of August to come. It seemed like I wished away the entire summer. Actually it's exactly what I did. All that mattered was the end of each month to see what my numbers would be. I was feeling better and better. With the exception of the weight gain and fatigue, the cancer was manageable. I just needed to be sure I went to bed before 10 or I was toast the next day. I would find myself napping every day, but I didn't fight it, you can't fight it. You have to listen to what your body needs. . I was anxious for school to start too. The year ended so abruptly and so negatively that I just wanted some normalcy again. Besides, I was a very structured person, and the non-structure that comes with summer had ran its course. I needed schedules. I don't know how people can wing it all the time. It would have driven me crazy.

Finally, it was the end of the month. Numbers day! As before, I went the previous day for my bloodwork so when I walked in, all she had to do was bring up my information on the computer. She showed me, the graph. My tumor markers were dropping like a rock. Unbelievable. I WAS IN REMISSION!!! I HIT REMSSION IN 13 WEEKS! Thank you God! I understood that I would always be stage 4, but now I was able to say, I AM IN REMISSION TO STAGE 4 BREAST CANCER. I cried. I was so happy. I knew the cancer was all through my chest and back, I knew I was in bad shape when this started. I couldn't wait to tell Bob and the kids. I couldn't wait to post it on facebook. I couldn't wait to tell everyone! Now on to the next step. I knew I would get here. What I didn't expect was is coming so fast. I really wanted a PET Scan at this point, I started the treatment at the end of May, but Dr. Jonas didn't want to at this point. She was happy with the numbers, I felt so much better, so I didn't push. She was talking about doing it at the 6- month mark. October. I would wait until then.

Since the plan was always first and foremost to get me into remission, the next step was to have a hysterectomy. Dr. Jonas wanted to get it done as soon as possible so I wouldn't have to have another monthly shot of lupron. Normally I would have the shot on the same day that I got my numbers, but she was going to talk to my gynecologist to see how soon it could be done. Dr. Jonas had recommended just to have my ovaries removed. Oh no... I wanted a full hysterectomy. I wanted it all gone. She argued with me, "Lorrie, the estrogen comes from the ovaries, there is no need to remove anything else." " Yeah there was," I told her. I had 5 years on tamoxifen, which basically did the same thing as my aromasin did now, which the exception that tamoxifen was given to women who were still menstruating. That alone put me at a higher risk of uterine cancer, even though I had a deep D&C done 2 years after my first bout with cancer. A deep D&C, obviously not the technical term, is when they cauterize the lining of the uterus to prevent excessive bleeding during a women's cycle. This being done only to women who cannot have or do not want anymore children. With the birth of Zach, I did have the tubal ligation. Having the deep D&C reduced my chances of a uterine cancer. But my argument was that in 2005, Dr. Jonas stated that I had only a 3% chance of my breast cancer returning. Look how well that worked out! Then I have to fight to get in and see her, only to be told she was "underwhelmed" by my scans and then 4 days later telling me she's very concerned. Why the hell was I still with her??? No, I wanted it all gone. No more. Finally, she agreed. Honestly, she had no choice. It was a perfectly reasonable request, I knew the insurance company would approve it and Dr. Silver would too. . I couldn't wait. I just wanted everything done immediately!

I wasn't home an hour before I received a call from Dr. Silver's office, my gynecologist. I had been with this office for so long and one of his nurses had been there as far back as I could remember. They had my surgery scheduled already. Knowing my situation and being my doctor for nearly 25 years now, Dr. Silver had gotten me scheduled for September 12! Ugh. The second week of school! I had no choice. I needed this done. I had to first have an appointment with him to get more blood work done, sign papers and talk about my options. He was a conservative doctor and I knew he would try to get me to understand that a full hysterectomy wasn't necessary. I wasn't budging. I talked to him about it years before but thought with a 3% chance, it wasn't worth it. What were the chances? I mean 3% reoccurance? I was 97% clean. Meteorologists don't give you 97%. So I didn't pursue it. My mistake. Maybe I never would have been in this situation if I did. Hind sight is ALWAYS 20-20!

I met with Dr. Silver, and as expected he did talk to me about other options. No. I held firm on this one. He didn't argue. So we were set for the 12th. I hated to miss the first days of school. Especially with the kindergarten classes. Poor babies are getting used to so much and I really like to keep the status quo. But, no choice. The lupron shots made menopause come on hard and fast. At least my body could start adjusting permanently. I wasn't worried about surgery at all. I never had any issues. I knew I would bounce right back. Usually doctor's orders are a minimum of 2 to 6 weeks off. No way. Maybe 2. I would get in more trouble sitting home. At least at school I didn't lift. I could sit if I needed to. Dr. Silver knew me all too well so he promised at least listen to me if I felt good enough to go back. I had lost the summer, the fatigue seemed to be getting better, I couldn't just cool my heels any longer. I was stir crazy.

The morning of my surgery came. Bob drove me and stayed for a while. This was the hardest part for him. I know he felt guilty about not being able to stay, but with a struggling business to run, he needed to be at the restaurant. He stayed with me as I was being prepped and then Gina came to relieve him. Followed by Lisa. My tagteam! No amount of argument from me would have kept them away. Surgery went off without a hitch. They biopsied the organs and did a specialized wash in the surgical area to make sure there isn't any sign of cancer. Thank God, none. I was clean.

I was expecting to go home late that afternoon. I would have to do the normal things required for release after outpatient surgery. Sitting up, go to the bathroom, walk, drink. Never did I have any issues coming out of anesthesia, until now. I couldn't sit up without becoming nauseous and vomiting. For the first time in my life I had to use the bedpan. What the hell was going on? Laying there, knowing full well something was wrong, I knew there was no way I was going home that night. Dr. Silver had given me the option as I came out of surgery. I told the nurses this has never happened. I decided to stay. I figured let them get me in a room so Lisa could go home. I felt guilty. I was still hooked up with an IV for saline and an anti- nausea drug. Then I heard the nurse as she was checking the IV bags. Commenting to another nurse, "We need to get her another zofran before she goes up to the room." " ZOFRAN? That's what you used, that's why I' m like this! " Zofran was the same damn anti – nausea drug that made me sick while I was getting chemotherapy. " Nomore! " I said to them. After being on it for several hours I knew it would take awhile to clear my system. They got me up to a room, finally, and I was starting to feel a bit better, although laying down for several hours had my back spasming horribly. My sciatica was down both legs. Surgery pain has never, ever been worse than the back pain I suffered from.

The hospital I had the surgery in was not my doctor's usual choice for surgery. Only because his office was attached to another hospital and that was where all the area babies were born. But, knowing that it was imperative that my surgery take place as soon as possible, he went out of his zone. The nurse on the floor I was put on was over run with patients. Having found out that she had been responsible for 13 patients, including me, on that shift. I knew I wouldn't need her much now that I figured out what my issue was, but I needed so pain medicine, badly. I was exhausted and just wanted to sleep but I was reeling in pain from my back. I was so thankful that Dr. Silver knew me so well, he immediately approved some strong meds and told the charge nurse that I'd I felt well early in the am, any time after 7 am, he would discharge me by phone. God, I loved that man. He made my life so easy!

I was still hooked up to the IV, saline only when the nurse walked back in. Intravenously, she gave me a pain medicine that immediately, and I mean immediately stopped all pain in my back. Holy shit, I was going of be able to sleep. Knowing I didn't need the IV anymore. I asked if she could please take it out of me. She unhooked me from the bag and then did something quite unusual. She left the tubing connected to the IV still in my arm. Her thought process was in case I needed anything they didn't have to put another IV in me. I was starting to doze off already. It could have been more than a minute. I just wanted to sleep. She left and I rolled over on my side, drifting off. I felt something tickle my arm. I brushed at it, with my eyes closed. annoyed, because I wanted to sleep. It was wet. I struggled to open my eyes to see that I was bleeding out! She never capped off the tubing. I'm watching my blood flow out of the tube onto the bed. I started screaming! I started pushing the nurse buttons. No one came! " HELP! SOMEONE HELP ME!!!!! " Finally an orderly came in and I said I need help! In broken english he's telling me he's not a nurse! Showing him my arm, screaming, "GO FIND ONE NOW!!!!!" She walked back in, like nothing was wrong, took out the IV and all I could think about is if I passed out, I would have died! With 12 other patients, I was low on the totem poll! With all that medicine in me, I swear, it took a good half hour for me to settle down. I got through the rest of the night, insisting once the shift change happened at 7am, to call Dr. Silver....I wanted to go home!

As promised, he released me soon after 7am. That worked out perfectly. Bob could pick me up, drop me off at home and I could rest. I really didn't feel too bad. It was my back that continued to be the issue. Asta and Zeppelyn were so happy I was home. Poor Asta had a bad night waiting for me. I worried about the stress she would suffer from because I wasn't home. But she was doing ok. The anti seizures medicines seemed to be working beautifully! I ended up taking 2 full weeks off from school. I would get tired quickly and I knew this was much more that just surgery. My body was going through some major trauma. Two weeks off wasn't going to kill me.

We were in the midst of a beautiful Fall. September was just gorgeous. But as the weather started to change I started to have more issues with my neck. Stiffness was getting worse, tingling and numbness in both arms and hands was getting worse. I was having a lot of trouble sleeping lately, being unable to find a comfortable position. As the end of the month approached, my numbers dropped even more. I finally felt like I was coming around. My stomach was swollen and very bloated, but there was nothing at all I could do for that for a while. I had to heal on the inside first and give my body a chance to get used to the post menopausal me.

Here I was, late September 2014, in the midst of the worst year of our lives, and I found myself so happy and grateful one Friday afternoon. I was going down to the restaurant for a bit, just to show my face. I wasn't down there too much anymore and I liked to go in and just see some of our customers that knew what I was going through. So many people would inquire about me and expressed positive thoughts and kept me in there prayers. It felt good. As I was driving, I had my conversations with God quite a bit. I said prayers, I said novenas when I knew something was coming up, but mostly now, it was like God was next to me. I just talked like HE was in the passenger seat. I started thinking how I need to pay this forward. Not sure what I could do, but I did know the person to contact.

In 2004-2005 when I first went through cancer, she worked at the boutique at the Regional Cancer Center. Bob and I had a wedding to attend and I was wearing a wrap around dress. I loved the series, SEX AND THE CITY, and I just happened to see the episode where Samantha had fake nipples. So I wandered into the boutique figuring where else would I go? Now, maybe you can figure out by reading so far that I am a bit loud, absolutely not politically correct and have a habit at times to just say it like it is. So much to the point that the first months of the restaurant being open, Bob would yell to me upon unlocking door to " PUT YOUR FILTER ON!" Imagine that, at 51, I needed a filter! I walked in, in full wig, and said, " Hi, I need nipples, and I know they make them because Samantha from Sex and the City had them on. She looked at me and howled. We became instant friends. Not close, like talking everyday, but we had a connection. Instantly. She was a sweetheart and through the years her position changed and was now a patient navigator. This was the perfect job for her. She was an amazingly upbeat person. And she cared. And you knew she cared. And I know I was not the only woman she connected with. She had a gift and anyone that had to deal with breast cancer and met her, was very lucky. So I called her. I was meaning to give her a call to let her know I was in remission anyway, but now, maybe she could give me an idea of how I could pay it forward. Volunteering? Maybe, but I knew I had to wait until the new year.

I called the imaging center, where her office was located, and like always, when the receptionist asked for my name, I was put right through. She was happy to hear from me, she told me that she was thinking about me and had every intention of calling me to see how I was. She had been on vacation, so I brought her up to speed. Upon telling her the reason for my call, she didn't hesitate. " I know exactly what you can do." Wow, I didn't expect this, not this fast." "What?" Then she changed my life. " I want you to speak at the Mayor's Breast Cancer Luncheon and Fundraiser in October.." Speechless, well almost…. I said, " Shit, I wish I called you next month!" We both laughed. I didn't know what to say. She told me I would be perfect for it. All that I have gone through, my positivity, my faith, my journey. I had never spoke in front of anyone before. I told her that I would think about it. Give me a week and I would let her know.

I went on to the restaurant, told Bob and he was immediately on her side. He said I had too. I knew until I found the words I couldn't make up my mind. Words came very easily for me. So I went home and started writing the speech. I had found out that it needed to be around 10 minutes. Not longer, this was done on a Friday, during lunch, and about 250 people took long lunches to attend. It was sold out yearly, and they would raise a considerable amount of money. The pressure was on.

How hard could this be? So I sat and wrote, and wrote and wrote. I wrote the guts of that speech in about 45 minutes. The following week I called her, yes, I would be honored to speak. Why is it, that you can make a doctor's appointment 6 months in advance and everything you need to do is on that day?! The luncheon was October 24th. My Sloan-Kettering follow up was, yes, wait for it....October 24th! Ugh! I called New York immediately and was lucky enough to get an appointment for the week after my appointment, October 30. Crisis deferred.

I remember waking up one early October morning to numbness all under my arm and in the mastectomy area. I hadn't had this issue since before my I had my diagnosis. I knew that it was probably due to the accident, but being in my present situation, I really was not in a position to make a mistake. It had now been 6 months since any scans had been done. I wanted to have one done, just to be sure. I called Dr. Jonas's office. As I was on hold, naturally, I noticed on my calendar that I didn't have an appointment at the end of the month, but mid November. Why did I do that? Did I do that? I was still going to have my blood work done at the end of the month, I certainly didn't want to put off my appointment for 2 weeks. I was on a cycle that worked, oh well, I thought, I'll change that appointment while I'm on the phone. I hit the prompt to make a new appointment, shit, right to voicemail. I called back again, and again voicemail. I left a message on Julie's voicemail, it was impossible to get through to this office. "Hi, it's Lorrie Markason, I'm having a lot of numbness under my arm and in my mastectomy site, I haven't had this since before my treatment started and I wanted Dr.

Jonas to order a scan. And I needed to change my appointment. " Later that afternoon, Julie called me back. " Hi Lorrie, it's Julie from Dr. Jonas's office. She wanted me to tell you that she doesn't want to scan you and that the numbness is from the accident." I couldn't believe this. " What?? I told you I want a scan!" Julie continued," No scan, if you want a scan you need to call your primary doctor." Now I was pissed. " Why the hell would I call my primary for a scan when I'm calling my cancer doctor to check on the cancer???" We went back and forth for a few minutes before I got so damn aggravated. " Fine, whatever. Oh, before you hang up I need to change my appointment." She comes right back at me, " No, that's when she wants to see you." Really? I have to fight about a damn appointment? Can I ever call this office without getting so aggravated and stressed? I told Julie that I wanted to change the appointment, period. "Well, I'll have to get back to you Lorrie..." Enough, I hung up on her. I immediately called my primary doctor, explained the situation to the receptionist, who's only response was a loud gasp. No one could believe that this was what you had to deal with every damn time you called. She told me to hang on while she checked if they needed prior approval before scheduling. I was placed on hold. While I was on hold my other line rang. I knew the number, it was Dr. Jonas's office. I took the call. It was Dr. Jonas. This was the back and forth. " Lorrie, it's Dr. Jonas, what's the problem now?" I thought I was just thinking it but it can out of my mouth, "What's my problem now? Really? I want a scan run because I need to be sure that this numbness is from the accident and not cancer." " Lorrie, it's from that accident, you know that!" "Really, I know for sure? I assume it is but I'm not in a position to have mistakes made. Remember, at first you were underwhelmed before you were very concerned!" She wasn't happy with me at all. " Well what kind of scan do you want, after all, we can't go on a fishing expedition!" I couldn't believe this is how a doctor, talking to a patient with stage 4 cancer is being treated! " Well let's see, a CT scan, PET scan, PICK ONE, YOU ARE THE DOCTOR, AREN'T YOU??" She finally agreed to a CT scan. I would have rather have had a PET but I just couldn't stand her anymore. " Oh by the way, I need to change the appointment so could you get me back to the receptionist?" " Well, I talked to the receptionist and she said that's when you wanted to come in." " Oh really? Because Julie just told me that was when you wanted to see me. " Silence. She switched me back over and I changed my appointment. That was it. I needed to find another doctor, I should have left along time ago. New York was at the end of October, I'll see if I could get a name of a doctor from them.

She got me in within a week for my scan, it was either Thursday or Friday, I can't honestly remember. It was a long weekend, Columbus Day weekend, so I wouldn't hear anything until at least Tuesday. Or I should say I would have to start calling on Tuesday because I knew they wouldn't call. The level of incompetence was staggering. We had decided to put our Zeppelyn down. We had looked for every reason to keep him alive. Now the weather was changing. It was getting colder and he wasn't going to be able to move in the snow and ice. As it was, he wouldn't move all day unless and until he had to go out, and most of the time that resulted in him having an accident in the house. My rugs were taking a beating. Even the kids had come to terms with it. They saw the suffering. When Ali had come to me and say, " Mom, Zeppelyn is in pain. I want to cry looking at him. I think it's time." It was.

The kids were all off on that Monday. The night before they all slept on the family room floor with him. He was so loved. We gave him such a great life. Returned to the animal shelter twice for being overly aggressive. Not at all. He was a german shepherd. He was an alpha male. He was the best shepherd we had ever had. It was brutal. Bob and I drove him up. He knew. They know. He was shaking as we got him into the car. He was a huge dog. I sat with him. I hugged him and cried. I knew Nonnie would be waiting for him. After all, she bought him for me during my chemotherapy treatments. Nonnie loved him. It was peaceful. I was on the floor with him. I told him I loved him. He licked my face. As life left him I wouldn't let him go. Bob was crying. The vetenarian gave us a few minutes alone. I didn't want to leave him. Bob literally had to drag me off the floor. It had to be done. We knew that. It just didn't make it any easier.

We returned home to an extremely somber house. The kids were so sad. Asta knew something was wrong. She was sniffing his collar and the leash. She wanted to go out, to come back in, she was running up and down the hall. She was looking for him. I could see the stress level in her rising. It never occurred to me. She would be alone now at home. Granted, it wasn't hours that she would be alone. Ali' s work hours varied. I was home til 11am. Bob was gone all day. The kids in school got out and home by 2:30. Still, I worried about the stress and seizures, which could easily trigger them. That entire week I wanted exact schedules for everyone. I wanted her to be home alone as least amount of time as possible. Everyday I would leave 5 minutes before I started at the school, so thankful we lived that close to work. At the end of my day, I couldn't get out of there fast enough.

About mid week, I got home and like usual, I laid down to rest on the couch. All of a sudden Asta jumps on me, licking my face, crying, very agitated. Something was very wrong. I got up. I looked around the room trying to figure out what was wrong. Walking into the living room I noticed something on the couch. It was wet. Foamy. Oh no. Please God no. She had another seizure and came out of it. I could smell it. During a seizure a very foul smell is released from the rectum. I remembered that all too well. We were 2 months clear of any seizure. Why now? I called Bernie. She was so familiar with this that I felt more comfortable speaking to her first. She told me that it was very common. It was called a breakthrough seizure. It happens. It probably won't happen again for a few months but it will happen again. I called the vet. She said the same thing. I relaxed a bit. Dear Lord, no more. I was instructed to give her an additional phenobarbital then and if it ever happened again.

It was Sunday morning and I had to run out to the store and make a return. Everyone would be home so I felt comfortable leaving Asta. As I was walking through the store, my phone rang. Naturally I'm frantically looking for it afraid that Asta had another seizure. But it was a friend that I had only been in contact with through facebook. Odd for him to call me. He told me how sorry he was over the loss of our Zeppelyn. Gave me some encouraging words regarding the year from hell we were having. Then he got to the point. He had a gorgeous male shepherd 4 ½ years old and he wasn't able to keep him anymore. He was busy, never home and the dog was just not getting what he needed. Knowing my love for this breed, he asked if I could take him. I was so not prepared for this and I told him hat we were going through with Asta. I knew the stress of losing Zeppelyn and a huge part of this and I couldn't stress her anymore. I hoped he would find a good home and he said he would keep looking. He just wouldn't him away to anyone. I felt guilty but I knew I did the right thing. I finished up my errands and returned home.

I just had walked in the door and within seconds Regina started yelling to me. Asta was head first in her closet, making biting sounds. It was the beginning of another seizure. It wasn't long lasting and she came out of it within a few minutes. Now what? I gave her another phenobarbital, as I was instructed to do. She was fine the rest of the day. My stress level was rising. We didn't have the money for another emergency visit. Just walking through those doors would cost us $1300. We just could not do it. I prayed so hard. Please Lord, don't take her from me. My baby. 3 ½ years old.

It started around 6 pm Sunday night. 3 hours later, it happened again. 3 hours later, it happened again. Two emergency calls to our vet at a cost of $50 per call. We were desperate. They couldn't do anything. We would have to transport her to the emergency vets office. We didn't have the money. With each seizure, I gave her more medicine. With each seizure, it took longer for her to come out. They were violent seizures. We all stayed up all night. They were coming every 15 minutes at one point. I knew she was dying. This couldn't be happening. It was early Monday morning. One week to the day we put Zeppelyn down. Asta, at one point sat up, she went through a 3 hour period with no seizures. I thought maybe all the medicine had finally taken hold. I was laying on the floor with her. Her face to my nose. I petted her face and told her I loved her. She licked me. She looked at me right in my eyes. I always said I thought she had human qualities. She always acted like she knew exactly what I was saying. She laid down and I laid next to her on the floor. I hugged her all night.

Morning came and with morning so did the seizures. One after another. She wasn't coming out of them at all. She was gone. She had to be brain dead by this time. I was hysterical. So were the kids. We had to take her up to the vet. Even if we had the money, at this point, we had no choice but to put her down. I couldn't go. I hit my limit. I was inconsolable. Bob went with Ali. I carried her to the car. She was limp. She was gone. Her heart was the only thing keeping her alive. I couldn't breathe. I couldn't eat. I couldn't sleep. All I did was cry. A deep, heaving cry that I haven't had since my father died. We, as a family, were beaten down. We lost 2 dogs in 7 days. October 13 and October 20. I was days away from giving the first speech of my life and here I am, my world in complete disarray. I was by far the worst. The kids didn't know what to do with me. I lost 6 lbs in a week. I had no will to fight anything. For the first few days I did nothing but cry. Everything was automatic. I walked into a store and ran into a friend who knew from facebook what had happened. He didn't say anything to me but made a sad face. That was all it took, I was hysterical in the middle of the store.

The next week was just brutal. Coming home to an empty house, no tail wagging at the door. No dog hair, my windows were clean. Everyone hated coming home. Zach and Regina would get off the bus and they would force themselves to look straight ahead, they always looked in the window to see Asta waiting for them. Tears flowed constantly. I couldn't throw her medicine out. Moving the dogs dishes was like a knife in the heart. My kids never lived without a dog in the house. I swore no more dogs. I couldn't bear this feeling anymore. But as I said it, I knew it wouldn't be true. We were dog people, but my heart hurt. Everyone's did. But she was mine. I found her, I drove to get her, I took care of the dogs. Being home a lot, I was mommy to them too.

My speech was written. I had to tweek it here and there. Words come easy for me, thankfully because at this point I couldn't function at all. I had practiced it a few times in from of my family. I timed myself alone. But this week with her dying, I didn't look at it at all. I would sit in the kitchen at the breakfast bar and feel for her under my feet. It was like I kept reliving it. The heavy, heaving sobs were uncontrollable. I didn't understand. I felt like I was, my family was, being punished. I said so many prayers, asked for strength in the face of the most horrifying weakness that I had ever felt. How many hits can one family take in the course of a year? We pushed through. What choice to we have? Do we lay down and die? Do we quit? Do we start hating others for their successes while we are drowning in our sorrows? Life isn't fair. I used to tell my kids that all the time. In their little worlds as children a simple, " no it's time for bed" would throw them into fits, crying that " it's not fair." Well we were living it. Bad things happen to good people all the time. There was no explaining it further than that. Realizations would follow. God works in mysterious ways.

My friend had called me again that week, on a Thursday, the day before my speech. I hesitated to answer because I prayed that he wouldn't ask me again about his dog. And his dog was beautiful. I had seen pictures through the years that he had posted. Absolutely gorgeous. He didn't mention it. He asked how I was, told me he was thinking about me and wished me luck on the speech that I would give the next day.

My kids took that Friday off from school. My inlaws were coming, Bob was able to leave the restaurant and I had several friends there. . Gina's parents were there too. Never having done this before, I found it odd that I wasn't the slightest bit nervous. 250 people had showed up to hear me this year. It was truly an honor to be asked. There were politicians, several in the professional fields, policemen. Everyone, unfortunately has been affected by cancer, one way or another. Mothers, fathers, children, grandparents, aunts and uncles. There is no adult you could talk to that doesn't have a story. That alone brings us all together. There was a lot of support for breast cancer. I was grateful for that.

The Mayor's wife got up to speak first. And then introduced her husband's secretary who is the one responsible for getting this all together. As it turns out, she is also a friend. She went ahead and gave a brief summary of me and I took the microphone. Deep breath in. I started in. I have a habit of speaking fast so I did my best to slow it down and still keeping it right around the 10 minute mark.

I did it. I nailed it….or so I was told. Looking out into the audience, I heard the gasps, I saw the tears and I heard the laughter. Walking back over to my family, seeing my inlaws, my husband, my kids and friends all in tears. All waiting to hug me. I felt good. I felt strong.

I went back to my seat to find the Mayor approaching me. Wishing me well and congratulating me on a speech well done. Gina's dad said it was very inspirational and I should think about being a motivational speaker. Bob just hugged me and was totally wowed. Over and over again, he just said," you nailed it". I appreciated all of the praise, not sure if I was really worthy of it. But it was obvious, the ability to write and speak was inherited directly from my mother. Finally! Something positive!

As I was finishing up my lunch, 2 women approached me. I could see that they were mother and daughter. The daughter, introduced herself to me and said that she had to come over because her girls are in Harts Hill School too! Small world! When I realized who her kids were, I remembered that in the beginning of the school year a second grader approached me. Quietly she whispered in my ear that her mom had cancer. I was sick for her. Kids impacted by adult illnesses that as adults we sometimes have a hard time dealing with. I hugged her and took her by the hand. I walked her away from earshot of any other children. I kneeled down, so I was eye to eye with her and said. " You know what? I have cancer too." My hope was if she could see me looking normal and there everyday, maybe she would not worry so much." It's such a hard line to cross with children and I didn't want to overstep my boundaries. Now, seeing this woman in front of me, a beautiful woman who I never would have thought to be sick. We held hands and talked for a bit. Finding out that she too had formerly had my doctor. More and more reasons to walk away. Things overlooked, um, sounded familiar!

I had gotten up at this point to use the restroom when a woman who was sitting at a table called out to me. I knew who she was because she was well known in the area. She held a doctorate in business management and was the executive director of the Women's Business Center of New York State. She had won countless awards for outstanding services in a multitude of business areas. Awards ranging from local to national levels. She had also written several books. This was a woman who knew how to get things done. Calling out to me, I stopped and her outstretched hand was offered to me. I held her hand and she congratulated me on my speech but she took it farther. "You need to write a book." She handed me her business card and said, " Call me!" I smiled and thanked her. I felt like I was in a very awkward situation and I didn't know how to respond. After all, me? I couldn't understand how I could write one? What would I say?

I was flattered with the offer. Actually, she had stopped me twice more before the she had left to tell me that I had to write a book. I took the card home. I kept it on my dresser, not really sure what do do with it.

It happened again! Being so heavy hearted regarding my dogs for the past few weeks I had realized that I still had not heard anything on the CT scan done the week prior to my speech. I was due in on the following Wednesday, the 29th and the following day I would be in New York. I would just wait. I had no other choice being the weekend.

It was Saturday, Bob was at the restaurant. I was home and so were the kids. My cell rings and I see its my friend with the shepherd. Again, I hesitated. I didn't want to be asked. The house was horrible. Too quiet. But I answered. He asked how the luncheon went, how my speech was and we continued with the small talk for a bit. Then he started," Lorrie, I know this is your dog. I know it. I don't want to give him to just anyone and I know how much you love this breed. You know not any dog owner can own a shepherd. You understand the breed." He was right, on all accounts. Ali had walked into the room because I started to cry. I told him I can't. I'm not ready. My kids weren't ready. I was so heartbroken over Asta that I couldn't imagine another dog in the house right now, no matter how horrible it was. Then Ali chimed in. " Mom, we've all been talking and we can't stand it anymore. We all loved Asta, but she's not coming back. We need a dog. We don't like coming home. Please, can we go see him?" I was shocked. I didn't see this coming at all. I asked if she was sure, Zach came out and repeated the same thing. I told him we would be over shortly to look at him.
That's all it took. We walked in to see this absolutely gorgeous animal. Ozzie, that was a sign. All our dogs with the exception of Asta were named for rock and rollers. I had Ozzie Osborne in front of me. He was a big dog, not quite as big as Zeppelyn but I knew he would be. Male shepherds take til 4 or 5 to really fill out. They get manes like lions. And he had Asta's colors. He was a combination of both our dogs. Can this be possible? In 3 weeks time we put down 2 dogs and have a combination of the two dogs sitting in front of us needing a home. Don't tell me this wasn't a divine intervention. There are no co incidents in life. Not like this, no way. I told him that I wanted Bob to see him. Our restaurant was not too far from his house. Little did I know that Bernie and Gina were on a mission to buy me a puppy.

Ready to spend whatever was necessary to bring me out of this funk. The kids and I drove over to the restaurant. Walking into Bob's office, he knew something was up. I told him about Ozzie. He shook his head. He couldn't believe that I would even consider it. The kids told them their feelings. He felt the same way. The kids went home and we drove back over so Bob could meet Ozzie. Bob had a soft heart for dogs. This was just a formality. The kids and I had already made up our minds, but it was good sometimes for Bob to think he had a say in things.

Trying to figure out an arrangement to take Ozzie, I had made it clear that the week coming up was filled with doctor's appointments. I had my follow up with New York and my appointment and bloodwork with Dr. Jonas. I was anxious for my CT results. Wednesday I would find out everything. I didn't want to take Ozzie all at once. Shepherds are horribly high strung and I wasn't going to put another dog into too much stress all at once. It wasn't necessary. I told him I would take Ozzie everyday for a few hours, returning him at night for that week, with the exception of Thursday, which was my trip to Sloan-Kettering. Friday was Halloween and I wasn't sure if it was a good idea that night or not. One way or the other, we would take care of him as of November 1st.

While I always considered myself with a deep faith, we all have points in our life that we just don't understand. I never questioned "IF" there was a God. I just wished I understood my path. The big picture, as we are told, is the picture that we cannot see. By faith we walk. Trusting God will lead us down the correct path. " FAITH IS BELIEVING IN THAT WHICH YOU CANNOT SEE."

It had been nearly 2 years of turmoil. Starting with the huge fight Ali was involved in on New Year's Eve heading into 2013, to Bob's emergency surgery, to the loss of his job, to the first business venture that didn't pan out, to my cancer, to my car accident, to the loss of our dogs, to the still in question success or failure of the restaurant which was still losing money monthly. Something had to give. I did question why God gave us all these trials. I knew God gave me the strength to continue my battles. In my prayers I asked for strength for my family too. All of us were battling. I knew the answer, instinctively, then, at that moment, like someone, God maybe, answered the question. The closer I became to God, the closer Bob became to God, the more the devil creates havoc. Trying to pull those who believe the most away. Wanting those to question and walk away from their faith. Through all of this, deep in my soul, I knew my family would be alright. Looking at all that I just wrote, all that had happened to us as a family, to me personally, anyone could look at me and question how, my God how I could still have faith? But I did. And it was deep. Bob and I were teaching our children faith. There is nothing like learning a lesson by living it. They saw the strength and determination in their father to work as hard as needed be to make this restaurant successful. They saw me live everyday, determined not to let cancer win. The devil created this havoc. And God gave us all the will, the determination, the strength to keep fighting. Cancer would learn that it picked the wrong bitch. We would fight through every obstacle that pushed its way in front of us. And we would defeat it. Everything, one by one. Together. We would not be pulled apart as a family. It really was a shame, our oldest, has missed an important lesson. I felt sorry for him. Everything in his world was superficial. Everything in his relationship was based on a lie. It wouldn't last. There was no stable foundation. He had hurt his brother and sisters deeply with his actions. I hope someday they could and would forgive him. Either way, the loss was all his, and it was a deep loss. But when you have to convince people what they have missed out of, it's not worth it. What a shame.

Chapter 11

The kids were so excited. I was going to pick Ozzie up right after I got out of school on Monday. By the time I would get home, they would be there too. It was good to see happiness again, the house really needed it. That Monday was gorgeous, a Bob was home due to the restaurant closing on Sunday and Monday. We decided to keep the schedule of 2 days closed in a row. Bob rarely had 2 days off in a row running all those restaurants for all those years. He needed to decompress, I needed things done around the house, and we figured it was best not to keep changing schedules around.

Ozzie connected with me immediately, I knew it the night we met. This moose of a dog was the biggest baby I have ever met. Horrible car rider. He cried and barked and whined. We got home and he sniffed around and I let him out into the backyard. Everyone was out there raking and getting things ready for winter. Zach started playing ball with him. He sniffed around, not looking too anxious, lifted his leg on every available plant he could find. I had a feeling this transition was going to be relatively easy. He came inside later on, walking around the house, getting his bearings. He knew exactly where Asta and Zeppelyn's favorite places were. He would stop and sniff. It made me sad. We took him back later that night, looking forward to tomorrow afternoon to get him again.

I did my blood work Tuesday morning, preparing for the next days appointment with Dr. Jonas. Fully intending to be battle ready. It was funny, Julie seemed to make herself scarce when I was around. She was probably afraid I would grab her by the throat if I saw her. She would have been right, she needed it. I walked in Tuesday after my school job ended, anxious for my results and numbers. Dr. Jonas walked in smiling, it was a shame, she could be quite pleasant, as long as you took her word for law and didn't question anything. "Well, I told you so." She says to me, nice way of starting out I thought, she threw the gauntlet down. " The numbness and tingling is coming all from your accident. Your CT Scan looks great! I was relieved. I knew it had to be, and I told her just that, but for the fact that I am not in a position to assume anything. It would be foolish to, especially with today's medical tools.

And the fact that I was 6 months into a treatment. She wasn't going to win with me. Period. My tumor markers were still falling. It was a great visit. Positive news. Sloan-Kettering tomorrow. I prayed that Dr. Camen would back it all up!

I walked out of there with an appointment for the end of December, she was ready to push me back to bi monthly appointments but monthly blood work. All I had to do was call in for my blood results. Great! Calling for numbers. She was so delusional thinking that was easier for me. She also was going to schedule a bone density test due to the aromasin could or would eventually cause some bone deterioration. She refused to PET scan me. I had made a decision, I was leaving, I would find a new doctor, I wasn't going to fight her anymore. Off I went to go get Ozzie for a few hours.

He settled in even better, spending most of the time indoors. I had a feeling that he was left outside a lot, alone, because he would not like to be outside at all unless people were around him. He discovered out how comfortable furniture was. But he refused to venture downstairs to the mancave, never having access to stairs before. I called my friend to remind him that I wasn't taking him the next day because of our trip to New York and I was going to drop him off around 8pm. He didn't answer, so I texted him. He texted right back, explaining he was a school for his son's something or other. He wasn't sure what time he was going to be home, so just leave him outside. No, no, no...it was freezing, it was dark. I was not going to leave this dog outside. I called Ali to find out what her schedule was for Thursday. We had to leave early to drive down near Brewster, NY to take the MTA line into New York City. It was a 3 ½ hour drive. Then about another hour on the transit line. We were hoping to get back home that night by 8-8:30. Ali was closing, not going in til 1:30. I had her ask if she could go in at 3, this way she was with Ozzie all day, Zach and Regina would be home at 2:30. He would never be alone and I wouldn't worry. I had it all set, I texted him back to tell him we were keeping Ozzie.

Our New York trip was always stressful. It's so much easier to do an overnight, but we just couldn't afford any extras right now. Down and back in one day, we missed the first train literally by minutes. Having to wait another hour for another train put us behind. We got to Grand

Central Station 10 minutes prior to my appointment. Running through that mammoth place, having no clue if we went out the closest door to our destination, we ran out and into a cab stand with about 20 people on front of us. I wanted to scream. I did scream, but this was New York, no one looked twice at me. I called the office to tell them our situation. They were so polite. We finally got there about 40 minutes late.

Bob met Dr. Camen, impressed at how young she was. Looking over my reports, she had nothing new since my first appointment back in June. Wow! Really? Dr. Jonas was supposed to be sending my blood results to her monthly. She walked back out of the office, a bit of anger on her face and had her assistants call for everything. She went ahead with an examination, remembering that we opened a restaurant, her memory was remarkable, honing in on little details that I would have thought would have been soon forgotten.

She finally had my results from July to October in her hand. My CT scan looked great. She questioned me about other scans. The PET scan in particular. I had told her the argument that I had with Dr. Jonas. Her mouth went into a straight line. I could see that she was holding back, not wanting to insult another doctor. "You should be scanned every 3-4 months." I told her that I had enough and was looking for a new doctor. I didn't have to be seen again until December and I had only made that appointment so no one questioned my motives. I wanted to be sure if something happened I always remained under the care of someone. Dr. Camen nodded her head. She told me to find a doctor I absolutely love and have him send me all my records. She also said that I couldn't be doing any better and it wasn't necessary for me to continue to drive all the way for this. God forbid anything changed, call and make an appointment. But until that time, there was nothing more she could do. She also went on about the 2nd biopsy. She reiterated that it was never sent to them like she had asked Dr. Jonas to do. Thankfully the node was not palpable anymore and there wasn't anyway to biopsy it. It was so obvious that Dr. Jonas's ego was in the way and more important than her patients results. I had waited way too long to change.

The following day, Friday, was Halloween, but me not being a big fan of Halloween, I considered it the actual start day to my Christmas Season.

Well, I had already put up the tree in our bedroom and the Nativity scene in the Living Room, but it became a tradition that as the kids were ringing the doorbell for treats that I would be putting up my Angel tree. This was a whopping tree with a span of close to 4 feet wide. Several layers went on it and it would take me literally 3 days, on and off to get it fully done. Ozzie was now a member of the family. He was acting right at home.

I went to school that day, very anxious to find the little girl whose mom had cancer. Having forgotten to ask Dr. Camen about referring someone, I thought I would see who she used. I got her number and texted her immediately. She responded right back and actually said that her doctor was referred by Memorial Sloan- Kettering! Can't ask for more than that. I planned on calling later that day, but with my usual schedule after school, I came home, ate and took a long nap. It was a long week. By the time I woke up it was too late to call. Monday. Monday, I had to call.

Monday morning I received a phone call from Dr. Jonas's office. I was scheduled for a bone scan. Ugh, another scan. I knew every one was necessary, hell, I asked for some! But I was so sick and tired of doctors. It wears on you. I already had started taking calcium supplements to counter any issues. All through this, I took a proactive approach. I had to keep my body strong. I kept busy otherwise getting ready for Thanksgiving. I remembered back a few months when I first got my diagnosis, I wondered if I would live to see this Christmas or was this my last? Those first few weeks were so difficult. It seemed like a lifetime ago. The months were flying by.

I called the new doctors office to make an appointment, unfortunately, there was no way they could get me in prior to the end of November. I was glad I hadn't said anything to Dr. Jonas about leaving. I was going to have blood work and call in for results. The new office told me have the blood work as usual and they would schedule an appointment at the end of December, but with the last 2 weeks of December being holidays, I was now looking at the first week of January. I would only be 7 days late on blood work. I figured that was alright. I couldn't put off this change any longer.

Thanksgiving week! The Christmas season was officially upon us! Things were a bit different this year. For the past several Thanksgiving, friends of ours would join us for Thanksgiving. One year they just decided that they wanted to go where they wanted to go instead of having to go with families. Both were close to their own, and everyone was ok with it all. So every year it was at our house or theirs. If it was at our house, I would cook and Tracy would do appetizers and desserts. . Then the following year it was at their house and the opposite would happen. But this year they had separated. It was hard on them but both Bob and I thought it was the best thing. We loved them both, took no sides and would be brutally honest about how we felt. Divorce wasn't going to change friendships. And it was made easier when they would be amicable towards each other. There were 2 girls involved, we were glad they really tried to be adult about it.

This year it would be just my in -laws with us. We would have friends stop over later. My traditions continued. I would put the movie " MIRACLE ON 34Th STREET" on, the original, as I cooked. I never watched the remake. Some movies are just better off left alone. We would eat mid afternoon, Bob had football on, we played some family games and after my in -laws would go, we would watch the movie "TRAINS, PLAINS and AUTOMOBILES." Bob and I watched that movie every Thanksgiving together since our first Thanksgiving together back in 1989. My house was completely decorated. My kitchen was all my childhood memories. I had all the character figures from SANTA CLAUS IS COMIN TO TOWN, RUDOLPH THE RED NOSED REINDEER and A CHARLIE BROWN CHRISTMAS. I was never able to find FROSTY THE SNOWMAN. But trust me, I keep looking! Over my kitchen cupboards I had Elves popping out of cups. The word BELIEVE, such a prominent word in my life, was reflected everywhere in my house.

Each room or tree had a different theme. The living room tree was angels. Creams, golds, green, bronzes, white lights. Very classy. My dining room was connected to my living room so everything blended. My family room opened to my kitchen so I kept that theme of colored lights. A whimsical look. Our family tree was made up entirely of ornaments my kids made through their elementary school years. Every year I would buy an ornament for each of us and ornaments that were family gifts. The kids trees actually matched their rooms at one point but I didn't update the trees because everything was hot glued on. Their trees, pencil trees, were easily picked up and stored downstairs in what Bob called my Christmas tree room. Our bedroom tree matched our room. Black, white, silver and gold all on a white tree. The mancave tree was all about Bob. All sports ornaments, team ornaments and his tree topper was a miniature Jets blinking helmet that I got from QVC several years before. When the kids were younger I had all the outside blow ups on the front lawn. The bus would drop them off and I would embarrass the hell out of them as everyone would look at the Grinch, Scooby-doo, a carousel, a snowman and if he won the championship, a Blow up of the Lowes 48, Jimmie Johnson's NASCAR ride! This year, had new meaning. I was so grateful to be alive. So grateful that the medicines had come so far as to knock cancer down like a house of cards. So many prayers for me. I was so truly Blessed. My work was not done on this earth. I was spared for a reason. God had plans for me.

It was morning, sometime in late November, I was in my bathroom, getting ready for school. I glanced over and the business card from Dr. Laino was sitting there. Dr. Laino was the woman who gave me her business card at the Breast cancer luncheon. I started thinking about all she said. I called her. Answering machine. Hell, what do I have to lose? Right?

Thanksgiving was late this year on the calendar, meaning there was only 4 weeks from Thanksgiving to Christmas. Again, I couldn't believe how fast these days were going by. Back to school the following week and wow! Blood work again! I went down Monday morning and then realized that I had not received a call from Jonas's office regarding my bone density scan that was done 3 weeks prior. Unbelievable. I knew it took a few hours for the blood work to come back. I waited until about 4pm and called the office. What a surprise! Voicemail! I left a message. "Hi, it's Lorrie Markason, I'm calling to get my tumor marker numbers that I had done this morning. No appointment for me this month, Dr. Jonas is seeing me every other month but told me to call for my numbers. By the way, no one ever called me on my bone scan results. So can you look that up too?" Nothing. By mid morning Tuesday, right before I left for school I called and left another message. Nothing. By 4pm Tuesday, I left another message. Nothing. Wednesday morning, another message. Wednesday afternoon I had enough. I called and hit the prompt for making an appointment. Finally I got through. I told the girl I spoke with that I had left a minimum of 5 messages. Unreturned. I want my damn numbers and the bone scan results. Her reply? " No one called you?" I was so damn aggravated! All I wanted was my numbers and I would ask for the fax number to have my records forwarded to the new doctor.

Julie finally had called back and I missed the call. I didn't hear my phone go off. I listened to the voicemail, " Hi Lorrie," oh how irritated she sounded," it's Julie, from Dr. Jonas's office," she sounded as though she was full of self importance," Dr. Jonas wanted you to know that you bone scan is normal and your blood work is good. " THAT'S IT?? That's all you tell me? I was more aggravated than ever. I called the office right back, going right through to the make an appointment prompt. Luckily, some one picked up. It was the one woman who was always nice to me. And I said to her. I waited for 3 days for a phone call, I missed it and I'm told as little information as humanly possible and then she hangs up? I asked for the fax number, I told her I needed to get some information over to her. The following day I went down to the restaurant and faxed a sheet over to her telling her that I have found a new doctor, and to please forward all my medical to the new office. I did this purposely on a Friday. Knowing they usually leave early in Fridays, I figured they'd notice it first thing Monday morning.

I felt so much better after doing that. I took control. No more. I was mad at myself for waiting this long. The following week the office called. They questioned who and why I was requesting my information to go to this doctor. I laughed, could they be that delusional in the office? I told her why, I told her Julie, on top of all the other issues in the office, needed to go. This area was way too small and I asked other people about her. She treated everyone the same. She had no business dealing with the public. And not just the public, the public dealing with cancer for God's sake!

It was the first week of December and I was home, Bob at the restaurant. He calls me to tell me that Dr. Laino stopped in. She got my message but was away for a few weeks. The message cut off and she didn't get my number. She remembered Papa Joes so she stopped down to try us out. She loved us! She loved the restaurant décor, she loved the food, she loved everything. She told Bob to have me call her, we needed to set up a meeting. As soon as possible. I called her the following day and she went on and on about my speech. She was so happy I called and she couldn't understand why we weren't busier at the restaurant. She had contacts, she had advice, she had the ability to put us out there. She wanted Bob to come to the meeting, she was going to go over everything.

We made an appointment for the following week. We went over some things for the restaurant. She talked directly at Bob, it was all him. Then she turned to me. I was so flattered that she thought that much of me, but I was honest, what do I write? I knew it was about cancer, but how do you make a book of just that? She took me through, talked about an outline, and what you are reading here, is the result of Dr. Laino. Talk about an angel coming into my world.

At the onset of my return of cancer, during those awful first months. My worries were everywhere. Me, the kids, Bob, the restaurant, our financial situation. The only thing I didn't worry about was our marriage, no matter what, we were strong. But everything else, unstable. We just needed issues solved. But everything was out of our hands. I was inboxed on facebook by a girl who used to date my brother so long ago. They were so cute together but my brother was so screwed up and she took off. I blamed her at the time not realizing the extent of my brother's problems and it was wrong. Years and years had gone by. She had moved away and through mutual friends, her profile came up on facebook. As soon as I saw her, I inboxed her and apologized for my behavior all those years ago. She was still as sweet and told me she understood. But I felt better telling her. She proceeded to tell me about a novena to the Blessed Mother. MARY, UNDOER OF KNOTS. It was a prayer to our Mother to untie all the knots in our lives. The first time I read it, I cried. It was perfect. It mirrored our lives. I said that novena for months, praying and praying to help us. We were planning on shutting down the restaurant at the end of December. We were out of money, only thing left was our retirement IRA. Then Dr. Laino comes into our world. We felt renewed. We wanted to continue, our feedback was incredibly positive. She begged us to continue. There were absolutely no prospects out there. Bob was signed up for job alerts. In all this time he was called twice for an interview. The second one just weeks before. It was for a national coffee chain. The man that called Bob was the regional manager, he told Bob that getting his resume was like a gift on Christmas morning. He called 2 hours after Bob posted it. He was set to meet with the district manager and this was for a store manager position, well below Bob's ability, but he would take it. One request was that Bob visit 4 area restaurants and preform basically a secret shopper analysis. Workers, signage, cleanliness, lighting, etc. This is what Bob did. He wrote up a very thorough report, commenting on things only a man that has held this position for so long would pick up on. He emailed it and had his interview with a guy 20 years younger. Bob walked out of there like he gave the interview instead of the other way around. The poor guy was selling himself to Bob. This was his life, he knew the restaurant business in and out. He was supposed to have a second interview, which never came. I'm sure the interviewer was so intimidated by Bob that he knew Bob was going to take his job. So, we had come this far, we made it through the first year, we had decided to go for it. We cashed in the IRA. Next year this time, we would be ok or we would be on welfare. I had a deep peacefulness in me. God would sustain us. 2015 was going to be a much better year. I could feel it.

Christmas was almost upon us already. I was able to have my yearly " POLAR EXPRESS" night early this year. I would make cocoa for the kids, hot toddys for the adults, popcorn and it HAD to be snowing outside! I just adore this movie. The theme. It chokes me up. To me, it was always deeper than Santa Claus. It was faith. From the first time I saw this movie. I welled up. I always took it as faith. My heart was full.

Chapter 12

So here I am, sitting in Memorial Sloan – Kettering's waiting room. Waiting to be called for pre-op. Yes, pre-op. Another biopsy. This time I'm doing it right. Something I should have done from the beginning. Hindsight is 20-20. Having things done in New York City may be inconvenient. But it's piece of mind. Between the car ride and train, I feel as though I should have a part in the movie, TRAINS, PLANES and AUTOMOBILES. This is hell on my back and neck. Actually, my entire body hurts. I popped my knee at school this week chasing a kindergartener who had just about enough of school and because of the surgical biopsy, I can't take any of my muscle relaxers or anti imflammatories. This has been so frustrating. Two steps forward, three steps back. All of this is absolutely necessary. Why another biopsy, you ask? Well, let me back up til the first of the year.

January 2015. My new beginning! It was a new beginning! 2013 and especially 2014 turned into the worst years that I can remember, especially 2014. Starting this year off with a new oncologist, so glad I got rid of Dr. Jonas, I was angry at myself for waiting as long as I did. We decided to push forward with the restaurant. This wasn't a hard decision, believe it or not. Our feedback, so incredibly positive, we had invested so much time, money and energy in it we had to go forward. We cashed in our 401 K. Our retirement. Our future. It was frustrating, our feedback was incredible. We had built some very loyal customers. But being in upstate New York, a lot of our customers were snowbirds. Gone south for the winter. So many would inquire about us. People cared. We were honest. We weren't there yet, we were still losing money. We would tell them, " By this time next year we'll either be ok or on welfare." We kind of laughed through it, but it was a completely honest statement. We had the weight of the world on us. Would it ever end?

Driving out to the new offices in Syracuse was so easy that it irritated me even more that I waited. Off the NYS Thruway, literally 40 minutes from my driveway, it was so worth my peace of mind. I prayed I really liked this doctor. There were no options in Utica. Well there were, but they weren't options in my mind. And the need for a local oncologist was necessary. . The one huge difference and the main reason I stayed with Memorial Sloan- Kettering was besides being world renowned, was that you were able to find a medical oncologist for your exact cancer. We finally mastered that trip down. We would drive about 3 hours to a little town called Southeast, NY. From there take the Metro-North commuter train to Grand Central Station. That was about an 1 ½ hour ride. Then a cab ride to the doctor, most times easier said than done. It was hectic, exhausting and back breaking. But we couldn't afford overnights so it was day trips for us.

I drove into Syracuse that January morning making good time. I checked in with the receptionist. I was given all the new patient paperwork and they put a paper bracelet on my wrist and told me a patient navigator would be with me shortly. Soon after I sat, I noticed a group of elderly people walk it. It was a miserable January day. Snowing and blowing and frigidly cold. This winter was brutal. Continuing my paperwork, suddenly there was commotion as one of the elderly gentleman lost his balanced and fell to the floor. I jumped up, as others did, to help, but the receptionist immediately stopped us. She called out a code over the loud speaker and what seemed to be a fraction of a second, an entire response team rushed over, evaluating this man. They were all very professional and I was extremely impressed to see how they handled an unexpected emergency. It couldn't have been more than 3 minutes after the response team came when a doctor walked onto the scene. He just happened to catch my eye, we smiled at each other and he continued towards the elderly man on the floor. Obviously he was either part of this response team or this gentleman's doctor. Either way, I was impressed. These were professionals. I felt as though I had made a good choice. I hoped I liked my doctor was much as I liked the way these people worked.

The patient navigator came to get me as I was thoroughly engrossed in the scene in front of me. My paperwork incomplete, we walked into a room, and she explained their procedures to me. Then she walked me to the elevator and we went to the second floor which were where the actual offices were. I was checked in again and then she said that I would have time to finish my paperwork. After leaving Dr. Jonas's office, how it always was so stressed and confused, seeing how well these people worked together, I knew I was in the right place. That is the best feeling! Feeling secure. Now I only hoped my new doctor was as thorough!

I was called, they checked my bracelet and took me back to check weight and blood pressure. The young nurse was very friendly, easy to talk to, we struck up a conversation about my boots and shopping. As we were talking, the same doctor that was downstairs, attending to the man that had fallen, walked by. He smiled at me and the nurse said, "That's Dr. T, (as I will refer to him) your doctor, he is so nice." I smiled. Things were falling into place. It's funny how things happen. Sometimes you just know you made the right choice. Anxious now to meet him, I was led to a examination room and waited impatiently for him to walk in. It didn't take too long and my impatience came from my excitement that I really found the right doctor. Dr. T walked in, introduced himself and shook my hand. He asked about my reason for changing doctors and his reaction, although it was muted, was noticeable as I explained all that I had gone through. He didn't question me but instead apologized for having to deal with all the unnecessary complications when I was going through a life threatening illness. I had originally got his name from a woman I had met at the Breast cancer luncheon. Ironically, she too had Dr. Jonas and had a very bad experience. So what he was hearing from me wasn't exactly foreign to him. Our conversation continued as he wanted to know all about me. I was extremely comfortable. He made it clear that my opinions and questions were welcome. He reminded me of my Sloan-Kettering doctor. This was a good move.

He told me that it was important for me to be a part of the conversation, a partner in my treatment. How I felt was a huge part of not only the diagnosis but my treatment. Then he shook his head and said, " If I saw you in Wegmans I would never believe you are stage 4." I thanked him for that. I told him that I was strong mentally because of my faith and I would do whatever was necessary to beat this damn cancer. He couldn't believe that Dr. Jonas had let me go this long without scans. He didn't understand. Before I left that day, I was scheduled for a CT and PET SCAN and he talked to me regarding the BRCA genetic testing. I thought about having this test done years back, I actually had a phone call from the doctor's office who would preform the test. Going through a series of questions, she didn't think I was a good candidate for the test. I let it go. Now things were different. I was worried about my girls. So after my appointment with him I stayed and waiting for his nurse practitioner to come in. She would explain the procedure and what it all meant. . All it was is additional bloodwork. I now met 3 of the necessary criteria for having this test done. My original cancer was before the age of 50, I had a reoccurance, and my sister had breast cancer too. This one I was worried about. This test was to check for a mutant gene. Specifically to test if I carried this mutant gene that made me more susceptible to breast cancer. Understanding that if this test came back positive, it meant that I was at a higher risk of developing breast cancer in my right breast. Right now I was being treated as a reoccurrence of the breast cancer that I was treated for in 2004-2005. If I developed breast cancer on my right side it would be a new cancer. I had already decided that if in fact this did come back positive, I would immediately schedule another mastectomy. This test wasn't a guarantee that I would develop breast cancer, just that my risk was higher. That was enough of a risk for me. I had a 3% chance if my cancer coming back, and it did, there was no risk worth it.   I was to see him at the end of January to go over all my results. He had me go in for blood work after my appointment. He was thorough. This was just what I needed. Thank God I changed.

I left that appointment elated. I called Bob immediately, I couldn't contain my excitement! This is so imperative to your care and treatment. Finally, finally this piece of the puzzle was coming together. It was after 5 pm that afternoon at home before I realized I didn't get my numbers! Oh well, I would call in the morning. Then, the most amazing thing happened. At 5:22 that afternoon, Dr. T called. He wanted me to know that my numbers were great! He wished me well and said he would see me at the end of the month for my follow up appointment.

It was back and forth a few times to Syracuse for all these scans. The good thing about it was that all scans were done in the same facility. Instant results, or results as soon as possible. I had my own little Memorial Sloan –Kettering in my backyard and I didn't even know it! I hated the scans. Being pumped with radioactive sugar. Fasting for several hours. Not to mention the stress of laying there, praying that things will be positive. Fighting cancer, there is no shortage of headgames. Brutal, just brutal. It can be tough to keep your chin up day after day. I had my down days. Honestly, they were far and few between, but it happens. We're human. Those are the days that I just bow my head and ask God to give me just a bit more. You have to carry on. We have to. The only other option was letting yourself give up. 6 feet under wasn't an option for me. Ever.

I was due to see my nurse practitioner, Cindy, in February regarding my thyroid. When the new year hit, I promised myself that now that the cancer medicine was in me for a while and that my hysterectomy would be 4 months past, I was ready to kick back into shape. I hated the way I looked. It was so hard to believe that the CHRISTMAS before I knew I had cancer that I was 25 lbs lighter. I felt incredible just before my world came crashing down! That made me crazy. I obviously had cancer through me and I didn't have a clue. I really believe that PET SCANS Should be a part of our physicals. It shouldn't matter if you are a cancer survivor or not. One scan, once a year, like a mammogram, a Pap smear. It's the same thing, isn't it? It's preventative. Think of the lives that could be saved. I think about that often, frustrated by the comments that "protocol for stage one cancer requires no yearly blood work." Bullshit. A simple damn test could have caught this early. Even Dr. T agreed with that statement. But it doesn't make sense. See, there, you caught me in a pity party. Have that party and then get pissed off again. It's simple, really. We all have negative thoughts that creep into our heads. Control it. As soon as they creep in, get mad and block them out. You can do it. You have to make your mind up and control your thoughts and were they take you. I've said it before. You can spin yourself into a funk so easily with any illness. Focus, control, pray, faith, getting mad. That's what my life consists of. Not necessarily in that order, someday it's all at the same time!

The week before I was to return to Syracuse for all my results, I received a large envelope in the mail. My BRCA genetic testing. I was confused. Was this a mistake? I didn't remember them telling me it would come to me in the mail. Then I realized I was holding my results. I couldn't swallow. I was afraid to open it. I was so sure, because this cancer came back with a vengeance that I already knew the answer. I opened it. It was an easy read on the first page before it got into all the

technicalities. NEGATIVE!!! I WAS NEGATIVE FOR THE MUTATED
GENE!!! Oh thank you God! That was a huge win in my book!

I returned to Syracuse the last week of the month to hear all the rest of
the test results. Deep breath in. This is so nerve wracking. I walk in,
check in, and have my blood drawn first, then wait to be called in for
the appointment. . Same routine. Dr. T walked in, I swear I think I
stopped breathing. "GOOD NEWS!!!! " Now this is how I like to start out
a doctor's visit! " Your cancer is isolated in your chest! Breathe! Yes! It's
shrinking! OH MY GOD! Thank you sweet Jesus! Then there was a
but.......you have some new activity in your chest. My heart started
pounding. I know he heard it. I couldn't concentrate. Breath, calm
down...LISTEN....LISTEN. WHY, WHY, WHY IS THERE ALWAYS ONE MORE
THING! WHY! He saw my face, he was so kind. He was compassionate.
" Lorrie, you have good news today. Your numbers are good. The
cancer is shrinking. Listen to me. Please." I was trying. I felt as thought I
had been through this scene before. I wanted Bob. I just wanted Bob. I
took a deep breath, closed my eyes momentarily and asked for
strength. "What do you mean activity? " He pulled up my PET SCAN
report and reading off of it, explaining to me that the scan showed that
some nodes increased in size and they were lit up. Questioning him
further, how big? What does it mean? Were they there before? I was
firing off questions faster than he could answer. Calmly, so calmly he
told me what I already new. Nodes can be enlarged for several reasons.
And, once he looked at the scans and retread the report, he questioned
it. "No, by cancer standards these nodes are within normal range.
Lorrie, be happy, you have great news today." I tried to show
happiness. I really did. But at that moment, I felt as though I got hit
over the head, again. He talked to me for quite a while. He never
rushed me. He was confident. He wasn't worried at this point. He
promised to rescan me in 3 months, April. He was so happy with my
scan results that he was willing to see me every 3 months. My head
jerked so fast that my reaction was unmistakable. He knew me already.
" You aren't comfortable with that?" A simple no was my answer. He
didn't flinch. Ok, if you want to come monthly, that's fine. Usually I
schedule my nurse practitioner to see patients every other month, but
if you would rather see me, that's ok too. I wanted to cry. Here this
man is, my second appointment with him. I have been in his presence
twice, maybe a hour total time, and I don't have to beg, to plead, to

scream, to get aggravated over anything. My well being was first. I had found the right doctor. The following month would only be blood work. I told him it was fine to see the nurse practitioner. I would see him in April, along with another PET SCAN.

I walked out of there shaken. I had some work to do. I got to my car. My heart still pounding. I needed to talk to my father. I needed to talk to God. I needed to talk to Bob. I called Bob first. I knew he was waiting. I know I shook him up. He asked if I was ok. I told him not really, trying to focus on the positive, but it's hard. I needed to put it all into perspective. I knew I would be by the time I got home. I told him that. That was one good thing about the ride, it gave me time to function and find myself. I hung up the phone and let my emotions take over, briefly. My conversation with God went something like this, " Dear God, you have Blessed me so much during all of this, all my life. I need you to carry me today. I need you to carry me everyday, but especially today. I know I had good news but the other news threw me. I realize there isn't any more cancer showing up, it's just activity which could be there for several reasons. Help me, please." Then I talked to my father. " Dad, help me." My father was around me all the time, my conversations didn't have to be long winded. Actually, my father was a "short and to the point" kind of guy. I know he knew what I needed.

By the time I pulled into my driveway I was ok. Perspective. Break it down. My battle was for my lifetime. I had to learn how to react and handle everything. I was getting better and better at handling all this stress. What did I know? The cancer once through my entire chest, under my left arm and crossed over to my nodes under my right arm was now isolated in my chest. I said that to myself again. That was HUGE. Dr. T was right. My cancer was shrinking. I was in full remission. Under different circumstances, if I had blood work, no one would even know I had cancer. I really had to keep thinking that. Nodes. Those damn nodes. That could be from anything. I have to keep calm and trust that God will see me through. Dr. T would tell me that he would base a lot of his treatment on how I felt. I felt good! I started a new workout, PIYO. This is a combination of Pilates and yoga. Since the car accident my neck injury and my back now wouldn't allow much. But a lot of this was stretching. My God, it felt good. No impact. I felt my body getting stronger. It was miserable outside so I was on my treadmill too. Walking will always be the best exercise. I would see the chiropractor too. It all worked together. And I felt the difference if I didn't do it for a while. I just had to continue on this path. My appointment for my thyroid was next. I was having some afternoon fatigue. I was sure that my thyroid was off again. After all I went through, no way it was functioning normally.

The end of January held a lot of hope for us in the restaurant. Bob had met up with a high school senior, a young entrepreneur, with a new concept. The concept was an on- line delivery service. A customer would order through their website from a selection of different restaurants. For a fee they would place the order, pick it up and deliver it to the customer. We were one of 8 restaurants that originally signed up with them. It was a win-win situation with us because there were times that customers had called and asked about delivery and we were unable to do it. There was a news segment on this story, in part because of the age of the young man. We were mentioned and a picture of the restaurant aired on the evening news at 6 and 11 pm. Free advertising!!! Then the biggest gift came. A local TV show that aired on weekends, each month featuring different restaurants along with other local businesses had contacted us. They also put out a monthly magazine that we had been purchasing advertising from them now for several months. Slowly it's seemed as though all our prayers were being answered. I wanted this to work so badly for Bob. Well, for all of us, but this was Bob's dream. His confidence was shattered when he lost his job, and he honestly felt that if he couldn't make this work, he just failed. He failed his family. It was the furthest from the truth. He had never in our life together failed me, or our family. But that was how he was, how he thought. He was old school and took the position of husband, father and provider very seriously.

The show and magazine were both highly rated among local viewers. They wanted to feature us for the month of February! This was an incredible opportunity! They came in for lunch midweek. Tried some of the favorites and interviewed Bob. He nailed it! Bob talked about his experience and how this opportunity arose. He talked about our mission statement. Homemade comfort foods, relaxed atmosphere and what was just as important as the first two, that we treated our customers like family. In our area, Italian restaurants are all over, we weren't going the gourmet route, we wanted to be family friendly. We wanted people to feel comfortable walking in with a work suit or sweats on. It didn't matter. What mattered was the " homey" comfortable atmosphere that we provided. We got incredible feedback immediately. Within the first few days 20+ people who saw the show, who never heard of us before walked through our doors. About mid month, I was at home and I received a phone call from the editors of the magazine/ tv show. They had received a check but the invoice got separated and they were making sure it was applied properly. As soon as I heard who it was I reiterated my husband's thank you's to them for our TV segment. We had such a pleasant conversation and then she mentioned that they had bought advertising and in return the television station had given them extra TV spots. We were on TV for a total of 36 times the month of February! We couldn't have afforded that ever! We lost count as to exactly how many people had walked through our doors. How can you explain this? This wasn't a coincidence. And that's what people think. All the coincidences in life aren't coincidences. They are prayers being answered. We felt as though we were overcoming the hurdle. I believed that God had heard our prayers. My novena to the Blessed Mother, Mary, undoer of knots, each and every aspect in are lived was starting to pull together. We still had a way to go, a long way. And we stayed honest with people. We had met so many nice people, and they truly cared. They would ask how business was and we told them the truth. We were struggling. We were building, but not fast enough. Word of mouth was spreading more and more. I remember talking about our restaurant in the beginning, people would ask what the name was, and there was zero name recognition. Now, it's "oh yeah, I'm hearing really good things about your place!" With all the stress of this happening, I remained so peaceful inside. It was unexplainable, but it was real. I honestly believed we were going to be ok.

As much as I was so sick of doctors, I couldn't wait to meet up with Cindy. She was a Godsend! It took me 3 years to find someone to treat me with the thyroid protocol that I wanted. She was holistic, something years ago I would have totally ignored. Ignorance. Basically, on my part. Why wouldn't holistic treatments work? Natural treatments, vitamins, herbs. It made a lot of sense. Simply put, as we get older, our bodies just don't have the nutrients that it once had. We need to supplement. The thyroid controls so many body functions. The heart, metabolism, digestion. When our bodies start to get out of whack there's a "snowball" effect. One thing leads to another and then to another. Finally we end up in the doctors office and they end up treating the symptoms INSTEAD of what actually caused those symptoms. This is all that I learned and to counter all adverse symptoms, we need to eat right, drink plenty of water, exercise. The cancer medicine now had me staying away from sugar too. Which in itself isn't a bad thing. Cancer loves sugar anyway. But I found out the hard way as the weight gain explosion that occurred over the previous summer with the Lupron shot and starting on the medicine. I seriously had to learn how to eat again. No sugar, no high sugared fruits, no dairy, no glutens. Was I perfect at all this? Nope? I cheated sometimes, I would try to give myself one day a week where I just ate whatever I wanted to. Other than that, I tried to say conscience of everything I ate. I was the only one going to suffer for it after all. The bloating I had was making me crazy. I needed Cindy to set me straight and then I could move forward, again!

The drive out to see her was a bit longer, about 1 ½ hours. Located out in Amsterdam, NY, out towards the Saratoga raceway. Her office was located at one of those small clinics but she was affiliated with Saratoga Hospital. There wasn't any Doubt in my mind that my thyroid was off again. It just seemed like an endless journey. When, when was I going to walk into a doctor's office and hear, "Everything is perfect!" NOT! Obviously this was never going to happen in my world.

Cindy walked in and we talked about my cancer, happy to hear that I was doing well, that last time I saw her was just after my treatment started the summer before. I told her that I'm not taking any weight off and I had been walking, watching what I ate, started doing Piyo. I was anxious to hear her thoughts and what I could do to get back on track. My Afternoon fatigue had returned which could be a clear sign of my thyroid was off. I had been blaming the hysterectomy for all the bloat but that was another symptom too. I suffered all month with sinuses...all signs were there. I wasn't disappointed at all. Cindy had ideas! She would do blood work first and foremost to check my thyroid levels. My body had been through hell. 25 lbs over where I was before all hell broke loose. I hated it. From previous appointments I had learned that eating by blood types worked. I was better off staying away from dairy products, glutens because of my thyroid and now sugar because of my cancer meds. She had also pointed me in the direction of a natural probiotic, KIMCHI. Basically it was fermented vegetables. One spoon full a day would help clear the bad bacteria in the digestive tract. She gave me directions for a 7 day cleanse. This was to help with LEAKY GUT SYNDROME (LGS). I had never heard of this. It was all about the digestive tract and the bad bacteria that is in it causing bloating, gas and other irritations. This was a proven cleanse, not a fad, that had results of a 5-20 lb weight loss. Hearing that I was anxious to try it. The only thing I had to order specially was a brown rice protein powder that was only $ 11 online! A bought a few to make sure I had enough. The rest was easy. I had to make a vegetable broth. I added fresh and/ or frozen fruits to add to my brown rice shake. Papaya, I had learned, was filled with enzymes to help clear the digestive track. Chicken, fish or turkey for dinner, along with brown rice and steamed vegetable. It was a very simplistic plan to follow. And best of all, I was never hungry! Actually, sometimes I couldn't even eat all that you were supposed to. It was sugar free, gluten free and dairy free. This was the last piece to my puzzle that I needed solved. This 25 lbs was going to go. That was my goal.

I finally got my phone call from Cindy just shy of 10 days later. Yes, my thyroid was off and she had to up my dosage. I was so happy! Not that my thyroid was off but that was what the issue was. I ended up dropping 10 lbs from that cleanse, now waiting on the increased dosage to kick in and I could lose this weight! That was one thing with Hashimoto's, occasionally you would go into hyper thyroid mode and be able to drop a few pounds. Unfortunately, it wouldn't stay off. This cleanse weight loss did. Now I just had to give the dosage time to work through my body. It usually took a few months before I started seeing a difference. I felt as though I was taking control again. It was a really good feeling.

2015 was definitely starting out better! I know that everyone makes their New Years resolution to get in better shape but mine was real. All the medicines and then the hysterectomy just screwed my body up good. Was this in part vanity? You bet it was. I hated the way I felt. Nothing fit right and I had just gotten rid of all the larger clothes that I used to wear before having Cindy help me with my thyroid. All winter I found myself wearing sweatshirts and yoga pants. I promised myself that I would get myself back into gear. With my thyroid medicine redosed, the cleanse, it was up to me to start moving.

March finally got here! February being one of the most brutal winter months that I could remember in a long time, we just couldn't wait for March. Not that we expected the weather to turn abruptly in central New York. If we had a mild March, we considered ourselves extremely lucky. But as usual, the "In like a lion, out like a lamb" theory went out the door. It was "In like a lion and out like one too. Winter wouldn't stop. By this time, we central New Yorkers felt as though we have gotten our brains bashed in. Constant snow falling, constant below freezing wind chills and temperatures. I needed Spring, badly. The older I got, the more I believed I suffered from that seasonal disorder. Being stuck inside for months at a time was horrible.

My March appointment was to be with Dr. T's nurse practitioner. I had met her at a prior appointment when she explained all the genetic testing procedures to me. One thing I wanted to go over was my actual numbers. While I remained in full remission, I just felt better knowing my numbers. Dr. T's blood work consisted of using different blood markers. Having no clue either way, trusting him completely, I never questioned it. Sloan-Kettering was fine with it, so I didn't question it. Gina, his practitioner, was a very sweet lady. Everyone was in this office. I asked her about my numbers. What was a normal range, where I was from January til now. I saw her face kind of frown. She acted nervous with the question. I felt that familiar stomach flip. Was she going to tell me bad news? I let her talk. She went on to tell me that these blood markers have a habit of waving up and down. They watch for trends to happen. Swallowing hard, I asked her what mine were. She was only able to give me January and February's since I just had done my blood work prior to seeing her. Normal turn around time for results were usually the next morning. Gina brought my numbers up on the screen. Now my heart is racing. I'm remembering the new activity in my chest and praying that nothing is going wrong. January's numbers were 21. Remission is below 38. A sigh of relief. February spiked to 33. No. No. No. PLEASE GOD NO! What the hell is going on??? Gina stopped me right there. " Lorrie, please, this is normal. Trust me." I did. I wasn't going to make myself crazy over these numbers. Gina asked how I felt. I told her that I felt really good. I told her that my thyroid was off and I just recently had my dosage increased. That was going to make a huge difference. Before I left the office I asked them to please call me tomorrow as soon as they could tell me what my numbers were. I knew they would call.

And they did, first thing. They were so happy to let me know that my numbers dropped back down to 22. THANK YOU SWEET JESUS! And it made sense. The entire month of February I battled sinuses. Never an infection, but to me this was huge. I refused in the early months of Fall and actually at every doctor's appointment to get the flu shot. I don't like some of these vaccines. Especially this one. Every year they warn everyone to get it and every year they start talking about a new strain that emerges and the flu shot won't work on. The fact that I could make it through the year, working with elementary kids, noses constantly running, hacking in my face and I didn't get sick at all told me that was my resistance strong. I know it's a fact that I have a compromised immune system, but that would make me sick. Part of my armor is the fact that I refuse to believe I am sick. As a matter of fact, just recently, at a doctor's visit, the nurse actually said that besides my cancer, I am very healthy! And that's exactly how I look at it. This is a lifetime disease. Like so many other diseases, it can be controlled and I plan on living a very long life. Mindset. Get there. Whatever you are facing.

April. PET SCAN. I was worried. I had a gut feeling about that damn new activity that was found on January's scan. I was relieved that Dr. T was proactive rather than reactive in his approach. It was a relief that I would find out on the same day this time. Having all the testing done at the same location made for a long day but at least the waiting time was shortened. I would go in for bloodwork first, then have the radioactive sugar injected in me and and then have to lay in the dark, quietly for an hour before I am brought in to the PET SCAN. Once that is over I would have to wait for just over an hour for my actual appointment with Dr. T to go over everything. Luckily, CROUSE MEMORIAL HOSPITAL had offices in the building next door, complete with a deli. I brought my iPad had lunch and played CANDY CRUSH for an hour. The night before the test I went to bed and asked God to please, whatever was going on, give me the strength to deal with it. I slept fitfully and when my alarm went off at 6 am, I did my usual snooze for about a half hour. My snooze button went off at 9 minute intervals. The second time, being set on the radio, Journey's DON'T STOP BELIEVIN was on. I couldn't believe it. Those exact words were on the radio as the alarm went off. I just sat up, startled and yelled, COME ON! Coincidence? No way. That was my message. I immediately relaxed. I knew then, what ever happened I was going to be ok. My message was don't stop believing. I wasn't going to. And if that wasn't message enough, the next morning I got another message. My morning ritual was the same, I would come into the kitchen, turn on the news and have my morning coffee while playing around on my iPad. Listening half heartedly, the news is so depressing, I caught the preview of a news segment that was coming up. Kids on a high school stage that had collapses during a concert. They had mentioned it a few times through out the morning and when it finally came on, something caught my ear. I played it over and turned up the volume. The song they were singing, the words spoken as the stage collapsed…. DON'T STOP BELIEVIN. Come on??? Again? Even if I didn't believe the first message, the second one made it perfectly clear. I was being told not to worry.

Dr. T was late. It was a long day, waiting for my results to come in. Having had to fast from the night before, it was after 1 pm before I got to eat anything. Coming back into Dr. T's room waiting anxiously, still having that feeling in the pit of my stomach but remembering my DON'T STOP BELIEVIN messages. He was always on time, or just a few minutes late…he was 20 minutes late. This is not good. Texting Bob, trying to remain calm, I imagined he was on the phone, consulting with someone, maybe New York. I could feel that inevitable pit in my stomach getting bigger.

He walked in, immediately apologizing for keeping me waiting. I could see it in his eyes. Oh my God. What???? He went on to say that the cancer has remained the same as it was in comparison to January's scan. It remained contained in my chest area. Whew! Ok, breathe…what else…? Nodes in the chest area had not only lit up but they had enlarged since January. Dr. T was pretty calm through all of this but he made it clear that I needed another biopsy. This was the bombshell. Because back in the beginning, still with Dr. Jonas, one of my original biopsy tests had come back inconclusive. And it was kind of an important one. The HER2 test. The test to determine my course of treatment. Dr. Jonas, while conferring with Dr. Camen in New York the summer before, had failed to mention this. Dr. Jonas, in no uncertain terms, had decided to call this a reoccurance of the cancer that I went thru back in 2004-05. Without the evidence to support it. When I had gone to Sloan the first time, Dr. Camen had asked me where the addendum to the biopsy report was. She was looking for the written report stating the HER2 result. I had no idea what she was asking for. It was then that I learned that Dr. Jonas had started me on a treatment without having all the information, and having conferred with Dr. Camen prior to me starting this treatment and Dr. Camen agreeing with the course of treatment, not realizing all the information wasn't in. Dr. Jonas had lied to Sloan –Kettering. This was unbelievable. Thankfully the treatment had been successful and the second opportunity to get a biopsy done had failed because Dr. Jonas, with a request from Dr. Camen wanted a re- biopsy done locally but have the pathology sent directly to Sloan Kettering. By this time, the node to be biopsied had shrunk considerably. The question was if there was enough of a sample to get a conclusive result. But, Dr. Jonas refused to send it to them. And I know this was the case because I personally said to the nurses after the biopsy that to please make sure this goes to Sloan Kettering. They looked at me and said, " No, Dr. Jonas ordered this." I corrected them. " Dr.Jonas ordered it for my doctor in NYC and the pathology was to be send immediately to them." I opened my iPhone and gave them names, phone numbers and addresses. They insisted they had to speak directly to Dr. Jonas. What happened? Her ego got in the way. She had a habit of not putting her patients first.

So now, fast forward to all this new area of concern. Dr. T wasted absolutely no time in speaking to a thoracic surgeon. That was why he was so late. By the end of daylight, I had an appointment with the head of thoracic surgery in 3 local hospitals. A lung surgeon had to get involved. Not because it was in my lung but the area was next to the lung and near my heart. A most difficult area to get to. Figures. Everything is complicated with me.

The following Thursday, I had a consultation with the Thoracic surgeon. He explained to me that an EBUS Bronchoscopy needed to be performed. He went on to explain that this was a procedure mainly for the diagnosis of lung cancer but was used frequently to identify other problems concerning the nodes in the chest area. It was an out patient procedure that was approximately 16-20 minutes long and I was to be given the same anesthesia as a person undergoing a colonoscopy would receive.   The bronchoscope would be inserted down my trachea and by using a needle aspirator they would be able to collect a sample of the node to biopsy. Then he said something that I was so thankful for. He said that the 3 biggest hospitals in Syracuse did not do this procedure with as much regularity as he would like. There fore recommending Strong Memorial Hospital in Rochester, NY. Another well known cancer center. At that point I had mentioned that I am already established with Memorial Sloan- Kettering. He put his hands in the air and said," Well, they are world renown! You can't get better than that."

Bob and I thanked him for his honesty. He promised to get on the phone with Dr. T immediately to let him know his findings. We drove home knowing that we would have to go back to New York. We got home about 45 minutes later and I immediately placed a call to Dr. T. He needed to call Dr. Camen as soon as possible to see how fast she could get something scheduled. I left a message and true to form he called me back later than evening, after 6 pm. We talked about the "what if" Sloan couldn't get me in quick enough. I agreed with him that I would go Rochester if that was the case. If my memory served correctly I believe he had been at that hospital prior to his position now. He made it sound as though he had the connections. Whatever. It didn't matter. I would go wherever and do whatever was necessary. And like him, I wanted it done yesterday. Dr. T was so proactive. I was so happy we were on the same wavelength. My appointment with him for May had already been scheduled. He wanted all the answers by then. My treatment was probably going to change. He wanted to move quickly. We were ahead of the curve. Right where I wanted to be. I couldn't help but think if I was back with Dr. Jonas that she would say to wait and see what happens. She just didn't get the fact that I wasn't a wait and see type of woman.

It seemed as though my life revolved around phone calls. I was always waiting for someone to call. But the call from Sloan Kettering came so quickly, before I was even expecting it. Dr. T placed a call immediately on Friday morning, the day after my consult. In the conversation, she completely agreed with the EBUS biopsy. Finally, I had a rhythm with both doctors. She was as thorough as he was. I knew they would get along. I would have loved to be a fly on the wall hearing the discussion about Dr. Jonas….you can't make me believe something wasn't said! The call came on that same Friday afternoon, 4:55 pm. New York had scheduled an appointment for Monday, 3 days away, for a consultation with a Sloan Kettering thoracic surgeon.

We were so sure we had this down pat. Driving down 3-3 ½ hours to the Southeast train station. Park and ride. Buying the tickets, getting on the MTA line. 1 ½ hours on the train. We hit everything on time. No traffic jams. We even walked out of Grand Central Station and got a cab immediately! My appointment was at noon and for the first time since all this had started, we got to the appointment on time! Could it be possible that this goes without a hitch today???? NOPE! The doctor was late…not just late, 1 ½ late. We thought we would get in and out. NOPE! After finally seeing him, setting up my surgery for May 15, my grandmothers birthday, now I had to go through the pre op…shit, I forgot about the pre op. Blood work, EKG, X-rays. This was going to set us back a few hours. It's was going to be another long day. But there was no choice, they had to have it then and there or they couldn't do the biopsy. Then, to make matters worse, as we were waiting in the waiting room, so many stories up, looking down, we notice that all the side streets were being cordoned off. What was going on? Yup! Just our luck, the president was in town and his security detail had the street, the street we were on, blocked. Wonderful. We aren't big Obama fans and then he has to be there on the same day…and I must say, the few other people I talked to, along with a few nurses, weren't fans either. Our day started at 5 am, we got home at 10:15 pm. Exhausted wasn't even the word for it.

Once the surgeon came in and met with me, the ball started rolling very quickly. He expressed his opinion on how he thought this was exactly what I needed to have done. He also said that this procedure is done approximately 200-250 times a year. Not too shabby. I was in great hands. His nurses were on point. X-rays came first, then the blood work and finally the EKG. Finally! We were done and ready to get to the train station. But because the president was there, traffic was still backed up and cabs were very scarce. Luckily, we had learned a very important trick. Ask the doorman to get a car service! We were able to make it to the train station and grab something to eat quickly, getting on the train, finally able to breathe and relax. We were on our way home. Only to be back in 10 days. I just wanted this over. Done. I wished away those ten days like you couldn't believe.

Options. What could be happening? A. The original diagnosis was correct and I am building up a resistance. B. Wrong original diagnosis, HER2 positive is now HER2 negative and that is a more aggressive cancer and that one usually hits the brain. Or, C. Another cancer altogether.

I would go over and over things in my head. I refused to believe that it was anything but the same diagnosis. Dr. T indicated to me he thought that was the case but in my given situation, I needed answers. I could have nothing left to chance. It was as simple as that. I kept remembering my messages...DON'T STOP BELIEVIN. That was real. My faith was going to sustain me. Again and again I would just ask to let this be the same diagnosis and let it be a resistance to the medicine. That was the best possible outcome I could have in my given situation. I remained calm for the 10 days waiting impatiently for the biopsy. My school job continued, May was a gorgeous month. Our anniversary month too. The 25th. My appointment to see Dr. T was slated on Tuesday, the 26th. Being the Memorial Day holiday weekend, we had decided to shut the restaurant down Saturday thru Tuesday. That worked well because Bob was coming with me to meet Dr. T for the first time. I really hoped Bob liked him. Bob was quick to read people and I always liked his take on people.

The kids were really starting to hit their limit with school. Boisterous, loud, difficult to control...welcome to Elementary School 6 weeks before school gets out. My usual job was recess. Now this time of year was my absolute favorite. Armed with shorts, a tank top, sunglasses, a whistle and baby oil, my sun worshipping days were here! We were outside with 1st grade, this group had a hard time listening, but 6 weeks out, forget about it. All bets were off. We would also take the few kids in the special education class out. Sometimes they required a one on one aide. She/ he would be responsible for that child. We would watch too, but it never hurt to have another set of eyes on these kids. Some of them were more physical and others were emotionally light. The simplest of things would set them off. And you never knew what it might be. I had been given an extra hour after my 2 ½ shift with recess to be just that, a one on one aide with a kindergartener. He was a sweet boy, his home life wasn't great at all, but he was extremely impulsive and just didn't listen. My left knee, my good knee, felt funny. It was just a dull throb. I worried, because of my back, I didn't always walk straight, putting more pressure on one side or the other. I blew my right knee out years ago. A soft tissue injury. Something that just really doesn't heal. It would flair up if my back had a bad episode or the weather changed. I was like a human barometer with all my aches and pains. We finished recess that day and I had about 10 minutes before I had to take him to gym class. During the Spring, the gym teachers would take them outside on the soccer field and play games. This is where we were heading today. I picked him back up after his snack and we walked with the class he was pushed into daily. That just means he spends some of the day in the regular class room and some of the day with other kids in the special education room. This year that room had approximately 8 kids in the room with a teacher and 2 full time aides. They got all the extra help they needed.

Walking into the gym, I noticed we had a substitute. A young girl. Sweet, obviously this was her career choice. I laughed to myself, she had no idea what the next 40 minutes were going to be like. I stayed close and helped her corral the kids a bit. It was hard when you were trying to keep control in a situation and then you don't know any names. We were about 10-15 minutes in and the kids loved being outside. But my little man decides he's going to run in the opposite direction. I took a step, called his name and POP! My kneecap pops. I hit the ground. Calling out his name again, I'm in severe pain. I can't put any pressure on it, he turns and sees me on the ground, thank God he ran to me. I had him sit down with me. He was so sweet. I told him I hurt my knee and can't walk," would you stay with me?" He sat next to me and we watched the other kids play. As the other kids lined up to go, I told the sub that I popped my knee and I wanted to get home to ice it. She offered to get me ice but I was closer to my car than the gym office to grab an ice pack. I lived 3 minutes from the school. She took him inside with the rest of the kids and I hobbled to my car. It felt the same as my other knee did. My right knee popped about 8 years ago in my back yard. Great, now both knees.

I got home and sat. Armed with ice packs I didn't move for the next 3 hours. I was hoping to alleviate some of the swelling and at least be able to put some pressure on it. Nope. It felt worse. It was throbbing. I couldn't believe it. All I did was take a damn step! I decided to get to urgent care. I gave up on emergency rooms a long time ago. We had a urgent care close to us that if you caught it right, up you could be in and out in an hour. I caught it right. But one thing I didn't think about, I left school with an injury. Workers comp case. Not what I want to deal with at all. No fault claim with my car accident and now a workers compensation case.

Just like the other knee, soft tissue injury. Ice, compression and elevation. I was given crutches. Wonderful. I got home, I called the school principal, apologizing that I didn't stop in the office. This was Thursday, they put me out of work until Monday. No big deal. The crutches lasted about 2 hours. I was putting so much pressure on my old bad knee that it was starting to throb too. . This had to get better. I had my biopsy in one week.

I had started saying my novena again. The novena to Padre Pio. This is one of the strongest novena's that I have ever prayed on. And the peace I get from saying it is overwhelming. I had to keep strong. And I was. Scheduling practices at Sloan did not allow me to have the time of the biopsy until the day before and then there was a 5 hour window. Anytime between 2-7 pm. We thought it was best to stay the night before in Fishkill, NY. That was about 20 minutes from the Southeast train station. The surgeon had said he was going to tell them to schedule my biopsy for late morning, early afternoon. They were so accommodating. A 5 hour ride back home after surgery wasn't going to be fun. Again, I just couldn't wait until this was over. Thankfully they called right at 2. Surgery was scheduled for 1pm. I had to be there by noon. This was perfect. We didn't have to rush to get there and we would have time to sightsee. Something we have never been able to do. My knee was starting to feel somewhat better. As long as I wore the compression brace. All that week at school I sat as much as possible outside. I could see all the kids but I needed to stay off of it as much as possible.

We left around 5 on the Thursday night prior to the surgery. Our kids were all old enough to take care of themselves. And God knows the threats we left them with if there were any parties at our house. I was more worried about our shepherd. He got so attached to me, and being as high strung as he was, I knew he was going to be stressed. That scared me. After my baby Asta and all the convulsions, I never, ever want to see that again. I told the kids that someone could sleep in our bed, or leave their bedroom doors open so he could have his choice. God, I just wanted this over and to move forward. It has to be the same cancer. It just didn't make sense. How could the Aromasin work, put me into remission in 13 weeks and be something different? Could it be a new cancer? Was that possible? Is cancer logical? That question I asked myself over and over.

We were up and out early the next morning. Leaving nothing to chance, we felt it was better to get to the city early and have the extra time there. We got to the Southeast train station in literally 25 minutes. Early enough to catch an earlier train into the city. Walking from the car to the station, an unmanned station, actually. The toll for leaving the car was a machine. We bought our tickets from another machine. And all the way from the car to the station, a good ¼ mile, I am smelling the most beautiful lilacs. I'm looking and looking around and I can't find lilac bushes anywhere. I said to Bob, " Oh man, do you smell those gorgeous lilacs?" He said no. It popped out of my head as the train arrived and we hopped aboard. An 1 ½ train ride until we hit NYC. By 9:45 we will be there. We relaxed a bit knowing that so far it was so good. I just hoped all went like clockwork. The doctor's office said I would have to remain in recovery for about an hour after I woke up. The anesthesia was a small amount. Approximately 30 minutes worth. I expected myself to bounce right out of that. As long as they kept ZOFRAN away from me.

We walked around for a while. Took in some sights until my knee started to bother me. We figured it was best to grab a cab and get to the hospital. Once there, I checked in and we went to the cafeteria. Bob, naturally was starving. Me? Oh no, I was still in fasting mode. It's always fun watching him stuff his face and I can't eat or drink anything. I posted a picture on facebook of him chopping on hamburgers as I sat patiently. With perfect timing, as we are walking back to the office, they were calling me. They were ready for me to get prepped.

Undressed and in the hospital bed, the anesthesiologist came in to go over everything. One bit of bad news. The surgeon doing my biopsy was delayed. There were complications with the first surgery of the day. Then, there was one more in front of me. Bob and I looked at each other. We were going to get home really late. Naturally we felt bad for the person in surgery, although we didn't have any details. I ended up going in an at 2:40 instead of 1 pm. One thing they did do, they bumped the other person ahead of me.

It went beautifully. I remember seeing the clock on the wall as I woke up, 3:45. I went in an hour ago and I was already awake. Fighting to stay awake. I had told Bob if he was there when I was wheeled into recovery to pinch me really hard to keep me awake. Man, I wanted to sleep. But I wanted to go home more. I immediately asked for water. That scope going down my throat made my throat raw. Then I asked for some crackers. I needed to get up and out and headed home. I was asking for Bob and couldn't figure out why he wasn't there. They wheeled me into another room. By this time I was sitting up, fully awake and ready to go. There wasn't any reason to hold me there. I was fully awake, I already went to the bathroom and got up and got dressed. Bob was walking in as I was putting my shoes on. There was a mix up and no one called Bob until then. All this time, he's thinking I'm still out cold and in recovery. The doctor had come in to speak to him already so he knew there was no danger. Thank God the biopsy went without a hitch. They got an excellent sample. We were good to go!

We left the hospital and we were able to get a car service right at 5pm. Rush hour in NYC is not fun. We were only a few blocks from Grand Central, but we had to change our tickets and I still hadn't eaten anything but crackers after surgery. We were lucky that we were old hats at this procedure now. We grabbed snacks, juices and headed to the train. We just made it in time. Unfortunately, this train was completely full and we ended up having to stand for about 45 minutes until it hit the first stop. Great. I was awake but still a bit groggy and all I wanted to do was rest. For the ten days prior to the biopsy I hadn't slept well at all because I couldn't take any of my muscle relaxers, pain pills or anti inflammatories before surgery. Fully armed with all my meds, I waited until we were about 20 minutes from our stop and I took everything. By the time we got to the Southeast station I was extremely woozy. Bob made me wait as he went and got our car. We headed home, about 3 hours away. I reclined the car seat and completely passed out. Waking only briefly as he stopped to go to the bathroom. We got home just after 10. It was over. I hugged everyone, including the dog. Walked down the hall, took more meds and hit the pillow, not waking until the next morning and feeling like a million dollars. It was the best damn sleep I had in over 10 days!

Now the waiting. My appointment with Dr. T was scheduled for the 26th. The day after our 24th wedding anniversary. . I was in my kitchen that morning after, again, smelling lilacs. I immediately turned to look out my kitchen window. Behind our pool we had replanted 2 good size lilac bushes that were formerly in the front of our house and on that same side, on the other side of my fence, we had a lilac tree. Looking out, they weren't in bloom yet. Then it hit me. Nonnie. That was nonnie! I had forgotten that I had the surgery on her birthday. The lilac smells were her, letting me know she was around. With tears in my eyes I turned back around and looked outside at the lilac bushes. On the left side of the bushes, right in front is a statue of a 3 foot angel. At that moment precise moment a cardinal flew and landed on the angel's wing. My visit from heaven. My grandmother was here.

I was really hoping that by the time of my appointment on the 26th that all information would be in. The surgeon at Sloan-Kettering had told Bob for me to call and make a follow up appointment with him in 2 weeks. I had no reason to. Dr. Camen, my Sloan-Kettering oncologist would get the reports, they would be faxed to syracuse, directly to Dr. T and then both oncologists could decide what the best course of action would be. It would be 11 days between the biopsy and my syracuse appointment. 5 days lost because of 2 weekends, one being Memorial Day weekend. Would it all be done in time? I hoped so.

I have to say that I was extremely calm during all that time. I had people messaging me, calling me, asking at school what was happening. I remember all too well this time. The waiting game. I was so proud of myself at how I was handling it all. The deep, deep, inner peace that I felt. The calmness that I felt, during every minute of every day was unreal. I was able to not even think about it. I didn't talk about it. I didn't worry about it. I didn't lose sleep over it. I know the Hand of God touched my soul.

I guarantee that some of you who have picked up and read this book question faith. Question if what I am telling you is real. Question if it could happen to you too. Well? Can it? Undeniably, YES! That is the entire point of this book, it's a journey of faith. I'm human. I sin. I don't go to church because I don't like some of the practices. I don't like what has happened and what has been allowed. BUT. My faith was, is, and will continue to be strong. All you have to do is ask for help. God hears! God loves us all. He wants you to call on him. He wants you to pray to him. And like I said, my prayers most of the times aren't real prayers. They are my heartfelt words to God. I'm not special because all these things have happened to me. My Blessings are real. My messages are real! And they happen to us all but so many aren't aware. They call things coincidences. AND THEY AREN'T! There are no coincidences. Have an open mind, pray to your loved ones that have passed on. They will come to you. As they sit on the Altar of Heaven, in the arms of God, they hear you too. I often say that I have more support from above then those living family members! Given the choice, I'd much rather have those in Heaven on my side.

Those 10 days passed with a beautiful Memorial weekend. The month of May was simply gorgeous. After the winter we had, we deserved it! We cooked out, had family and friends over, bonfires and s'mores. And yes, I cheated and ate s'mores! Sometimes you just gotta say, what the hell! Tuesday morning came and Bob and I were on our way to Syracuse. Now that we were on our way I was anxious as all hell to find out everything. Then my cell phone rang as we were approaching the thruway entrance. It was Dr. T's office. They had received nothing from

Sloan yet. They had tried the week before but was not able to get through. What the hell was going on! They called to tell me this because there was no reason for me to drive out. The appointment was to discuss everything. And right now, there was nothing to discuss. I was pissed. I hung up the phone with Syracuse and told them I was calling NYC myself. I got through immediately and spoke to one of Dr. Camen's assistants. They have always been very helpful towards me so I questioned what had happened. Well first of all, the pathology lab shuts down on weekends unless it's an emergency. Shit. What I was afraid of happened. All those days lost did interfere. Dr. Camen's office was going to call pathology to be sure nothing had come back. They had promised to call me back immediately as I told them we were sitting at the thruway entrance. I called syracuse back to hold my appointment until I heard back. After 20 minutes I called Sloan back. Yes! Results were in. They were faxing them to Syracuse! We were on our way! I called Syracuse back again to let them know. I was so grateful. I wanted Bob to meet Dr. T and visa versa. I wasn't nervous about these results, but I wanted to get the ball rolling again.

We got to my appointment just a few minutes late and I went through the ritual that I knew so well. Bloodwork and the scale. This time the scale wasn't too bad. I was 10 lbs away from my weight loss goal. I felt and was starting to look like myself again. We walked into the exam room and Dr. T walked in shortly after. "Well we don't have all the results." He says to us. What? Why? Sloan didn't mention to me that all the testing wasn't complete. Our trip was still basically wasted. I was so aggravated. At least Bob had gotten to meet him. The one result that came through had positive results. The test came back showing that the cancer was consistent with a Breast cancer. THANK YOU JESUS!!! Knowing that I had no breast tissue on my left side, knowing that these nodes were not breast nodes, it was the same cancer! It had to be! We could do nothing more that wait. I had a rescheduled appointment for 2 weeks later. June 11, sixteen more days of waiting. That would delay any new treatment. But, being logical, where I was right now, compared to where I was one year ago, I was so much better off. If they had found my cancer where I am right now, I probably would have been staged at 3. But it is what it is. One thing I didn't ask for was my numbers. I knew that if this was a resistance that was in fact building up then my numbers were probably up too. I refused to get myself into a funk over one piece of this puzzle. I needed all information before I could process this. Really. At this point in time, my mind set and my ability to stay positive even amazed me. The power of the Lord. I BELIEVED!

Bob wasn't going to be able to make my next appointment. I knew it bothered him. But he had to be down at the restaurant. We were determined to see this thru. We were starting to see double digit growth numbers. Word of mouth was really spreading. More and more new people were in every week, along with our regulars who were incredibly supportive. They had told us more than once that they tell everyone about us. Money was running out, we didn't have much time left, but again, we believed so deeply in this. Our feedback remained very, very strong. It would have been so much easier if everyone hated us. But they didn't. We focused so much on not only making sure that our food was hot, fresh and delicious but we went after that personal side of it too. Bob had always said that in our area, restaurants were everywhere and I will tell you that we have some of the best Italian restaurants around. When people have a choice, they have to have a reason to come back. We talked to our customers, we opened doors for them. We would make accommodations for them. We were in this business to service customers. We had no reason to say no to any dinner request if we could do it. Simple as that. And it was working. We weren't out of the hole yet, but we were definitely seeing positive results.

Waiting for the next appointment wasn't hard for me at all this time. Having this much peace and calmness inside of me, like I have said, I knew God was with me. It is absolutely impossible to have the deepest of confidence, the deepest of faith, the deepest of peace on your soul without God's Blessings. I don't know why, but God has Graced my family so many times over the years. I'm always humbled by it all.

I just got home from school on June 10th, did a few things around the house, it was hot that day, I love heat but I think the aromasin doesn't sit well with the heat. There are some days I feel like I am in slow motion. I wasn't sleeping really great. Since I blew my knee out, as soon as I get into bed both knees start throbbing, naturally because I was putting more pressure on my bad knee. Add my neck, shoulders and lower back. I really was a hot mess! I know we needed a new mattress, we needed a lot of new things but we just couldn't afford it. I picked up the phone and called my primary care doctor, I had seen the nurse practitioner a few days before and I forgot to ask her for pain medicine. I used to be on a pain medicine called Tramadol but it honestly didn't help much, so I stopped taking it. When I went to urgent care for my knee, they gave me Hydrocodone. I'm not a huge pill taker but I slept so well with this and woke up normally, not groggy. In a previous call to her, she refused to give me anything. I was a bit aggravated so I called the doctor himself. I am so sick of fighting with the medical community. My doctor called me back and I explained the situation. He was well aware of the cancer but I honestly didn't know if he knew about the car accident. But, here I am, stage 4 cancer, knowing of all things I need my rest. He prescribed them immediately. That was it, I was done with her. I changed my 6 month follow up to him. I refuse to deal with these people anymore!

My phone rang again, noticing it was from Dr. T's office. This can't be good, I thought to myself as I was answering it. It was one of the nurse practitioners letting me know that my results STILL were not in. " WHAT????" I'm fairly certain that the neighborhood heard me loud and clear. She continued," We have been back and forth all day waiting for them to return the call from pathology, and if we don't get the results, it's futile for you to come out here in the morning." Now. I'm. Pissed. This wasn't going to happen again. "Let me call them." I hung up with her, looking at the clock, 4:25. Great, I may not reach anyone and my appointment is 9am the next day. I took a chance and one of Dr. Camen's assistant's answered immediately. I wasn't exactly pleasant to her. " Jonna, this is Lorrie Markason. Who the hell has my results from the biopsy that was done nearly one month ago????" She stuttered before she could get the words out. "I'm sorry Mrs. Markason, we are waiting on pathology to get back to us." I continued with my whiplash tongue. " I have been patient. I haven't called, I haven't made a big deal out of having to wait this long. But do you understand where I am in life? Do you understand that I have stage 4 cancer and there is new activity going on and I have to probably start a new treatment and I am going to be delayed because of this. "NOW I WANT MY RESULTS!" She promised to call them again and promised to get right back to me. That was all she could do but I was prepared to go a step further. I called the surgeon's office who had actually preformed by biopsy. They would get a copy too. I spoke with Karen, a woman that I had spoke to several times as I was setting up the biopsy. She was extremely polite to me, very helpful and answered that phone on the 3rd ring, each and every time! She didn't fail me now. " Karen, Lorrie Markason, I had the biopsy done on the 15th of May and I spoke to you several times?" It took her a second , then" oh yes! Lorrie! What can I do for you?" I explained the situation again and she was emailing the doctors nurse practitioner to find out what was going on. She promised to get back to me. She never did. I called Dr. Camen's office again. By this time I was beyond livid. Someone had to have answers for me. Jonna answered on the first ring. I could here the apologetic tone in her voice. I knew it wasn't her fault, but she was catching the heat. She immediately apologized. "There has been a huge mistake, " I hesitated but didn't speak. I let her continue. " The HER2 test was never ran." Before I could contain myself I started screaming at her. Can you imagine? The most important test wasn't run! " Now what!!" She explained that the test was going to be run immediately and I will have my results tomorrow. Maybe not first thing but as soon as possible. The lab was opening early for this test. I was concerned about the sample. Was it still viable? Yes, the sample was viable. She promised to call me by 9:15 the next morning to update me. I left her with one comment," we drove 5 hours to have this done. I expect this level of incompetence up here, not down there!"

There was nothing I could do. I cancelled my 9am Syracuse appointment.

Jonna did call as promised the next morning. The test was complete, she was waiting for it to be read by the radiologist and then it would be faxed up to Dr. T's office. I was now so anxious to know. I wasn't worried. But it was time. I placed a call to Dr. T's office to give them the heads up. I also begged Dr. T's nurse to please ask him to make an exception and give me the results over the phone. I went to school and waited impatiently. Just as we were lining up kindergarten to go back in, Dr. T called. He apologized for all the mix up, and continued on. "It was just as we thought. HER2 positive. You are developing a resistance to the aromasin!" Oh my God! Thank you Lord! You heard my prayers! My results, for where I was, was the absolute best news I could have gotten! We made an appointment for the following week. He wanted to talk to Dr. Camen, he wanted a new baseline CT scan and we would go over choices. He wanted me to be a part of it. The week couldn't have come fast enough. I went in, had my blood work done, drank the nasty drink for the scan, 45 minutes later I took the scan and I took myself out to lunch until I had to go back for my appointment. One thing that I really liked about these offices was that Dr. T was always on time. Except for that one time. Then I knew something was up. But, true to form, he walked in 2 minutes after my scheduled appointment. Deep breath in... Here it comes, ready or not.

He shook my hand as he walked in. Sitting directly in front of me. Your CT Scan shows no change from April! NO CHANGE!!!!! Again, my thanks to the Lord! We were still ahead of the curve. He talked about different treatments. He had conferred with Dr. Camen and they had agreed that the best choice for me was putting me back on aromasin and adding to it another drug called Afinator. This, when used in conjunction with aromasin, was extremely effective. " ok, side effects?" At this point I was 6 lbs away from my weight before the nightmare started. I wasn't going to commit harry- carry if I gained the weight back again! No, weight gain. A small amount of hair loss and the worst side effect, fatigue. Ugh! I hate fatigue. There was nothing I could do. I had to deal with it. I was now to wait 2 more weeks to get insurance approval on this. I wasn't worried. It would go through. I just wanted to get back on track again.

Chapter 13

Just when I thought we were back on track. The two week turnaround to get insurance approval seemed like forever. I hated not being on something, but it was worthless to stay on the Aromasin at this point. It wasn't working. Adding the Afinator to the Aromasin was talked about at Sloan as the next approach from early on. . But unfortunately, this step came quite sooner than expected.

 It was within that 2 week period that suddenly I felt myself become winded. Walking and talking became difficult and I had some pain and discomfort in my back and chest. I went a few days with this issue and then it was a Friday. Well, not wanting to end up in the emergency room, I placed a call to Dr. T's office. True to form, I received a call back within 20 minutes. " We need to see you. We need to scan you." Oh, man, really making myself regret this call…" Why, what do you think is the problem?." They went on to explain that any pain and being winded was a huge concern. First and foremost they needed to rule out a blood clot. Not realizing that this now was a common side effect for where I was with cancer….great. And the hits just keep on coming! I drove up immediately and they did a CAT SCAN, thankfully ruling out any clots. But what they find was a good amount of fluid surrounding the left lobe of my lung. It has to be removed. Soon. Unable to schedule me at the office location, they were affiliated with CROUSE- IRVING hospital and able to get me an immediate appointment for Monday. This worked well, the restaurant being closed and them advising me not to drive. Bob was able to take me up.

The procedure itself was a simple one. I had talked to others in the medical field and some expressed that it was extremely painful. Not what I wanted to hear. We went in on Monday, headed to the outpatient surgical unit. The nurse took one look at me and stopped. " I'm sorry, I don't mean to stare, but you certainly don't look like one of our regular patients for this procedure." I smiled. How can you get sick of hearing that? I told her that my oncologist tells me that every time I walk in. I was brought into the procedure room. There were 4 women in the room with me. I didn't even have to get undressed. My shirt was lifted, my bra unhooked and we all had a very pleasant conversation regarding everything. Cancer, my doctor, dogs, kids, jobs. My God I talked through the entire procedure! It didn't hurt at all. Except for the end. With just a little fluid left, it felt like they were sucking my lungs out of me. They stopped there. Taking just under 2 liters, 3 lbs of fluid from around my lung. Unreal. They gave me instructions on how not to try to breathe deeply at all. My lungs had to expand and it took time. By the time I left, within a half hours time, I felt a bit better. But breathing deeply didn't happen for a good 24 hours. I could breathe easier, but to inhale deeply, still hurt. I still couldn't believe 3 lbs of fluid was taken out until the next morning and I stepped on the scale...I was 3 lbs down.

Returning home, I had a missed call from Dr. T's office. Due to all this, he called the insurance company and was able to get me approval to start immediately on the new therapy. Good. Because If I didn't get that call from him, he was my first phone call.

I had to drive back out to Syracuse on Wednesday. This drug, Afinator, was not something I could pick up at the local drug store. This had to come from the pharmacy at the doctor's offices. This was serious shit. I had to go over all the side effects with the nurse practitioner again. The Afinator along with the Aromasin was targeted directly at certain cancer cells, while the Aromasin went after any estrogen. Between the two drugs, they have had great results. I was happy with the choice. I believed it would work. But I wouldn't know for 3-4 months, it took that long to show any change. It was now the end of June. School had ended and it was a good time to start a new treatment. I was told that the side effects that I encountered would last. They wouldn't go away. Everyone was different, so I had no way of knowing what to expect. They came hard and fast. The first thing I noticed was the mouth sores. Within days, I had canker sores on my tongue and hot spots under my tongue. Brutal. I couldn't eat anything acidic, chewing was another issue. Dry mouth. Ugh. It was horrible. They prescribed "magic mouthwash" which was a mix of some pink liquid and lidocaine for the sores. It did help, quite a bit actually. But I had to keep water with me at all times. Dry mouth made it worse.

I have to say, during this period of time was the hardest. Knowing that these symptoms were to stay with me. I had no choice. I just prayed for more strength. Just get me through this. Please.

We planned on closing the restaurant for almost a week over the 4th of July holiday. We would be open on Friday the 3rd closing the 4th thru Thursday the 9th, reopening on Friday. Bob needed this time to recoup. He was there morning til night, day after day. I don't know how he kept up that pace. But he continued. He would never quit. We were a good team.

He got home on that Friday, exhausted and looking forward to just days around the pool. He didn't know it, but I had a bit of a " honey do" list for him. I went to bed around 11 pm that night, only to be awoken an hour later by my screaming daughter. Running into my bedroom, hysterical, a call from my niece, my nephew's wife who had been battling a rare cancer, leomiosarcoma, had collapsed. Ali was needed to run up to the house to take care of the kids. My niece had left her house so fast she didn't tell her husband. I jumped out of bed and ran to the hospital as fast as possible. What the hell was going on???

Some people are just very private. As was she. Not letting on to even her closest friends how ill she was. I never will understand that, but it needed to be respected. Not all of us are comfortable putting our lives in print. The September before, she was diagnosed with a fibroid tumor. They thought it ovarian cancer. They thought it was contained and they removed all of it. Treating her preventatively, she was hit hard with chemo for several months. Clean bill of health in March, only to have it return with a vengeance in Late April-May. This cancer it turns out, wasn't ovarian cancer, but a rare cancer, unresponsive to chemo and other treatments. They don't have a lot of information on this cancer. Having gone to Sloan- Kettering and Dana Farber in Boston, they did all they could do. At 37, with 3 children under 12, my nephew turned off the machines that night that were keeping her alive. She didn't want to live like that. There was no life to live. Machines were pumping air into her. Her own functions were inadequate. This was God's time. If she was to live and respond, she would have then. God was in control. This was unreal. This couldn't be happening.

The next few days were indescribable. I found out things that I had never known. My niece, so close to her, hadn't realized how bad. My niece would take the kids with her, pic them up with school and my sister. Thank God was there too. And everyone respected her wishes. She just didn't want to be seen. She would text but Danielle, who loved her like a sister and respected her wishes. And honestly I was grateful that my sister was there too. With all the bad blood, I knew she was always there for the kids. The night in the hospital, I hugged her. Now wasn't the time or place for anything but prayer and support. Sometimes you just have to put feelings aside.

Her last month was filled with pain. All she wanted was my nephew. And he took care of her until the end. Hearing what my nephew did for her brought tears to my eyes. They had a love that was so deep, so consuming. Watching my nephew grow up I worried. He was walking down the same path as my brother. Then they found each other. She was younger than he was, by 7 years, but she changed him. He was an incredible father, a loving husband and her rock. I was never so proud of anyone in my life. Seeing the pain in all of their faces was too much to bear. Those kids, without the mother bear that she was. Her family was her life. And so, we are left to understand why. Why did God need her? Surely her family needed her more? How do we understand this? It's so easy to talk about, having faith, but now it's directly in our faces. But the power of faith is incredible. We cannot question. We have to believe that we just don't know everything and why it happens.

Her wake wasn't for a few days. In-between this time I had received another call from Dr. T's office. The fluid that was drawn out of me came back positive for cancer. That wasn't really a surprise to me because the actually cancer was in my lymphatic system. But now it hit the lining of my lung. It wasn't in my lung, per say, this was still breast cancer, but it took a turn. I was so pissed. All this as a result of Dr. Jonas's error the year before. If she just scheduled another biopsy as soon as my results came back inconclusive, then I could have jumped from one treatment to another. The resistance STILL would have happened, but I would not have lost the 5-6 weeks in a treatment that I did. On top of that, my bloodwork showed that the Aromasin/ Afinator treatment that I was on dropped my platelets to a concerning level in 10 days. Less than 10% of people on this treatment have this issue...here we go again. I would end up missing the funeral because they needed me off this medicine and they scheduled an appointment for that day.   I insisted I stay on all my meds until I got to the appointment. I wasn't willing to go off anything again. I knew where this was heading. Chemotherapy. And I was alright with it. This is cancer. You have to hit it harder than it hits you.

Her wake was huge. Her parents, originally from the New York City area had a lot of family still there. Along with a huge family business in the area, friends, the kids football teams, it was obvious how much she was loved. She was just a good person. A beautiful young woman with so much in front of her. It didn't seem real. It still doesn't. I had found out the day of her wake my news. As much as I didn't want to tell anyone, they had to know why I wasn't going to be there for her funeral.

We got there right as the wake started. The line was out the door. We could have come earlier I guess, as family. But I respected them all too much and let them have their time alone. The casket being closed as per their wishes. In talking to my niece that night, knowing that my sister, Corinne, called a priest and he prayed over her, giving her last rights that day, praying over her as she took her last breaths, I had a thought. Maybe she did really change? My niece insisted that she did. Living under the same roof with a young, beautiful woman, watching her fight, listening to her faith, has to change you. I couldn't think of that now. The night she died, I walked into the trauma room. I said a prayer, told her I loved her. I told her that I would pray for her, for everyone. Pray for everyone to have the strength to handle this. Her face, so thin, it didn't even look like her. But a few days later, My niece had relayed a story to me about how the funeral home had questioned her about her appearance. They had asked if she had lost a lot of weight. Yes. She had. No work was done on her face, it was full, and beautiful, never needing the tricks that undertakers use. She was in a STATE OF GRACE. She immediately went to Heaven. There was absolutely no doubt.

The following day, I had a graduation party to attend. Life goes on, as horrible as it may be. We have to continue. Leaving the BBQ restaurant, I got into my car, my closest friends now hearing everything that went on that week. Between my news and my niece's death, the week was sheer exhaustion. They walked me to my car. I look up to the sky to notice a massive cross. Formed, obviously by 2 airplanes that crossed at some point. This was no coincidence. She was home.

To say that her death threw me into a tizzy that week, doesn't even describe it. Watching her family, like robots, just responding, in full shock, not fully hitting them yet, seeing myself in that casket, seeing my kids in a fog, Bob standing next to me...how can you not see that under my circumstance?? I prayed a lot that week. In part because I felt a horrible guilt that I was still here. In part that I had several options in treatments. In part that shf never stood a chance. I had to pull myself out of this funk. Now! A downward spiral was not what I needed.

Bob and I went to the appointment while my kids went to my nieces funeral. Dr T. was direct and to the point. Just the way I liked it. We were completely on the same wave length. Up to this point we were ahead of the curve. But, he explained, that sometimes breast cancer does something unusual, as was the case here. Because my platelet count dropped, not to dangerous levels, but because they did and it would take 3-4 months for any results to come in, he wasn't willing to wait, nothing left to chance. Bob and I fully agreed. We would move on to chemotherapy. When I asked if this was the most aggressive treatment I could do, Dr. T looked me directly in the eye and said," Lorrie, we are throwing the kitchen sink at it. " I loved his attitude. In talking to him, knowing that since April, I had been out of remission, I hadn't asked for my numbers. In part because I didn't want to get myself caught up in numbers. Dr. T looked at the entire picture. How I felt, my energy levels, everything. Then he told me my numbers. My tumor markers were at 57. Remission was 38. I couldn't believe it. Those were good numbers. I felt invigorated. Bring on chemo and get this friggin cancer out of me!

Dr. T thought it would be good for me to have a port put in. I was only able to have blood taken out of my right arm due to the mastectomy and nodes removed. Any bloodwork or blood pressure taken on my left side would give me lymphedema. A port would make chemo easier and there was no doubt that my veins would start to collapse. 10 years ago, on my 4th round of chemo, they had the worst time getting the needle in. It was painful as all hell. That chemo needle was huge. I didn't need to be convinced at all.

I was scheduled for the port to be put in on a on the following day, but they wanted me off all meds again to allow for my platelets to rise back up. Which they did, in less than 2 weeks. Chemotherapy was scheduled on a Monday, Bob was my co pilot this time around. I know it had always bothered him that he wasn't there the first time I went through this. He wanted to be there.

Preparing for chemo this time was a bit different. The office literally goes over everything, all side effects, talking things out, answering any questions that I may have. Doctor T wanted 3 full months of treatment. 6 rounds. Then a scan. If I hit remission, I was done, if I didn't, I would continue. Since this wasn't my first rodeo, I had an idea what to expect. I was clear with my intentions. If I was nauseated, I planned on using pot. I told them about what I had learned with the steam, drawing all the toxins out of me and drinking literally 80-100 ounces of water daily through chemo week. It was just a matter of figuring everything out. Unfortunately, it would take the first round of chemo to see what and how I reacted to everything. All my adjustments would be made during the subsequent rounds of chemo. 3 months to be exact. 6 rounds I believe. Then I would be rescanned. During this exam, including a physical exam, they still found a bit of fluid around my left lobe of my lung. Not a lot, but it was there. At least it didn't increase. That was a very good sign. I wasn't having any trouble. Thank you dear Lord!

The chemotherapy infusion unit was located in the same building as Dr. T's office. I just loved having everything right there. This way, I see basically the same people each time. And they were all so friendly. The unfortunate situation I was in health wise was made easier by these professionals. They were good people! We walked in and were asked if I had a preference to where I sat. Yes! Near the window! Please! My nurse walked over. He was very sweet. For each treatment, I was told to rub this lidocaine cream on the port area to numb it about 30 minutes prior to getting there. He immediately flushed the port and hooked up the IV line. Simple. This chemo was scheduled in a 2 hour block. Much less than last time. As the treatments went on and school started I wanted to avoid the loss of any work time. Juggling would have to be done. Once the port was flushed I was given saline, an anti nausal drug and something like a twilight drug just to relax me. I brought my iPad, Bob brought his laptop and we just hung out for a few hours. Once chemo was hooked up it literally was done in a half hour. My appointment was at 2:30, we walked out of there before 5 pm.

Home by 6. Now I only had to look forward to this week and what would occur. There was no way of knowing what symptoms I would suffer from.

Once we got home I immediately went into the steam. Staying hydrated was absolutely essential, especially going into the steam. You could dehydrate very quickly. I would spend 10 minutes, 2 times a day for 3 days. Morning and night. Flushing the chemo out through my pores. I had such good results back in 2005, I figured that was my ace in the hole.

Organization. This is key. Preparing for all you can prior to the side effects hitting. Mentally preparing yourself for a long week. Praying that it's not too bad. Knowing that " THIS TOO SHALL PASS. One day at a time. One treatment at a time.

Monday night was uneventful. Maybe a little nausea. Nothing to get excited about. I slept well and waited to see what Tuesday would bring. I felt good! A bit more nausea, I took a few hits of pot. It was gone. Ok. Last time side effects hit 36 hours out. None really yet. I was told Wednesday, Thursday and Friday may be the bad days. I just held my breath and waited. Wednesday afternoon I started getting some leg pain. Above my knees, in my knees, in my calves and into my feet. That was the worst. I felt achy all over. My back, lower back, throbbing. Then it got worse.

Wednesday night came and I was in serious pain. It would hit in waves. A dull, constant throb through my body and then suddenly it would elevate to a level that I have never had before. The pain of this made childbirth seem like a toothache. I didn't sleep at all. Laying down hurt, I couldn't bend my knees. Every inch of my body felt like it was beat up. By Thursday morning I couldn't even talk. During the middle of the night I went and looked over my paperwork. Comparing my side effects with those listed. Pain. Muscle and bone pain. Yup. There it was. The only real thing that caused an issue. I was able to counter the nausea and the fatigue. I was able to keep myself totally hydrated. I was taking Hydrocodone for my pain and it wasn't touching it at all. Thursday morning I called the office 3 times in a hour, begging them to call me back. They did. They wanted to see me. I put my foot down. No way. I can't drive and I don't have a ride. Well, if I really needed one I could get one. I wasn't going anywhere. They understood and didn't give me a hard time about it and called in a prescription of steroids. I was instructed to double up on the hydrocodone. It worked. There was relief. Until it wore off. The pain was still unreal, but it was manageable. Only because my pain tolerance is very high.

Friday and through the weekend kept me down pretty much. Leg pain would be ok until night time and then flare up again. My taste buds became bland. I felt as though I had a film over my teeth and tongue. Nothing tasted right. I was even choking down water. I was bloated and uncomfortable. Then neuropathy hit. My left hand would become weak and my motor skills were minimal. I couldn't hold a pen and I had zero strength in my hand. I had heard about this and with all my nerve issues already from my accidents, I didn't need this. All I could do was rest. Let it pass. It was a tough week. But, I had also learned a lot about this chemo. I could now figure out how to counter some of these symptoms.

ONE DOWN. FIVE TO GO. ONE WEEK CLOSER TO REMISSION!

I had a Followup appointment with Dr. T's office to go over everything and talk it out. This was helpful and informative to them too. We talked about the steroids helping a great deal. Now I knew that next time I would start with the steroids right and pain meds   immediately after my treatment, for a 5 day period, keeping me ahead of the curve. The water worked, along with the steam. I was happy with the information we found out. All I was waiting for at this point was my hair to fall out. According to this chemo, 90% of all patients lost their hair. I laughed. Every time I was in a low percentage, I came through in the clutch. Maybe I would get lucky? Yeah, right!

Preparing for hair loss like this is traumatic. I remember going back to the first time. I didn't care what body parts were cut off during surgery, but you are taking my hair. It was ok once it was over, but leading up to it, like anything else in life, fear of the unknown is worse than the actual reality of it all. But, getting back to my original point. IT IS TRAUMATIC! It isn't a vanity issue. People react to hair loss. I didn't want pity from anyone. I was pretty much prepared for it all. I met an incredible woman who I purchased my wig from. The woman who I used last time had died this sometime during the 9 years In-between my cancers return. I wanted to go with a " real hair" wig this time. Dr. T's plan was 3 months of treatment and then to scan me. Praying for remission at that point. If not, continued chemo for another 3 months. But I prayed for the best but prepared for the worst. Real hair wigs last forever. I would buy one and I'd be done. The only problem was the expense. They are expensive. I went to the St. Agatha's foundation to help me out. This organization was there for those in financial need. I couldn't believe this was our situation. But we just didn't have the money. The restaurant was building, but August hit and it was a lousy month so far. Back to school, back to college, more vacations happening in August. We heard every excuse. True or not, we simply couldn't afford to have business slack off. It threw Bob into a tailspin. He tried to keep his worries to himself. But I knew. We were at the end. September was going to be it. We had no choice. There was just no more money. We didn't know what the hell we were going to do. All through this time he still was sending out employment apps. Nothing. Zip. Zero. Nada. It was unreal that all this was happening to us.

My hair actually started to fall out before they said it would. The first Monday after chemo, exactly one week to the day I noticed a difference. Just a few strands as I washed my hair, but definitely more than usual. It was so hot that week so I just kept it up in a pony tail. No one thought anything different because I always wore my hair up around the house. By Thursday I could run my hand through it and more would come out. It was here. It was happening. Even though I was ready to deal with it, my kids weren't. Ali and Regina cried, Zach was just sad. They really didn't remember the first time. I told them that it's alright. It's temporary. But like I said, the anticipation is worse than reality. Earlier that week I decided I would have Tracy shave it over the weekend. Make a party out of it. Let the kids see I was ok. But by Friday night, as I was getting ready to go to the restaurant, I knew it needed to come out. I put it up in a bun, making sure none was loose, and I went down to the restaurant. I stayed completely away from the kitchen. I greeted and seated and made sure our waitresses were set. As I left there, I said to Bob that I was going to call Tracy and see if she could shave me tonight. I could see the sadness in his eyes too. " You ok?" He asked me. I was a bit melancholy but I was ok.

I called Tracy when I got home and left a message. If she couldn't do it now, I knew it would be tomorrow. No big deal. She called right back. She hated this. Not shaving me, but going through this again. She had buried her brother and her father, both with cancer, a few years apart. This wasn't easy for her either. Regina wanted to come. She cried. I hugged her and told her that it was all ok. Heading into August, the heat, humidity...me without hair. I could live with it! We drove over to her house, literally 3 minutes away. We had a glass of wine, talked, Regina just sat there, quietly, completely unlike her. I knew she was scared. How I hated cancer. How I hated to see the fear in my kid's eyes. All the more reason for me to stay strong. They could never see me falter. My faith was so deep. I was so sure this was going to work. I had absolutely no negative thought or fears at all. I just wanted to start, to finish.

"Ok, Tracy, let's do this!" We got started. I took my hair tie out. Or tried to. It knotted and pulled and it was so obvious that it needed to be shaved. And Tracy said that much. Regina sat there, tears running down her cheeks, curled up in a ball on the kitchen chair. Just watching that scene. That made it real for her. Tracy confirmed it. " Oh yeah, it's time." Just lightly running her hand over my hair took so much out. She cut it down and shaved it close. Not forgetting to put my 48 in the back of my head! Less than an hour later, I was done. We had another glass of wine and I hugged her. Tracy was always there. We went home and by this time Bob and Zach were home. He kissed me and rubbed my head. Zach's eyes lowered. Regina started to cry again. I told them both that I was ok. It was all ok. And it was.

My head, literally was in such a different place from where I was 9 years earlier. I was ready to embrace my bald head. Thank God, ok, maybe a bit of vanity here, I had a nicely shaped head! I had my wig, and it was gorgeous, but it was too hot out. I didn't want to wear it. I bought some really pretty baseball hats with all sorts of bling on them. I was able to get a NYS TROOPER hat, not an easy thing to do. They just don't give those out, but my contacts were policeman and they knew my father was too. That one became my favorite, naturally, it had special meaning. Then my friend Gina had told me that a lot of the cops would put their name and badge number on the back of the hat. I wondered, could I get my father's name and my father's badge number on mine? I didn't know his badge number. I do remember my mother having my father's retired badge, but I had no idea where it may be or what his badge number was. I contacted a good friend, a retired policeman and asked him if there was any way to find out. It took about 3 weeks, several emails to Albany, and some very decent people going back 30 years to look for it. I was so honored. And it was done. My hat with ARCURI 192 on the back of it.

The time I spent on facebook varied. It was something to do. I stayed upbeat, positive, talked about my faith alot and got such tremendously positive feedback. I was getting messaged by those who not only told me that they prayed for me but thank you for inspiring them. I would always say that everyone is going through something. Whether it's an illness or some other issue. I felt better putting my life out there. To let people know that aren't alone. It was therapy to and for me. Then I got in touch with an old friend. I knew him from way back in the 80's. He was a DJ and just an incredibly good man. Several years had gone by and I didn't see or speak to him. Then he appeared on face book. He had an organization that aided children going through cancer. We met up and talked, learning that he had gone through his own bout with cancer back in the 90's. What he told me next was so upsetting to me. He said that he went through his illness alone. Yes, he had family, but with all the people he knew, no one supported him. He too, with an incredibly strong faith, prayed and asked God to give him the chance to pay his Blessing forward. And did he ever. When we finally met up again and talked I was amazed that our message was the same! I felt as though it this cancer was given to me for a reason. I felt that I needed to pay my Blessings forward. But he was on a level that was incredible. Just as our relationship restarted, he had organized "A RIDE FOR JOE". This was a ride, named for his brother who had passed away and it supported law enforcement suffering from leukemia and other cancers. He vowed to ride in each and every county in the state. And during this time of so much hate and protest against law enforcement, here was a black man putting himself out there. He himself was inspirational! I was in awe of all he had accomplished! Was it all starting to come clear? I fully believed that God was showing me the way! When I posted a picture of myself without hair with him, the response was incredible! I didn't need a wig, or a hat, or a scarf for that matter. I was strong. I didn't want pity. I smiled widely at those who walked by me in stores. I embraced my baldness and was proud that I wore nothing to let everyone know that cancer was not going to make me hide. Bullshit! I was going to continue to live my life! Chemo may slow me down temporarily, but it wasn't going to beat me. NEVER.

Chapter 14

The 3 weeks in -between chemotherapy went very quickly. It was already time for round 2. August was so hot this year and I didn't miss my hair at all. As a matter of fact, I was on a mission to tan my head as much as the rest of me! The only time I had to stay out of the sun was chemo week. I would get extremely overheated. The back of my head would literally start to heat up. I really didn't get hot flashes, thank God! Those stopped very soon after my hysterectomy.

Having one chemo under my belt I could now utilize what I had learned and apply it now to this chemo. I would now start the steroid the same night as the chemo and continue for the the 4 ½ days. Along with double Hydrocodone, I was hoping we could get ahead of the pain and keep it manageable. So my chemo routine was the same. Steam immediately after and again that night and for the following 2 days. 100 oz of water for the next 5 days. A lot of rest. I had other symptoms that I just couldn't do much about. Temporary loss of taste buds, neuropathy in my hands, legs and feet. Agita...commonly known to non Italians as heart burn, bloating and some weight gain because of the steroids! It was frustrating to say the least. Before this I was about 6-7 lbs away from where I wanted to be, now I was rollercoastering back up. I just had to keep reminding myself that it was all temporary.

My second treatment went a lot easier. Taking the steroid and hydrocodone immediately did get on top of the pain. It was still there, but manageable. The secret really being to continue to do all that I was doing to counter everything AND relax. You need to shut your body down. I cannot stress that enough. It makes a ton of difference.

We were struggling big time at our restaurant. April, May, June and July we started seeing double digit growth. Bob was cutting labor down and working so many hours, just trying to save as much as possible. He was a work horse, but I could see the physical toll it was starting to take on him. I don't know how he continued as he did. But he did, and he would until the end. We had a gorgeous summer, once it started. August was hot, sunny, very little rain and each and every weekend was gorgeous.

Perfect for those that loved bbq's and their camps. Perfect to get those kids off to college, perfect to shop for back to school, perfect for vacations. Horrible for lunches. We took a horrible hit. We lost a ton of money. If we didn't have a miracle come September, we were done.

Follow ups/ bloodwork out to Syracuse may have seemed like it would be a real pain. I mean the convenience of having your doctor around the corner, a lab to draw your blood at several different locations around the area may be enough to keep you here, but when you know the level of care is so extremely different, it was so worth it! That ride was a tremendous comfort. Having to go back to Syracuse every 3rd Friday, 3 days before the next scheduled chemo was very important. It was a follow up to what had happened and to check blood levels to make sure my white counts were good enough to continue. I felt very strong. Very confident. I was coming through these chemo treatments good. Dr. T was very happy with my results and he was already talking about different treatments after chemo. After my 2nd treatment I looked at him and said, " I know I'm healing!" He looked me straight in the eye and said," Lorrie, you are preaching to the choir!" How I adored his attitude. When I met with his nurse practitioner, I told her how the neuropathy was in both legs and feet but only on my left arm and hand. Dr. T was on his honeymoon right now but that didn't stop emails from going through. This man was committed. I left that appointment waiting on answers to if he wanted to cut back my chemo prescription a bit to ease up on symptoms. He was a little concerned that I was only having issues on my left side. Although he was fully aware that the year before I had suffered whip lash in a car accident. But, being as thorough as he was, it wasn't 20 minutes into my drive home that I got a call back. They had already scheduled a contrast MRI on my neck and upper back for the next day. I knew what his intent was. He was making sure that the cancer hadn't hit my bones. He didn't say that, but you know.

Driving back out there the following day for the MRI was nerve wracking. Deep in my soul I knew the cancer was pushing back. My lungs were crystal clear, I had no cancer pain. My energy level was up. I didn't have any medical proof, yet, but I could feel it. Still. This was another test that I never had before. The constrast MRI was considered a closed MRI. For those who had never had one it is terribly confining. You feel as though you are in a coffin. You only have a few inches above your head and they give you the choice to hear music or they will give you earplugs. The machine itself makes a jackhammer noise. I have learned to deal with it but it is hard. After 30 minutes or so, they pull you out to give you an IV. It's almost like 3D. It's layered. These tests are amazing. I basically spent nearly an hour in there. And I have to be honest. You start worrying! I did. I find myself saying THE OUR FATHER and HAIL MARY over and over again. You find yourself hearing that little voice say, " What if, what if? THAT'S WHEN YOU HAVE TO STOP IT! RIGHT THEN AND THERE! I had a silent, motionless fight with myself at that moment. You can't move because the test will take longer. But right then, in my head, I said, NO! The negative thoughts, those damn devil thoughts are not going to control my brain, my body my heart or my soul! I refuse. I know better! The power of the Holy Spirit is stronger than the devil. I knew my path and the devil wasn't a part of it. Period. I got through it, came home and within an hour received a call. It was all degenerative changes due to my accident. No cancer in my bones! Thank you sweet Lord!

My 3rd chemo came as we headed to our yearly back to school meeting. Faculty and staff of the entire district would meet for a 3 hour period. It was a formality. I really didn't enjoy going, but this year was different. I couldn't wait to get back to the routine and see everyone. Most of the people I worked with I hadn't seen since the end of school. They had no idea what was going on. My only fear going back to school was seeing the kids. I didn't want to frighten them. Some, very few kids, because of knowing parents, knew what was going on. Most didn't. They had known me for all their lives as Mrs. Markason with the big hair. Now I had nothing. My wig was gorgeous, but it was too hot. I was comfortable without it and I knew once the kids saw me, realized nothing changed, it would be ok. But it was a genuine fear. I spoke with our school principal, asked her advice and she agreed that maybe the teachers could talk about it before they would see me. Taking a bit of the shock value out. I thought it was a great idea. She sent an email to the faculty and staff regarding my situation. Asking them to talk to the kids prior to recess. Explaining the situation to the kids in the best way possible. As I would run into parents I had asked them to talk to their kids about me and tell other parents. Whitesboro was a small, tight knit community, if I could get to a lot of these kids before hand, I would feel better. Something positive had to come from this. Unfortunately, we can't shelter the kids from cancer. It's hits home to every family. I had zero problem talking about the cancer. I wanted the kids to see me, hear me, know that with the exception of my hair, nothing was different. I would be ready to talk to them about anything they wanted to. But I would let them come to me. I wasn't pushing myself on any of them.

They were amazing! Little by little. Groups would come up to me. I think they just wanted to look. Some asked to see my head. Some wanted information. Some just hugged me. As a matter of fact, lining up 3rd grade, after recess, that first day of school, each of the 3 classes walked by me as I dismissed them, holding my hand out, as usual for my high 5, nearly every one of them hugged me. Yes. I was reduced to tears. The love that came from those kids just amazed me. It was something I never expected.

I always wore a hat to school. By this time I was completely bald. I kept losing even the tiniest pieces of hair through the summer. I had a few patches of longer hair. It made me crazy so I just shaved it bald. I looked like Kojak. Anybody remember him?

September picked up at the restaurant where August had left off. Horrible. The absolutely picture perfect weather continued along with road construction at the main thoroughfare. Traffic backed up and detours just killed our lunches. Nothing. This was the end. We had to face it. There was no way we could continue. We would need money to survive. We had to give ourselves a bit of a cushion until Bob could find a job. We didn't say anything to anyone. We were praying for a miracle still. New people were still walking through the door. Our feedback was still extremely positive. It would have been so much easier if our food was lousy, service was terrible and everyone hated us. That wasn't the case. I could now really see the physical and mental toll on Bob. He was limping, having twisted his knee. He wasn't sleeping good, and he was exhausted. He had no simple pleasures. No quality of life. I felt as though he was back to the last days of WENDYS. He was going to drop dead if he didn't stop. His blood pressure was up. Why not? He gave every minute of every waking hour to making this restaurant work. I knew him. He would think of himself as a failure. Well, I wasn't prepared for him to do that. This man, my husband, was the most loyal, hardworking, honest man that I had ever met. This would never in my mind be considered a failure. He had his chance at a dream. His parents gave him his inheritance to do this. I regret nothing. I didn't want him to either. Those were his parents, their money and their son's dream. I fully supported it. But my heart broke for him. Still, how many people actually get the chance to live their dream? We met so many good people through this journey. It will always be reflected back positively! But we had to move on.

We had to break the news to our employees. No one took it well. Everyone was sad. They were beyond employees. They were family. Brian, our chef, was one of our closest friend's son. Our nighttime waitresses, one started with us and the other shortly there after. Our daytime waitresses, one was a personal friend, the other, a good soul. This was hard. Bob had to tell our landlord. We'd had guaranteed one year on the lease but had a 5 year agreement. We had always been very honest with him and in turn, he had been a wonderful landlord. We hated putting him in this position, but our back was up against the wall. Bob called him and told him. He was shocked. He thought we were doing better than that. He offered a months free rent to keep us going. I could see Bob doing the math in his head. Can we do it? Give it one more month? When those words actually came out of his mouth I Yelled! No!! We can't do this. We had to stop the bleeding. We had to have money to survive. So the last week in September we announced to our customers this was our last week. Saturday, the 26th of September we would officially close. It was a horribly emotional week for Bob. He went out and thanked personally everyone that walked through those doors. More than once ending up in a hug with our customers, everyone crying. That final weekend was the busiest we ever had. All our friends had come in to say goodbye. Our support was overwhelming. Our final Friday was the busiest ever. I can't tell you how many tears were shed, not only by us, but our loyal customers. This was hard. Bob was heart broken. We closed our doors that Saturday night, Bob's dream was over. These next few weeks were going to be very difficult.

Sunday and Monday Bob was able to have a normal few days. We were closed those two days so it really hadn't sunk in yet. Tuesday he would find himself back down there with Brian and Ringo, he was a Bob too, but he resembled Ringo Starr so Bob dubbed him Ringo years ago. We had a ton of work to do. Going into the month of September, Bob kept the ordering very light. Knowing full well this just may be the end, he didn't want a lot to have to bring home. Naturally the first thing I did was get all my wall décor. Amazing, the restaurant décor fit beautifully in my house. We would unload in the garage and work out of there. You know how things are. You change one thing on the wall and it has a snowball effect, everything got moved around. Within a 2 week period we pretty much got everything home, trying to sell the equipment that we purchased. This all kept Bob pretty busy. This was the hard part from him now. He didn't have a schedule again. He struggled with this first being out of work. He just didn't know what to do with himself. Going from working 60 hours a week to nothing was pure anxiety in his mind. In a perfect world I wanted him to have a month off to get the restaurant closed up. Have time to breathe and move on. He would wake up and here's me, Mrs. Schedule, "What are you doing today?" Oh he would get angry at me! I didn't mean it in a " you lazy thing" kind of way. I was trying to get him to think about schedules. Routines. I thought he would feel better.

After the first 2 weeks, he was in a better place emotionally. Our Regina, during those last days, happened to walk into his office at the restaurant and found him crying. She had never seen her father cry before. She didn't know what to do. On that first Sunday, Bob got a surprise call from an old friend. Light years ago, he lived in the area. He was a very talented singer and song writer. One of those guys that had enough talent and no way he couldn't make to the top. He made an album and Bob, back in the early 1980's was his financial backer. He didn't make it big and through the years he decided to move south. He knew how it felt to have a dream not come through. He was the perfect person for Bob to talk to. God works in mysterious ways. He hadn't talk to him in months. With in a few weeks, Bob had gotten himself into a routine. He would spend sometime every morning checking alerts for jobs. This was a completely different world now in the job hunt. No longer do you walk into a business and fill out an application. Now you have to "market" yourself. Resume online. Job alerts. Emailing contacts. LINKEDIN, head hunters. Everything on line. It was an uphill battle. His 55th birthday had passed in June. His experiences in the restaurant only added to his skill set. Numbers man, numbers cruncher. Running a business. I had a deep peacefulness inside of me. He didn't. He worried. Not that I didn't at times, but I just believe that everything happens for a reason. I also knew that we had enough happen to us. Better days were ahead.

I was able to not miss work during my chemo. My job as a teacher's aide, covering recess, inside and outside, allowed me to sit if I needed to. Our principal was so accommodating. I would schedule chemo before school and go in and work my shift. September, being gorgeous and hot, had me sitting in the shade. Heat sensitivity was one of the only things I couldn't figure out. So I just sat in the shade. I kept a Power Ade Zero with me at all times. I refused to miss any of school that I didn't need to. When the side effects kicked in, and they remained minimal, I still had to take it easy. Those side effects could become worse at anytime if I pushed myself. The neuropathy in my legs and feet would increase if I was up and walking too much. But I knew, deep inside of me, the peacefulness, the calmness, the way I came out of chemo every time. My bloodwork remaining normal so far, that there was a healing happening inside of me. I couldn't wait for my tumor markers numbers to be ran. I had a scan scheduled for October 22. I knew I was going to get good news!

I would have to make the trip out to Syracuse every third Friday for my bloodwork. They check the white blood count to make sure that haven't dropped. If they do. They hold off on chemo for a week or so, until they get back up to normal levels. . Driving out that Friday before my fourth chemo, I knew they were running my tumor markers. My appointment was first thing in the morning, which I wanted because this particular test took about 6 hours to get results. I should have them by day's end. I would have a quick visit with Dr. T's nurse practitioner, just to go over everything. They were so thorough. She promised that I would get a call on the results if they got them by day's end. Remission, remission, remission. That's all I wanted to hear!

What a surprise! I got the call that afternoon. No remission but my numbers dropped! I started chemo at 58. Normal range is 38. My results came in at 49.6! THANK YOU GOD!! I still had so many people praying for me. So many people in my corner. God heard. God hears. Pray. Pray. Pray!!!!

I was praying that once I got through the 6 rounds of chemo, which would be the first week of November, that my scans would show remission and I would be done. My last visit with the nurse practitioner we talked about going forward. They saw the positivity in me and they felt it too. We talked about moving forward after I hit remission. Not if I hit remission, when I hit it. Thinking about it logically, if the scan and bloodwork showed remission numbers, but I was just below the magic number of 38, maybe it would be better if I continued chemo just to knock it back further? I thought so. As much as I wanted this over, I had to be realistic. My next appointment I would see Dr. T. He was out of the office for the past month, he had gotten married!

Since we were getting head on into October, naturally Christmas decorating was on my mind. I needed to pick up this particular type of lighting for my trees. Random sparkle. I loved this. They twinkled beautifully, in a calm way. It was relaxing to watch. Well, for me, sitting and watching any Christmas tree is relaxing to watch. Especially with a glass of wine! With tunnel vision, I ran into the store. It's very hard for me to walk by CHRISTMAS decorations and not buy anything. Honestly, with 12 trees I put up, 30+ bins of decorations and now the decorations from the restaurant, I didn't need anything. But not wanting to be tempted, I remained focused! A friend of mine worked there. We weren't close friends but we had a good friendship. She went on an incredible cruise about a month before. Italy, Spain, Turkey. It was unreal! She saw me and said not to go anywhere, she had to give me something! When she came back, she handed me a small bottle, about an inch and a half tall and the Blessed Mother on it. She had visited a Shrine in Turkey which was located on Mt. Koressos. . It was called " THE HOUSE OF THE VIRGIN MARY" it is believed to be the place that St. John took Mary to live until her assumption. The Shrine also known for the running water, now a fountain, has been continually running since the time of Mary's earthly life. These waters have been said to have great healing powers. I was so overwhelmed that she had thought of me! I hugged her and couldn't thank her enough! What a gift! Every day I would put a little on my left side of my chest. I would ask for healing. My fifth chemo treatment went off without a hitch. I was wishing away the entire month of October. I wanted to get those scans under my belt. My bloodwork was perfect. The only thing that was truly making me crazy was the weight gain, other than that, I was so thankful. By the fifth chemo, bodies start breaking down. I refused to let myself get run down. You have to become the priority in your life. Period. End of story!

Finally! It was the day of the scan! Like before, I had everything scheduled for that day. Bob being home, came with me. I had bloodwork scheduled first, then about an hour wait to drink that wonderful concoction that would light up the cancer in the CT SCAN. After the scan, another hour until my appointment with Dr. T. I would have all my results except my tumor markers. Bloodwork wasn't done until after 1pm so there was no way it would be done. I would find out on the next day, Friday. This all made for a long day but I walked out of there with all the information. So much different from a year ago. No stress. It was wonderful!

Bob and I were sitting in the waiting room. My appointment with Dr. T was late in the day. 4:15. The waiting room was cleaned out. Only a few of us remaining. Usually Dr. T ran pretty much on time. The only time he was late was when he was consulting with another doctor on me. So my history with him was if he's late, I was getting bad news. I told Bob this. See, there it is….those damn negative thoughts creep in your head! I yelled at myself in my head. Just then, the man who works at the desk walked over to me. He must have seen me getting anxious. He said, " I just checked and your scan results aren't in yet, that's probably why you haven't been called." I thanked him. I needed that! But I was amazed that this gentleman, who I see every month, was kind enough to take it upon himself to ease my tension. And he did. Then I saw Dr. T's patient navigator. She was the sweetest thing. Always smiling, positive attitude, and that can't be easy working in a place where I'm sure bad news happens every day! As she walked by me, she saw me and smiled! " Hi Lorrie!" I immediately said," where's Dr. T? Every time he's late, I get bad news!" I was going to carry on with this now! What an ass I was! She told me no, he's late because another patient had him in there for a long time. Typical Dr. T, he would sit with someone for as long as they needed it. Ok, the anxiety lessened. Then I get mad at myself. Be logical will you??? Your numbers are down, you feel great. There is no way you are getting bad news today! I have more conversations with myself than anyone would realize! But the best part of it is that I have learned to turn myself around quickly!

FINALLY!!!!! They called us in. They promised Dr. T would be here soon. About 5 minutes went by. Ugh. Waiting. Nothing worse! I pulled out my phone and started playing CANDY CRUSH SODA. I needed something to pass the time! Then he popped his head in and said," Don't get nervous! Scan results aren't in yet. The lab has been running behind all day! Don't worry! ". He walked in about 5 minutes later with a smile on his face! The tumor has shrunk considerably!!! YEAH BABY!!!!! He went on to say that we couldn't have gotten any better news and he was thrilled how small it got! Bloodwork wasn't in, so we got right into the plan for moving forward. As I thought, he wanted me to continue chemo for a bit. One to three months. Rescan in about 6 weeks to see where we are. His thought process was since this is working so well and I am tolerating the side effects so beautifully, let's kick this down further. Going forward would be another oral treatment but since those treatments take up to 3 months to show if it's working, he didn't want to give the cancer a chance to grow. What I didn't tell him but I could feel was that there was a Healing happening inside of me. One of my future scans was going to show that no cancer was in me. There wasn't a doubt in my mind. But for now, we continue as planned. I totally agreed it was the right course of action.

Friday the 23rd, the day after my scan, I called the office for my results. You get the nurses voice mail and they promise to get back to you by day's end. And they do! I hadn't heard anything all day. I knew in my heart that I was in remission but wasn't willingly to say it until I had those numbers. I went into school that day and I knew the staff had heard because our principal, had told everyone. One woman I worked with in particular, one of the sweetest women I have ever met. A woman of faith and family, she was one of my biggest supporters. Always praying for me, always giving me these little gifts. As I walked by her room, I popped my head in and smiled. She popped up out of her chair and ran over to hug me. As she got closer, I saw a sadness in her eyes. I stepped back. " What's wrong?" I asked her. She broke down a bit, her newborn grandson, 3 weeks old, was hospitalized the night before. The flu, she thought, 105 fever. I hugged her back and said I will say a prayer for the baby. The I remembered I had the Holy Water with me in the car. My schedule wouldn't allow me to run out to the car at that moment. I had to wait until I had a 10 minute break in-between the grades coming down to recess. As soon as I had the chance I ran out to my car. Walking back into the school, perfect timing! She was just leaving school to get to the hospital. I stopped her and told her about the Holy Water. I told her to please bless the baby. She hugged me, thanked me and promised to bring it back on Monday. I wasn't worried.

I had to be back at school by 5 pm that night for the annual Fall Fest. The school would do this the Friday before Halloween week so it didn't interfere with the real Halloween. The kids get dressed up in their costumes, so do all the teachers and staff and they go trick or treating through the school. The lights are off, spooky music through the sound system, the kids love it. This year, faculty and staff were all to be Minions! I had missed the last 2 years due to the restaurant. I ran into Patty, her daughter and her grandchildren that night. Patty's two grandchildren, sister and brother of this little baby came to trick or treat. Patty's daughter hugged me and thanked me. I told her, the baby was going to be fine. What I didn't realize was the baby didn't have the flu, but was being tested for several things, including spinal meningitis. The Fall Fest was only an 1 ½ long. But while I was passing out candy, Dr.T's office called. I missed it. Damn! Now I have to wait until Monday! This was an easy wait, I wasn't nervous. I knew I was at remission, but not willing to use that word until I had those numbers! Monday came and I forgot before I left for school to call. My mind was on Patty's grandson. I walked immediately to her room, she was waiting for me. She grabbed me and hugged me. "How's the baby?" She was beaming. " Lorrie, I put the Holy Water on his forehead, lips and chest on Friday night. I get there Saturday morning and ALL THE SYMPTOMS WERE GONE!" What she said wasn't registering...." All the symptoms were gone? The fever, everything?" I asked her. Oh my God." We had a miracle. They sent the baby home!" I had chills. Even me, who believes so deeply, was completely overwhelmed. Then, I go outside with the first group of kids for recess, still completely blown away! Then, one of the kids handed me a rubber bracelet, the ones that are sold as fund raisers, you know the ones. No one lost it because we just came out. It was breast cancer pink. And when I turned it over, it said BELIEVE. My mouth fell open. Co-incidence? No way. Huge sign! I couldn't believe all this has happened. I never doubted that Patty's grandson was a miracle baby, even in those first minutes, but it's so amazing, that you can't grasp it immediately. God wanted me to understand. So he sent me my word. BELIEVE. It went through the school like wild fire. One of our kindergarten teachers approached me, another Patty, another huge supporter. Another woman of faith and family, and a dear friend. She told me that one of the other kindergarten teachers wondered if she thought I would mind if she asked me for the Holy Water for her father who was dying with cancer. I immediately went to her room to tell her I would bring it tomorrow. And I did. This was going to be shared with anyone I felt needed it. It was that important that I shared it.

With all that happened on Monday, I completely forgot about me! So Tuesday morning I went onto the patient portal to ask the question regarding my tumor markers. I really had to start using this. They actually got back to you faster. But I'm old school, I like talking to people. They responded quickly! I got the news I wanted to hear! REMISSION!!!!! I dropped from 49.6 to 34.18! Thank you sweet Jesus!! It was an amazing feeling!

We were having an incredible Fall. Warm days and cool nights. The perfect combination for gorgeous Fall foliage. Bob was starting to embrace these days. He got himself on a schedule. Spending the first few hours of the day checking emails, job alerts, sending resumes. It was a different world. Marketing yourself blindly. I liked the old school way better. It was more personal. But, to my delight, several things were getting done around the house that needed to get done. The Fall clean up, putting away all the lawn furniture. His office, work room and other areas got a healthy clean out. We took advantage that we still had the dumpster at the restaurant. We had some ceiling damage from a roof leak a few years back and he got that done too. He needed this time.

Halloween has never been a favorite of mine. I enjoyed it as a kid but as a parent, viewing it from an overprotective mother's eyes, I didn't like it. I saw it as a night for all the wackos to come out in costume. Yet, since so many of my kids from school lived in the neighborhood it was a fun night. Everyone who was familiar with ringing my doorbell knows full well they would see me putting up my Living room Christmas tree.

My Angel tree. Yes, and again this year, my angel tree topper was pink! I decided to wear my wig so I didn't scare any kids. I would make up around 100 little bags because I never knew how many kids would show up. This year, being a Saturday and good weather, I figured I'd go through the majority and what was left over would be devoured by my kids. I went through about 75 bags that night. Usually by around 9 it was over and the neighborhood lights would go off. It was close to 9 when my bell rang again. I answered it to find 7-8 teenagers yelling BOO! None of them looked familiar, but they rarely do at that age. I figured I was going to have some fun with them! I looked at them calmly and asked if it was my turn now to scare them? They giggled and said, " yeah, ok!" Well I whipped my wig off so fast and said, " BLAHHHHH!" Well, I wish I had a damn camera! If you could have seen their faces! I told them that no one else was going to do that to them tonight! They all high fived me and wished me well. Good kids, all of them. Hey, I was just getting wiggy with it!

My 6th Chemo came at the beginning of November. My schedule for it would change. I would prefer it in the afternoon after school. That wasn't always available. As was this chemo. We had to be there by 8:15. I liked getting there about 15 minutes earlier to check in and give them time to get the prescription for my abraxame all set. I wanted to be in the chair, IV's in me and ready to go. While the chemo treatment literally took 2 hours, I had to get home, get into the steam and be at the school by 11:20. I have always said that I enjoyed my trips to Syracuse for my check ups, usually I was alone with Bob at the restaurant. I would get so many signs during that time. Whether it was crosses in the sky or songs on the radio. It was my private time to thank God and talk to my father. We were driving out and I was texting my niece. As I was waiting for her to answer. My phone in my hand, talking to Bob. I looked down at my phone as it lit up. I was confused. It said " I LOVE YOU" I didn't understand why she was telling me this, then I realized it was in my bubble. Like I typed it. But I didn't. I looked at Bob and said look at this! I didn't type it. My fingers didn't move. And even if they did, I cannot type out a text without making a mistake. It was perfectly spelled out and spaced. My fingers are too big. It was a message. Then I realized it. It was my parents wedding anniversary. My father's message to me.

Chemo finished in time and I was able to get to school on time. Weather was incredible, low 60's! Incredible weather for early November! I wanted to try something different. Between the steroid I would take and the chemo. I had bloated up nearly 20 lbs. so far. Yeah, I know, I'm still bitching about it. But it was more than just vanity. I was uncomfortable. I refused to go by new clothes. I wanted to try to go through the week without the steroid. I would take my pain meds but that would stop the bloating. I decided to kick up my steam treatments 5 minutes more each time and throw in another day, drink 60 oz of Power Ade zero in addition to the water and pray for the best. Well, I had an incredible chemo week. Controlled pain. Minimal pain. My taste buds never faded. Even my neuropathy was better and didn't last as long. My God, this was unreal. With each chemo treatment, I got stronger. This just doesn't happen. People would shake their heads at me, unable to believe, yet believe, because I was I was in front of them, functioning. I had possibly 3 more treatments to get through. I was re-upped and ready to go!

The following week I started wearing my wig. My head started to get cold and I would get a chill on the back of my neck that would go right down my spine. Even though weather was above average when the wind kicked up, there was that unmistakable November chill. I knew walking into school was going to throw all the kids off. Especially the kindergarteners. I walked into the cafeteria. I stopped as I walked in and said as I always did, " HELLO LITTLE PEOPLE!" Silence! They couldn't figure it out for a second! Then I had to start explaining. "No, my hair didn't grow over the weekend, no it's not a hat, my hats are at home, no, I'm not going to take it off right now, my head was cold so I put my wig on!" How funny they were.

I always started my Christmas decorating early. But this year Bob told me he really was excited about the decorations. I looked at him oddly. I have never heard that come from his mouth. I knew he loved the decorations but this was different. Something changed. Our youngest, Zach, was born on the 5th of November. Bob was very melancholy lately. His parents were getting on in age. His mom, suffering from dementia, still knew us all but was severely limited with short term memory. Every time she saw me she would ask me about my lack of hair. I felt bad for my father in law, it was hard to deal with it day in and day out. She was becoming very reclusive. I was glad that they had moved into a retirement community, at least he could and would have contact with others.

The change in Bob was a subtle one. I'm sure no one else could see it. It was just things he said to me. Between his parents, the closing of the restaurant, his worry about finding a job and the financial situation we were now in, and don't forget my cancer, that was enough to cause worry. Yet I remained calm. I just believed it was going to be alright. He would tell me over and over," please, keep staying positive, you are the only thing keeping me going." Oh, I had my moments of anxiety, trust me! I had my pity parties. I couldn't dwell on everything because if I did it would become an obsessive thought. An obsessive negative thought that I didn't need to overplay in my head. We tried to do everything right through out our life. We weren't perfect, and never claimed to be. But how did we get in this situation? There I said it. I would say it, then let it go. It didn't help reliving that any more than me being angry for cancer coming into my world. I can't change the past. Remembering the Serenity Prayer always kept me grounded. It was just common sense.

 Bob had become closer to the kids. That was his one regret all these years. He was such a good father, always, but his jobs always took away from me and the kids. He was cherishing the time he had now with all of us. He would tell me he loved me at least 4 times a day. He wanted to find a 9-5 job. He wanted weekends off. I wanted that for him. He wanted to spend time with the kids. This would be the first Black Friday that he wasn't worrying about restaurant sales. Anyone who has never ran a restaurant, fast food or full service has no idea the stress and hours it takes. It was not only physically exhausting, but mentally exhausting. And he ran 9 stores in the WENDYS franchise. He deserved a 9-5 job now.

Then it hit me. With all that I had gone through and continue to go through, there had been changes in me. Now, suddenly, there were changes in him. Was this part of God's plan? Did Bob have to realize that he wasn't balanced in life, that earning all that money took him away from us? It's almost an unfair thought, I mean, he had to work, he had to provide, but, making a lot of money in Bob's mind was most important. He was old school. He wanted to provide, he wanted nice things, he wasn't afraid to work for it. He loved us all. We always had a very old fashion marriage. He was the bread winner and I took care of everything else. And while it may not be the politically correct way now adays, it worked and still works for us! When I realized the change, I walked into his office and sat down. He had become more religious through out my battle. He would tell me that he prayed everyday for God to heal me but he didn't want to ask for the restaurant too. He didn't want to ask for too much. I knew the feeling. There were so many days when I would just walk around and talk out loud to God just asking for help. I was afraid he was getting sick of me! But I said to him. "Do you realize the change in you? Your relationships with the kids, finally you have that closeness you always wanted and you are realizing the importance." I knew now things would happen. God works in mysterious ways.

Bob's grandparents, both deceased, had passed down to his father and uncle, camps on a river about 45 minutes away from us. Bob, as a child loved going there. His uncle, had made it his hobby and had remodeled everything, adding several decks and upgraded everything to make it more of a home than a camp. Bob had decided he wanted to take Zach out of school for his birthday and go up to camp along with Bob's father. It was something he had never done. Well, let me rephrase that. Bob never had the opportunity to do that. Between running the WENDYS franchise for all those years to running the restaurant, he had never had any time to enjoy simple pleasures like that. Simple pleasures. Quality of life. He was embracing this time for as long as he could. 3 generations. All 3 went up, it was a gorgeous Fall day as our crazy Spring like weather continued! They spent the entire day. I have never seen him happier or more at peace than he did when he got home. Bob couldn't stop talking about it. Neither could Zach. I could see him questioning all he had done through the years. He was always a good husband, father and provider. How he wished he could have gone back and relived those years giving more of himself to his kids. But he was doing it all now.

Chapter 15

With my 7th chemo treatment I was able to back off a week. It would have fallen during Thanksgiving week. My treatments were always on a Monday, leaving my worst days for Thursday and Friday. Given the option of delaying it a week, I jumped at it.

Even though I had a handle on the side effects, I still would get tired and I would try to just shut down by 7pm and just watch tv in bed. Ozzie would stay with me constantly. Always right up against me. I needed him as much as he needed me. I was able to back off on the steroid and with the added fluids and steam, it seemed to counter it well. Getting through this many treatments with minimal side effects and perfect bloodwork was truly a blessing. I couldn't wait for my next scan. That would come at the end of January. December 4th turned out to be my 7th treatment. Because of Thankgiving the week before, my schedule was a little screwed up. My appointment was actually scheduled for Friday this time, my bloodwork was done just before chemo that day. I would then have my followup with Dr. T's nurse practitioner. By the time I met with her, my blood results were in. Chemo went off without a hitch.

In between all this I had a scheduled appointment with my primary care doctor. He was also a heart doctor. With all my issues, I felt better having him as my primary, besides, it cut down on one less doctor. First thing they do, naturally, is the blood pressure. Mine was through the roof. 190/111. " What?? Are you kidding? Take it again, that can't be right!" Well, they took it again and yup, 190/111. I guess that's why they call heart attacks the silent killer. I didn't feel stressed. But let's look back. Cancer, restaurant closed, Bob can't find a job, Christmas looming, no money coming in. Any reasons there to be stressed? Ummm, maybe? He upped my meds and had me come back the following week. No change. Now I was getting frustrated. I felt as though I had cancer pretty much under control and now this. Why? Why was it continually one thing after another with me? This was unreal. I went from not thinking I was stressed to being extremely stressed. Now dealing with weekly appointments until I get all this under control. Christmas week, night appointment. Add another pill to the list of high blood pressure meds. As he is putting in the order on his computer, under his breath I hear him say, " You were on this a few years back, why did you go off of it?" He was actually talking to himself but I answered. "I wasn't on this." Completely forgetting the incident with the pill that I swelled up all through the groin with. That didn't hit me for a few weeks yet! Anyway, it was too late to grab it from the pharmacy when I got out, I figured I would pick it up the next morning. Running into the store the following morning for the prescription, I was told there was nothing there. I called the office, yup, he forgot to call it in. No way I was running back later to Walmart. I would just grab it the next day, Wednesday, the Eve of Christmas Eve when I went shopping.

I guess I shouldn't have been surprised when I found out my blood pressure was so high. Bob was getting so aggravated. He had sent out a good 20+ resumes and was hearing nothing back. It was the worst time of year to look for a job. No one was hiring in the 4th quarter of the year. Especially in an economy this bad. He knew he was going to have to take something, anything. We needed money coming in. Times were getting desperate. My friends would ask every so often about throwing a benefit for me. I always said no. I never thought bad of anyone who had benefits. God knows I knew the bills that hit us. Bankruptcy was looking more and more probable. Unbelievable. How the hell did we end up here?

I did my shopping on the eve of Christmas Eve, forgetting to take the medicine. I wanted to take it with all my other pills so it was easier to remember. I figured it would just take it the following morning. Christmas this year was just different. I cut down on a lot of what I cooked, vowing to enjoy more. By nighttime, I was exhausted. Getting undressed I noticed how swollen my feet and ankles were. I was actually swollen right up to my calves. Reaction to the medicine no doubt. I tried to look for the insert but the garbage was already taken out. So I brought it up on WEB MD. A severe reaction was swelling to the feet ankles or legs. Great! Now what? I'm not calling the doctor on Christmas Eve. Certainly not on Christmas Day either. I figured I would just wait until Monday and call him then. I pulled myself off the meds then and there.

My 8th treatment was on Monday, December 28th. I know, right before New Year's Eve. We really didn't have any plans except for a few friends that would come over. I was just trying to take it easy, resting and hoping that me just sitting down would allow me to get through it. On our way out to Syracuse for chemo, I called the doctor and told him I pulled myself off the meds because of the swelling. He wanted me back on. He prescribed a water pill and made an appointment for the first week of January. Guess what? It didn't work. My legs started swelling. It was getting worse. I pulled myself off it again. For the first time since my first chemo treatment, I had a bad week. I think I ended up with a stomach flu. Everything was the opposite of every side effect that I had. Ugh. One more after this. My body was tired. Thank God we had the week off of school.

I just knew that 2016 was going to be better. It had been 3 long years of stresses that consumed every aspect of our lives. It had to be over. I begged God to please, please, let us have some peace. We needed these stresses to go away. I continued to stay positive. Mostly in part because I felt so good and I knew that I was heading for complete remission! I wanted to hear " THERE IS NO CANCER IN YOU!" I BELIEVED! When I went in for my bloodwork on the before my treatment on the 28th I had been seen by a different nurse practitioner. Vacations, everyone was on vacation. I hadn't had my tumor markers done since October. So I asked. " Were my markers ran today?" She looked on the computer. " No, they were actually run on December 4th. You dropped to 18.8!" I couldn't believe it! I never asked and no one told me! I wasn't angry, these people had been too good to me! I was at 18.8. Last numbers in October were 34.8! They were dropping like a rock! Thank you sweet Jesus! MERRY CHRISTMAS TO ME! I couldn't wait to get to the end of January. I was due to see Dr. T for the next follow up right before that I thought to be my last chemo! 2016 was going to be a good year!

I had a feeling Bob was going to be offered a job by the new year. And I told him that. He was getting more and more discouraged. Between his age and the impersonal way of filling out applications and resumes was now, you had no chance to make an impression. But my prediction kind of came true when he received a call from a restaurant, a franchise, asking if he was available for a phone interview on New Years Day.

Naturally he said yes. But who interviews on New Years Day? A restaurant that is open 24/7, 365 days a week. That's who. He interviewed well, but they just didn't seem like they were managed well. It took the entire month of January to go through the hiring process. He got the job, naturally. Not what he really wanted, but we were out of options. We needed money coming in. He would keep looking, more than anything, after all he, we, have been through, I wanted him to find the job of his dreams. This wasn't it. Maybe, this silver lining wasn't showing itself yet. I refused to go negative. Everything has a reason. Faith. You have to keep the faith.

I went back in to see my primary doctor the first week of January. Again, pulling myself off my medicine. With everything going on with cancer, I refused to deal with all this swelling. This certainly can't be good for me. That's when it hit me. I took this drug before my diagnosis of cancer. I swelled up. The nurse practitioner had argued with me and then I found out I had cancer. It was the swelling from the cancer that caused my heart issues to inflame. I told them I had a reaction to this medicine and they put me on it again??? Seriously? For some reason, I think they viewed this medicine as some kind of wonder drug. They were insistent that I remain on it. Now giving me lasex. A stronger water pill. I gave it another try. I gave it a week. Nope. Not working. Once again I was on the phone with the office. I was on a very low dose of the lasex. Normal dosage I found out was a minimal of double that I was on. The nurse practitioner called me back, I didn't realize my doctor was out due to his own surgery. Do you know what she told me? Basically to suck it up, get off my feet and go buy compression stockings! I went off the wall! I screamed at her. With all I had going on, suck it up??? She doubled the dosage. I gave it a few more days. It didn't help.

In the meantime. I had my follow up with Dr. T. The following day was to be my 9th treatment. He refused to say this was my last, pending my scan which would take place in 2 weeks. I could see the smile in his face. He told me, " Lorrie, you are making my job too easy! " he knew and felt what I felt. That scan was going to show incredible news.

I got through my last chemo. I remained swollen, now the swelling was the way up to my thighs. My legs felt horrible. The water pills weren't working. Nothing was. I could feel the skin stretching and it hurt. My feet were double the size. My ankles, well you couldn't see my ankles. This wasn't right. Enough. By the time I pulled myself off the medicine again, it was the day after my scan.

I couldn't wait for this day. Since October, when he asked me to agree to 3 more. I reacted so well to the chemo and he wanted to kick this back as far as possible. I agreed. I didn't want to but it was the right move. It was over. Bob and I got up there. I had my blood work, then the scan, then my follow up for Dr. T to give me the results! I felt incredible, with the exception of this dull ache in my back, under the rib cage. I've felt this before but I don't get myself worked up because with all the back and neck issue, me seeing a chiropractor twice a week, I figured it was all muscular.

He was late. I started to breathe heavy. I reminded Bob that when he's late, I get bad news. I tried to stay positive. He finally walked in and immediately said to me," how's your breathing?" Panic filled me. " WHY?" Omg, what's wrong? What the hell could be wrong. I felt like I was spinning. He asked he to sit on the table so he could listen to my breathing. He finally sat down and started talking. " Your scan looks good. No change since October. The cancer is very small." Then came the BUT…. " The scan also showed that you have a bit of fluid built up in the lining of the lung again. Like last year, although it's not as much. It's minimal. I don't even want you to have it removed at this point " How the hell could this be possible. We were blindsided. He was blindsided. " I think you developed a resistance to the chemo and the last 2 stopped working. My jaw dropped. How is this happening again? Bob couldn't say anything. What can you say? Here you are fully expecting the best news possible and you get Wally Wonked across the head. You can't even think of a question. After a few deep breaths, I mentioned my adema from the heart meds. He thought about it briefly but said, I just think it would be on both sides, not just the left side. I was crushed.

Regroup. Time to regroup. Everything changed in that moment. My treatment. My mindset. I was thrown. Oh God. Please. Help me. I would not be going on an oral anti estrogen treatment. I would be going on another chemo pill. SON OF A BITCH. I was scheduled for the following week for another appointment for the " chemo teach"

We drove home mostly in silence. I called a few people to let them know. I put a status on facebook. So many people waiting to here me give the Hercules yell that I was cancer free. It took me a bit of time to process it all. Actually, my news wasn't that bad. My numbers were 18.8 as of December. Much better than 6 months before. The fluid build up was minimal. I had a bit of a cold but he couldn't really hear anything bad when listening to my lungs. When I got home I hugged Bob. I told him, " look, this is a lifetime thing for me. We are going to have bumps in the road. We just have to deal with it." But it bothered me. I decided now after all week with adema that enough was enough. This couldn't be healthy for me. The more I thought about it the more it made sense. The adema was up to my thighs. My Lymphatic system on my left side is compromised. Maybe the fluid build up isn't on my right side because it didn't have a chance to get there. This just didn't make sense to me. This can't be a coincidence.

By Tuesday morning, I was absolutely convinced Dr. T was wrong. I didn't tell him the full story. By now I was off the meds for 4 days. My ankles were STILL a bit swollen. Don't tell me this isn't affecting my compromised lymphatic system. I walked in to see the nurse practitioner. I really adored her. She was sweet and kind and honestly listened. That's what I counted on. When she walked through the door and sat down I told her I had to talk to her. To please, hear me out. And I told her the story. And she listened. She told me that Dr. T was beside himself with my scan and the fluids. He never saw this coming. When I explained the situation, I asked her if I could be rescanned the following week. I wanted time to have all this out of me. She agreed! Holding off my treatment til the following week. If I was right, I would go on tamoxifen. An anti estrogen drug. If I was wrong, it would be the chemo pill. I thanked her. Do you know what she said to me? " Lorrie, it's so important that you are on board with any treatment we prescribe. If you have any questions we will do whatever to all alleviate your concerns. It was amazing. I was actually listened to. It just goes to show you, don't be intimidated by anyone with letters after their names. You know you better than anyone! Be your own advocate! I asked for a rescan the following week. I wanted the fluid to have time to subside. It did. Within 10 days of coming off the heart meds I lost 10 lbs. I felt vindicated! That's why my blood pressure was through the roof. The fluid. My rescan was coming up and I felt more confident that the fluid was going to be gone. I wasn't having trouble breathing which was a good sign. I waited patiently for the scan. My blood pressure returned to normal.

I was wrong. SHIT. The fluid had actually increased a bit. Not a whole lot, but enough to be clear that I had, once again, developed a resistance to the medicine. This was so frustrating. Seriously, it was 2 steps forward and 3 steps back. Back to chemo. Pill form. Back to chemo teach.

February 2016. Xeloda. My new chemo pill. An older drug, about 25 years old, but used with great success with some patients. It was a shell game. I was grateful that there were so many choices with breast cancer meds because now this had happened twice. A resistance to medicine after a 6 month period of time. What if this continues? Will I run out of options? Then what? That was too much to consider. Time for a trip to Sloan-Kettering. Dr. T agreed. I called and made an appointment for mid March, asking if Gina's brother Joey would and could drive us. Yes, he and his wife, Mary, would make the day trip with us.

I had finally given in and accepted the benefit my friends had wanted to throw me. We were out of options. Bob started his new position the 3rd week of February training with a Denny's franchise. Not what he wanted to do. Weekends, holidays, 24/7 operation. Obviously badly run, no support from upper management and at least 2 months of training to learn every position before being handed the reigns to run it fully. We both knew this was a stepping stone. It was obvious there was no growth potential. Bob had to learn the procedure of this company but running a restaurant was running a restaurant, and my husband was more knowledgable than the people he answered to. It was frustrating on his part. And while now money was coming in, we were taking in about 50% less than what he was making while running the Wendy's franchise and now we had a huge hole to dig out from. The benefit was necessary. And I was humbled at the amount of people willing to volunteer and donate. We had close to 300 people through the door, so many of my Harts Hill family came to help with tickets and raffles. I talked to just about every person that walked through that door, at least I tried. It was an overwhelming, emotional day for me and my family. The support was unreal. The generosity beyond belief. I will never forget it for was long as I live. Neither will my family. It took the immediate financial strain off of us and allowed us to put money aside for taxes, personal debts, and hospital bills. To say I was grateful wouldn't even come close.

I wasn't sure how I felt about starting this new treatment. I mean I knew it was necessary but the last chemo pill was hell. Dr. T wanted me to try this because it was actually a bit of a break for my body. My hair would grow, but the list of side effects was there and it was a wait and see thing how I would react. I was started out on a very high dose, 5 horse pills morning and night. Dosage, 2500mg with each dose. I was to take this for a 14 day period then I would have a week off of them, have blood work done during this time to check levels and pick up the next round of pills after that. One caveat. Neuropathy was a huge side effect and if it got too bad before I hit the 14th day, stop the treatment and call. They would make adjustments for the following round. Now me being stubborn and just wanting this damn cancer gone, I had it in my head already that I was going to tough it out. Bob, knowing me well enough, blew me in. " Well she won't call so I'm going to have to because she won't admit it and I know she won't call." I shot him a look that he knew instantly I was calling him an ass for blowing me in. The nurse practitioner was a new one that I had never met, so she told me not to be stubborn, this is the was these meds are adjusted. And that she would be very surprised if they weren't adjusted. I promised I would call if there was a problem. And there was. The first few days I was tired, I felt like I was in slow motion. But I wasn't sick. No nausea, diarrhea, constipation, headache, mouth sores. After the first couple days I bounced back. I got this! Then bam! About day 8 my feet started hurting so bad that I had trouble walking. Now I had nerve damage from my back injury so burning in my feet to a certain point was normal. This was way beyond the norm. I made it through day 10. On the 11th day I called.

The follow up thankfully showed that the chemo pill wasn't affecting me like the afinator did the year before. My blood work was good. One thing about me is if the meds are going to work, it's always immediate. And the same for if they don't. I know immediately. I had a good feeling. If we could just get the right dosage down where I could function, I could handle this. When that neuropathy kicked in, it felt as though I was walking on nails. It was brutal. By the 3rd round my dosage dropped to 4 pills in the morning and 3 at night. As long as I had on sneakers for support, it was manageable. Towards the end of the round, the neuropathy would increase but I had to deal with it. If this worked, it was well worth it. I wanted to live.

Right around the time my cancer came back I was noticing that I had cardinals around a lot all of a sudden. 2 of them, male and female in my backyard constantly. I was told a story after telling a friend this, that cardinals are a visit from heaven! I had never heard this before and it was funny because I started seeing them everywhere. On Facebook, on tv, on cards people sent to me. I would see little stories about people that had lost loved ones and suddenly cardinals were all around them. It was funny because that was exactly what had happened to me. Signs. I would get signs constantly. All in different forms. I used to believe in coincidences. I don't anymore. I believe that God and our loved ones can punch through this world to send us messages. Open your heart and soul to God. He hears. He answers. Sometimes it's in ways we don't expect. Since 2013 our lives were in complete turmoil. I knew 2016 was going to turn around.

My trip to NYC to see my doctor went perfectly. With Joey driving us, he turned a 4 ½ hour trip into 3. He was amazing, knowing exactly where to go. It made the day hours shorter and more fun. Joey and Mary are just great company. While waiting for Dr. Camen to come in, Bob and I were quietly talking. Her computer was on and it was flashing a series of winter scenes. They caught my eye because of the beauty. Then a cardinal came on the screen. I looked at Bob and said that he had to know that this was going to work. My messages. I'm not alone. My father was there. He was and always will be my male Cardinal. And the female, I knew, was nonnie.

Dr. Camen liked the protocol I was on and thought I was doing perfectly. The cancer was still there, not growing, smaller than ever and she felt that I had a good chance with this medicine. While older, this medicine has produced great results and she was very hopeful. Once again she told me to make an appointment any time I felt the need to. She received all the notes and blood work from Dr.T's office on a regular basis. He never hesitated to call her or tell me to go visit her if I felt uneasy. It was so much of a change from my first doctor. Still, I wanted to kick myself for taking so long to make the change that had yielded me nothing but positive results. I don't hesitate to tell anyone, facing any type of cancer to get out of this area.

By May, the weather had turned. My scan was scheduled early in the month. I felt amazing. No pain, no trouble breathing. Nothing. I felt healed. Bob came with me that day. As always I said a little prayer and asked for my father to watch over me. Lately, every time I drove to Syracuse for a scan or results I would notice a cross in the sky. Now I'm outside a lot being recess monitor with kids for a 2 ½ period every day. I never see crosses a lot. How unusual is it for 2 planes to cross? As we drove the 40 minute drive to Syracuse that morning, I was scheduled for blood work, followed by my scan, followed by my follow up appointment. Blood work was quick and then I would head down for the scan. It took about 10 minutes for my blood counts to come in and then I would drink the contrast drink for my CT SCAN. From there it took about 45 minutes for the drink to circulate through and the scan itself was less than 10 minutes. Having to fast until the scan, we would always go to lunch and be back in time for my follow up. That morning, texting back and forth with my niece in the car. Holding the phone in my hand, waiting for her to answer, I look down to find the words " I LOVE YOU" in the message box. Confused to why she would say that as it didn't fit into the conversation, I asked her. She never sent it. A message from my father, that's who sent it. Ask, and you shall receive.

My scan came back beautiful! Fluid completely gone, no enlarged nodes at all. Tumor markers at 28. Cancer, very tiny. I was done! Dr. T was pulling me off of the chemo pill! OH MY GOD! After 11 months of chemo I was done! There it was. My father sending me that message!

At first I was told to finish off that chemo round. 3 days left, then actually Dr. T told me to throw them out! Happily, I did so. Now what? The first anti- estrogen pill, aromasin, worked for 7 months, then I developed a resistance. There are 2 types that I know of regarding anti estrogen blockers. The aromasin blocked the estrogen from entering the body. The other type Tamoxifin, which I was on for 5 years after my first round of cancer, was now approved for women who were already through menopause. Not sure if it worked or not, because no one knows when exactly my cancer came back, Dr. T wanted to try it again. It would take a few months to kick in. The only different between this drug and aromasin is that Tamoxifin acts as a shield over the estrogen receptors in the body. Both of these drugs have been very positive for cancer patients and there are other drugs that do similar things but both of these drugs were considered cream of the crop. So I started my daily dose of Tamoxifin, worried that last time I had a 15 lb weight gain. Having not lost the weight put on with the chemo treatments, I was determined to eat properly and wanted to start back up on the treadmill, hoping that the neuropathy wouldn't linger. I was due back in a month to check numbers. Finally, thank you God! I was here. 2 years to the month of my diagnosis, I wasn't cancer free, but I was, my doctor was, and God was in control.

Through the last 24 months I had continually prayed for God's will was for me to be healed. While I felt it, not one bit of pain or discomfort related to my cancer was evident. I wasn't healed yet. I started to wonder if it was God's will. My trust in Him was solid but I had learned over the years that He would lead me down the path I must follow and everytime I thought I had my path figured out, there was another turn. So we must rely on our blind faith in God to show us the way. I call it blind faith because I believe in the saying "FAITH IS BELIEVING IN THAT WHICH WE CANNOT SEE." Faith in this country isn't as strong as it needs to be. We are now a country of instant gratification. People had to realize that we live on God's timetable, not our own. So with all of this this, all that I know, It didn't really upset me because I knew and accepted that this disease was and is controllable. Like diabetes, heart conditions or any other chronic disease, as long as it's managed, the doctor and patients stay on top of it, a long life is very possible. I had accepted all of this as the path for me to follow. I also have accepted the rollercoaster ride of this disease. I will have setbacks. But I trust in my doctor and that is so important! I trust him to be on top of things. I cannot do any more.

I was so excited for summer! I was off chemo, my hair was growing back thick as ever, my energy level was through the roof. After owning the restaurant and treatments, financially and physically we had 3 years of just not getting anything done around the house. No upkeep. Money was tight but we could get caught up on little things. It felt good to have the time, will and energy to get it done. The school year had passed so quickly, after February break time flies. The school, the families and the kids were so supportive of me that I knew saying goodbye would be hard. Twice during the course of the year, the 5th grade had approached our principal and asked if they could have a "Support Mrs. Markason" day. Both times a complete surprise because I always forget my password to the school email so I have a tendency not to hear things before they occur! I walk into school to see a sea of pink. Pink hair, pink shirts, pink socks, sneakers, hats! You name it, it was pink. I would spend the day crying. It was unreal. Hugs, high 5's, t shirts that were sold as a fundraiser for the school kids that had a heart in the middle and said HANDS TO HEARTS, HARTS HILL HELPING MRS. MARKASON. I had kids receiving their First Communion mention to their teacher about my cancer and the entire class made me cards. Inside recess days, the first, second and third graders would make me cards with I love you on them. They had me in tears all the time. To be that Blessed, I keep saying it. I was overwhelmed by the love of these kids. Yeah, the end of school this year was going to be tough.

June came and as I figured the last day of school was filled with tears. That day a learned that one of the kindergarten teachers, one I had become so close to, who prayed for me constantly, had decided to retire. Her daughter had given birth the year before and lived out of town. She wanted to enjoy him and no one could blame her. She was young, healthy and could afford to retire. Live life and enjoy. She made the right decision, but the rest of us cried. She was an amazing teacher who had touched so many lives. When I first met her I thought that no one could be this sweet, it had to be an act. It wasn't. Never in the 11 years I worked with her did I hear her raise her voice to the kids. Even when she wasn't happy, she was amazing. She was loved by her kids, their parents, and all of us. Her room would never be the same. And so the walls were cleaned off, the rooms packed up and we said our goodbyes with a luncheon for faculty and staff catered by a local restaurant and held in our cafeteria. I was happy for summer but already missing this place.

My June follow up came shortly after the school year ended. Blood work and a visit with the nurse practitioner. I would see different ones with people changing positions. All were sweet and caring. It didn't matter to me. I was in good hands, and I knew, if it was my choice, I could have seen Dr. T at any time. In and out. Same questions. No pain, no problems, energy good. Ok, see you next month….

Not so fast.

My appointment being first thing in the morning, I expected that my tumor marker numbers would be called into me sometime in the afternoon. I wasn't worried at all. So when my phone rang and HOA showed up on my caller id, I wasn't surprised. What did surprise me was hearing Dr. T's voice on the line. My heart fell into my stomach. I could literally feel the drop. " Hi Lorrie," he says to me in a very calm voice. " what's wrong?" Blurted out of my mouth, not even a " Hi Doc!" from me. No way, I was all business. He only called when something wasn't right. Shit! Shit! Shit!

" Your tumor markers shot up to 93 from last month, last month with your scan you are at 28." Son of a bitch! " Are you freaking kidding me?" I asked, like really, did I think he called to make a joke? "Yes, I want to get you back in next week for a rescan. I want to see what is going on." He continued, "don't get nervous, it could be anything. Your scan was great last month, it may just be cancer cells exploding as they die off and they run through your blood stream, or it could be inflammation. Let's just get you in and scan to see. You know I don't rely on just numbers so I don't want you to worry. I'm not, but we need to be sure and a scan is concrete evidence." God how I adored this man. He took no chances with my life. I trusted him. But I told him I can't wait till next week, can't we get in sooner? He thought for a moment and said he would have someone look at the schedule, he asked when I could go and I told him whenever I needed too. I appreciated him so much. No argument, anything to ease my nerves.

As promised, I received a call back in less than 15 minutes. They had an opening the following day. Perfect. I'll be there. And I was. The only problem was that I could get in to see him until the next day, Friday. Not a problem. I will drive back out, I told them.

Here we go again. The rollercoaster. Higher than high a month ago. A beautiful scan with zero enlarged nodes, cancer very small and zero fluid in the lung lining and my lung lining had actually returned to normal size. Now what. Driving out for the scan I just prayed. Please. Not another setback. Please, God. Tears of frustration. Knowing full well that what ever was happening that I was ready, willing and able to deal with it. So half way out on my drive I notice a plane flying straight ahead, traveling in the same direction as I was with the jet wash leaving a line in the sky, it looked to be straight up and down. Within a second, I swear, a second, a second plane crosses right through the middle. There it is, my cross in the sky. I pulled over, I started crying. This isn't a coincidence, no way. I was so much in awe of the power of God that I couldn't drive. I started back up and the second plane's jet wash line was already disappearing....just as it was almost faded, here comes a second plane to complete the cross again. I started crying and called Gina. I was sobbing so hard trying to explain what just happened. She couldn't believe it. But she did. She knew these things happen to me. But I know some must question. Let them. They are the ones that don't believe in signs. In meanings to simple things. They believe in coincidences. Not me. Ever. I walked in to that scan, drank my drink and waited. Taken in on time, I remember to take my St. Michael out of my bra this time. I laid there for the brief time it took and as usual said my Hail Marys and Our Fathers until the scan was done. Tomorrow I would find out. I left there in peace. Total peace. No fear. God sent his message.

Friday came and I walked into the exam room still with the grace of God's peace in me. My scan was exactly the same. Dr. T was right. The cancer was dying and causing inflammation. He wanted to pull me off the Tamoxifin and restart me on the Xeloda again. The chemo pill. I questioned that I had almost 6 months of it, and with my history did he think I would develop another resistance? No. He was confident. He also wasn't willing to say that the Tamoxifin didn't work. It may have needed a bit more time, but he took no chances with me, always erring on the side of caution. I agreed. Let's get back to it. Rescan again in September. I knew I would feel it one way or another. I knew my body.

I got through summer. And it was hot. Being on this chemo pill at the end of winter months and early Spring was completely different as I got through the summer months. Humid, sunny days, days that I love most, I couldn't take. I had to be in the pool. Just sitting in the sun would have sweat pouring down my back. But all in all, this was easier to deal with than having to shut down a week at a time. On top of all this, we were planning on my in laws moving in. My inlaws sold their home the year Bob lost his job. They moved into a senior complex and enjoyed it. As time went on, the dementia that my mother in law was suffering from was getting worse. My 91 year old father in law was trying to care for her by himself. She had become more reclusive and wouldn't go to dinner most nights. On top of the memory loss, my father in law, a somewhat social person, was becoming isolated too. The stress had begun to build and Bob and I were concerned that he was going to drop before she did. There was only one thing to do, move them in.

It wasn't as simple as all that. The hall bathroom had to be gutted and redone to accommodate elderly people. That bathroom was already in need of a remodel having a tub from 1954 in it. It was a very deep tub and no way they could step into it. That was the first thing to complete. Then moving the kids around and painting. All had to be done by August. With June just ending and having until August, well, while it seems like a long period of time, it really isn't. We got it all done and they were moved in by the second week of August. The move itself was relatively easy. Minor adjustments for everyone. The hardest part is that we didn't realize how bad his mom really got. Not only the short - term loss of memory, but long term also. Some times she seemed right as rain, the next minute she was asking for cigarettes. She hadn't smoked since the 60's. My heart broke for Bob. His father too, but his father had been around this for a while, and we hadn't really seen to the extent it really was. She didn't recognize our home. It is just such a horrible disease and I wanted the kids to be as ready as possible. They weren't babies anymore, but still, it is hard to watch.

With all that was going on my father in law thought this may be too much for me. It was to be the first and last time he woud show any concern for me. As I knew, 2016 was turning around for us. We weren't financially on our feet yet but the benefit took the immediate strain off. Bob was working but hated it. The company and an owner of a franchise that the one and only thing he cared about was his profit. Hey, it's his company and he has a right to his profits but at the restaurant level there was literally no support. Not for managers. As a manager, Bob is all about supporting his staff. That is why he has been so successful. People honestly love to work for him. Don't get me wrong, he is no pushover. He expects results, a true self motivator. He would come down on you for not doing your job but he was very quick to praise a job well and explain to those what was needed. He was still looking for a new job but there just wasn't a lot out there. I never lost faith. I kept telling him that his job just didn't show itself yet. I had to keep reminding him we are on God's timetable, not ours. But my health was improving and we had money coming in. My novenas to the Blessed Mother, the undoer of knots, was heard. I was sure.

After the heat of the Summer, I was so looking forward to Fall. I love Fall weather but Summer had other ideas. It wanted to hang on a while more. Day after day of upper 80's and high levels of humidity. I found myself finding shade during recess. Pounding water and Propel water packets to keep the electrolytes up,   I refused to let it beat me. Before I knew it, it was scan time again. It's amazing how fast 3 months go by.

Dr.T always made a big deal about how I physically felt. I could pretty much differentiate my aches and pains from the whiplash and nerve pain, lower back and the neuropathy that would effect my feet. I felt amazing. My energy level was great and I didn't have an ounce of pain in my back that could be associated with the fluid build up. My BP was perfect, finally, everything health wise was good. I honestly felt as though I had no cancer in me at all. Zero. What would this scan show?

 My scan date fell the week of Labor Day. Because of the shortened week, I was unable to have my scan read the same day. I had to make a trip back there the following day. It wasn't a big deal. Dr. T was adamant about the date of my scans. He wanted it EXACTLY 3 months apart. There was never a time during the past year and a half that I have spent with this doctor that I didn't feel he had every inch of my back. I was his first concern. I didn't have to beg, plead or scream. He cared, and it was obvious.

The scan went off without a hitch and I returned the following day. I was so confident, but there always comes that bit of doubt that enters all our minds as we sit and wait. Just like the mammograms, you sit and wait...and wait. Naturally if Dr.T walked in late my head would start to spin. That's when I get so mad at myself. There was no reason at all to believe anything other than it was gone.

Deep in thought, Dr. T comes quickly through the door, I almost laughed because he resembled Kramer, from Seinfeld as he whipped through the door. He immediately asked how I felt... I smiled, remembering the scan a few months back that blindsided us. I refused to believe that was going to happen, so I told him," I feel amazing, so if you tell me there is something in that scan you are going to blindside me again!" He smiled. "I'm not."

Speechless. I was speechless. He continued," you have a tiny, tiny spot in your chest. I don't think it's anything. I think all the cancer is destroyed. That's why your tumor markers are up a bit. They go through the bloodstream. I'm not concerned in the least. You have no enlarged nodes, and no fluid around the lung lining. "

I wanted to cry. OH MY GOD! THANK YOU! We talked for a bit. He wanted to keep me on the chemo pill for a bit. I could see the happiness in his eyes too. He handed me the report that I never read and went to go grab by chemo pills on the other side of the building. I couldn't wait to call Bob. As I'm sitting there, I opened my report and glanced down. My eyes immediately were drawn to the big letters on the bottom of the page.

THERE IS NO INDICATION OF A METASTASTIC DISEASE.

Let me say at again.

THERE IS NO INDICATION OF A METASTATIC DISEASE.

I don't think it fully hit me as to what he told me. The cancer was gone. My cancer is gone. I was healed. God healed me. After 2 ½ years, I was in absolute remission.

I cried and cried and cried. I cried for 24 hours. Everything made me cry. The sky made me cry. There was nothing I could look at without crying. I was looking at the world again from new eyes. One by one,

God was healing our lives. All of us. Our family. We stayed strong. We didn't falter.

I look back to May 25th, 1991. Our wedding day. We were so full of hope and plans for the future. We never thought in terms of cancer, losing a son to a destructive woman, job loss or financial strain. Life isn't fair. Its as simple as that. But we have to continue. We have to have hope. We have to have trust. One by one I watch the turmoil in our lives dissipate. It hit me not too long ago. I am stressless. I AM STRESSLESS. I have so much peace in my heart. I know it will all be ok. I trust in God. After all, I've been living in his hands all my life.

As September was winding down, the only prayer that hadn't been answered was a new job for Bob. The stress of this job was hitting him. He could handle the job, he was developing his staff. After only 3 months running the restaurant, his numbers were better than those that had been there so much longer. What it came down to was lack of support. Not only for the managers but the entire staff. Turnover was huge. Then I received a message from a friend who had been one of our suppliers with Papa Joes. I had known him forever, Bob meeting him during this time and they hit it off. He mentioned that the business he worked for was hiring. He had passed Bob's name to the Director of Sales and told Bob to give him a call. If Bob got this, he would be heading a department. Working hours of 8-6. Weekends and Holidays off. We had never had that. He would be in an office. No more late night calls. No more covering shifts. No more restaurant aggravation. Real dress clothes. Casual Friday's! Oh! We could actually go to a happy hour! God please let this be it.

The interview was 4 hours and included lunch? Good sign? I think so. Then the waiting process had to begin. Praying that no one interviewed better. I knew they couldn't find anyone better. My faith in Bob was always clear. This was a smart man. This was a loyal man. This was a man that I knew very early on in our relationship would take care of me. Even in our darkest moments of despair and worry, my faith in him never wavered.

October 4th, 2016. Bob gave notice to his District Manager. He got the greatest night's rest in a long time he told me the next morning. That's what you call peace. I wish it lasted. This position would quickly turn into a nightmare.

Chapter 16

October was suddenly upon us. Bob had landed a new job, directing a department for a local, well known company. He had never worked in this capacity before and he would be overseeing a group of salesmen selling products to restaurants locally and throughout the state. The most exciting thing for him was that he would be, for the first time in his life, be able to have nights and weekends off. He was looking forward to starting and learning the process. Bob was always a quick study, brilliant with numbers and had a great attitude working with customers. He was truly a people person. Everything seems to be falling into place.

I had an appointment with my nurse practitioner scheduled out in the Galway, NY area. Right outside of Saratoga. I continued struggling to take off any weight, actually I kept gaining. I now knew for sure my thyroid was off. I was 35 pounds above where I was when I started the intravenous chemo the prior year, napping every day. In bed early, never enough sleep. Bloated. Bloated. Bloated. That damn steroid made me gain weight so rapidly, within a 3month period of time. I was hoping that once I stopped it, I could take off the weight. It didn't happen. I had my thyroid bloodwork done the year prior but all was normal. I was hoping my body would just readjust. How I hated this. I had worked so hard to get back into shape and I had to start all over again. Right then and there I decided that it didn't matter how much pain I was in never again would I use steriods.

I was very familiar with all that I had learned concerning my thyroid. When the body is inflamed your body just won't function correctly. Our bodies are no different than a machine, a car, anything. Maintenance. More so as we get older, the more we have to put into our own care. Inflammation can cause so many issues. I had my thyroid bloodwork done a week or so before my appointment. It never made sense to me to have an appointment scheduled, then have bloodwork done and have to either go back to the doctor or carry on a conversation over the phone. This way, I was there, she was there, my results were there. But as it turned out, I was right. My thyroid was low. She upped my armour thyroid, we talked about inflammation in my body and she agreed that my thyroid was causing the inflammation and could very possibly be affecting my tumor markers. I left there feeling better, knowing now that in 5 weeks she could retest my bloodwork and see if any other adjustments to the medicine needed to be made. Now came the patience I had to show. It would take 5 weeks for this to cycle through and see if it stabilized my thyroid. I wasn't a patient person. But, this would be very telling as my 5 week recheck would be right before Christmas. It would also fall in line with my next scan and subsequent tumor marker check. If it was inflammation causing my tumor markers to rise, I just may see a difference, even a small one, by then.

As we headed in the end of October, my excitement naturally started to build. CHRISTMAS!!! My decorations had already begun to go up. I used my mother in law being there, and how much she would just absolutely enjoy the beautiful decorations that I had spent years acquiring, as an excuse to may be put them up a bit earlier! In all actuality, I just couldn't wait. Halloween was around the corner, my school kids would bombard my house, naturally expecting to see me put up the tree as I handed out the candy. I just loved this, even though Halloween was not a favorite of mine, but seeing all the school kids just made my day. We were settling into a routine with my inlaws. Not without issues. A lot of issue, actually. Thankful that the house was big enough so everyone could have space, but the winter months were long anyway and with my tendency to become affected by the seasonal disorder syndrome, I hoped for a mild and early end to winter.

Winter actually started early that year. By Thanksgiving we had snow on the ground. I could live with that, snow during the Christmas holiday season was perfectly acceptable to me! And during that 5-6 week period of time between Thanksgiving and Christmas would go by so fast that you really didn't have time to stop and breathe. Bob for the most part was happy but a bit of frustration was beginning to set in, there was no training program. His immediately supervisor was one of those people who liked to hear himself talk. To him, training was letting Bob listen to him all day. Bob was attempting to establish new accounts as the department had been failing recently, but Bob's biggest issue was that he had never been in sales, he was a numbers guy, but they knew that when they hired him. He wanted to look at charts and trends. He wanted to see what went wrong and why. He wanted to find the weakness in the department. But he couldn't. Not because he couldn't figure it out, but because he wasn't given the materials to do the job. Sitting and listening to someone talk all day isn't a training program. He tried to remain hopeful, attempting to learn on his own. His hours were great, he was happy that his parents were with us. They had spent so many years going to Florida for half a year that he didn't see them or spend as much time with them as he would have liked to. They were Blessed with health for the most part of their lives. His dad, turning 92 in March and his mom, with increasing dementia, was 86. I was glad he had the opportunity to spend the remaining years of his parents life close to them.

As it seems, the older we get, the faster the days go by. Christmas week was here! No matter how prepared I try to be could always use just one more day! My scan was this week. And I also had to have my thyroid bloodwork done. I wasn't nervous at all. I felt great. No pain related to cancer at all! I was sleeping well. Still taking naps mid afternoon. I was actually more curious to know what my thyroid levels were. I knew there was no cancer in me. Well, let me clarify again. As you are staged 4, I will never be restaged and will remain stage 4. Even though my scan may come back once again with no evidence of a metastatic disease, it was there, dormant inside me. But I knew who was in control. I knew who remained in control. I knew who was leading me down the path to find my health and wellness. God. He provided me the tools. And now it was up to me to take advantage of it all.

My scan appointment was 2 days before Christmas Eve. Usually because my scans are exactly every 3 months they are able to schedule everything in one day. Bloodwork, scan, appointment. Makes for a longer day but at least I leave knowing exactly what is happening. They spoiled me in that regard. If tests can literally come back within a matter of 2 hours then why are some people forced to wait longer periods of time with the stress, anxiety and worry it causes. This just made sense. There were just so many positive aspects of this office. Unfortunately, because of the loss of time off during the Christmas season, scheduling becomes a bit trickier. So my bloodwork and scan were on one day and the following day I would return for my doctor's appointment. I had also put in a call to my nurse practitioner's office for my thyroid results. I was hoping to have a very Merry Christmas full of good health news! Scan news came back as I expected. Thank God! My Blessings continued. A part of me was so hoping that I would be pulled off the chemo pill with those results. Another part of me felt as though I tolerate this so well, even though the neuropathy during those last days of the cycle were nightmarish, it was like a security blanket. Does that make sense? I trusted Dr. T's judgement and I knew that he would contact Memorial –Sloan Kettering if I had questions or if I was unsure or even if he was unsure. I was so comfortable in that fact that he put my health over his ego. We talked it over and he felt that I was tolerating this extremely well. My blood counts, platelet counts had remained stable, my tumor markers dropped slightly and as long as I could deal with the neuropathy, then let's just go 3 more months. Rescan in March and go from there. He had offered several times to write me a prescription for the neuropathy. I refused. In part because I was really sick and tired of taking pills. Between my chemo pills, thyroid meds, high blood pressure meds and my supplements, I was taking about 35 pills a day. Besides, I wasn't willing to add another pill to stop one thing and have 5 more side effects start. There HAD to be something out there to help.

My nurse practitioner's office never got back to me during that Christmas week. By weeks end, I had forgotten too. It happens. So I called first thing on Monday morning only to find out that she was away during this week! Ugh! Come on! I did not want to wait another week to find out. If I needed another adjustment on the meds, she'd have to call in the prescription, and then it would take another 5 weeks before bloodwork could be done. I know it doesn't sound like a very long time in the scheme of things but I was completely over this weight gain, the bloated feeling and naps. The sooner my thyroid came back into a normal range, the sooner I would be able to get myself back on track. Thankfully another nurse practitioner was able to reach her and she called me to say that my thyroid numbers were good. Thank God! 2017 was just days away and my News Year Resolution was the same as so many others......weight loss and a healthier new me. As frustrated as I was having to start all over, I knew I could and would do it. But it still took time for everything to start working again. But I was on a mission. During the week in between Christmas and New Year, we received a surprise call from friends that live in Washington State. Craig, was a longtime friend of Bob's who had lived out west for a very long time. They would stay in contact through phone calls and texting but we hadn't seen him and his wife, Bonnie, since our friend had past away a few years prior. They had a family business that they were closing up after several years, Craig's dad having passed away the year prior. They carved out a bit of time to stop and see us. Craig served in the military, holding medical administrative positions. Once out of the military, he remained in that field. Bonnie was a computer programmer. They had a great marriage. It was good to see them. As the conversations bounced from one thing to another we talked about my treatments and my neuropathy. She began telling me about a friend of hers who suffers from neuropathy, although for different reasons. She told me about a " painstick" that her friend swore by. Made with bees wax and infused with cannibus oil, and promised to mail it to me. I was ready to try anything. Some weeks were better than others but with Christmas, the cooking, the shopping, the wrapping, so much to do, so much of it on my feet that neuropathy right at that point, was kicking my ass. I had mixed emotions on the legality of medical marijuana. I knew it worked because I used pot during my 2005 chemo treatments. It took the nausea away immediately. Not knowing how the system worked, I thought it was good for pain but how many people were just looking for an excuse to get high? That was my problem. I would soon change my mind.

Within a few weeks, as expected, they sent me this pain stick. It was double the size of a chap stick, both in height and width. My worse time was at night so I figured in order to make it last I would only use it at night. I did not expect results to happen immediately. Well, ok, not immediately. 20 minutes later. The burning was gone. The shooting pains were gone. The tenderness lessened. For real? This was actually relieving it? I slept so good that night. Usually I was up half the night, feet out of the covers, trying to sleep as when it felt like someone had a blow torch on my feet. It was brutal. It got so bad that at one point I was going to bed with an ice packs on my feet just to relieve the incredible burning. Dr. T didn't want me to continue doing that because I could permanently destroy my nerve endings. I began using it nightly, dealing with the pain during the day. Making sure I always had sneakers with memory foam in them. It gave support. If I was home and not leaving I would wear the gel socks. Always making sure to keep a lot of lotion on my feet. I was told to use UDDERLY SMOOTH, a hand cream also used on cow's utters. No, I am not kidding. The container looks like a cow, being black and white. It worked really well. I had to keep my feet and hands hydrated because I would get calluses, horrible calluses which turned into deep cracks. And boy did they hurt. Especially on the feet. I would have to sit in the hot tub or give myself foot baths to soften it up, then gently use a pumice stone to remove the dead skin. It was like a part time job. My hands didn't suffer as bad but there were times that I would have to smother my hands in the cream and sleep with the aloe gloves on because I would wake up with stiff, hard palms.

I remember in December, early December being so frustrated that I couldn't find something to relieve the neuropathy pain. I remember in one of my little conversations with God, (it's a wonder HE hasn't started to ignore me) why can't I figure this out??? Then Craig and Bonnie come. These aren't coincidences! I used to believe in them, not anymore. This is God's way of fixing the problem you are facing. It doesn't always come in the form we expect. But it does show up! Then, right after the first of the new year, I received a message from a friend. She had undergone health issues the previous year, serious issues. She started researching her symptoms, saw several doctors, and started eating differently. She started looking into essential oils, researching them and contacted me specifically about frankincense. Now my only reference to frankincense was that this was one of the gifts, along with gold and myrrh, given to Baby Jesus on January 6. The Epiphany. And this was the day I received a sample gift of frankincense from my friend to try. With so many healing properties, pain relief, cell regeneration, could these oils seriously work? I started believing more and more about holistic forms of medicine. After all in Jesus's lifetime there wasn't any synthetic medicine, yet they did have medicine. And I understood fully after having gone through all the arguments with so many doctors who absolutely refused to remove synthetic synthroid and replace it with the armour thyroid. The original and natural form of treatment for hypothyroidism and hashimotos disease. And I'm glad I never gave up looking for someone to treat me, because I was right.

And it turned my life around. Once again, being your own advocate can be tough, but it is necessary!

I was told to put the frankincense oil which was blendedwith fractionated cocoanut oil on the bottom of my feet. By doing this you are letting the oils go directly into your blood stream. It then hit me. I am using cannibus oil and I work in a school. While there was no drug testing on us, if ever they decided to, I would quite possibly fail. This wasn't good. New York State, the year prior, had passed the medical marijuana law allowing people with certain medical conditions to become certified. I thought this was the way to go. To protect myself and my job and seeing further what the state had to offer. Unfortunately we didn't have all that some west coast states had, since they were legalized earlier, they had time to develop and create choices.

I called Dr. T's office to basically tell them this was what I wanted. Hoping he didn't give me a hard time. There was no doubt that just based on my diagnosis of cancer that I would be eligible. But it had to start with him. It then again, some doctors and pharmaceutical companies have their deals and they will push pills rather than having their patients attempt a natural solution. Within a day I received a call from the new doctor's office who would be able to certify me. There weren't too many around yet, having this law in effect in 2015. I would have to travel back out to Cazenovia, a suburb of Syracuse. Actually, I was able to schedule my appointment right after my blood work appointment so I didn't have to make a second trip out in one week. The nurse practitioner was able to certify me which was a very simple process. Your referring doctor contacts the office where the certification will be done. They then send over your medical history for this office to review. They make that determination prior to you even being in contact with them. Once they review your information, decide if you meet the necessary criteria, they contact you. From there it is just paperwork and naturally a $300 filing fee (you just have to love NYS, their hands are in everything!) that insurance usually doesn't cover. You then have to go to the states website and register. With in a week period you will receive your medical ID card. I felt better having done this. I presented the paperwork to the school principal for my files. It was the right thing to do. Now I had 2 choices. Cannibus and frankincense, both holistic and both successful in treating my issues. I now had to decide what choice to use when it came to the medical marijuana. New York State only offered 3 choices. Unfortunately, this pain stick wasn't one of them. We were so far behind the west coast on this and that was depressing. I was kind of hoping that now that I was certified I could order this pain stick but that wasn't the case. I could ask my friend to keep sending me this. It was illegal. It was ridiculous really when you think about it, the certification should be a national policy. Instead, if I was in Washington state, without a certification, I could walk into a store and purchase this. Yet here I am, certified and I cannot order it and have it sent across state lines.

So what were my choices? How do I make the decision on which one to choose? For me, what I needed was the most cost effective, longest lasting choice there was and insurance didn't cover these costs either. So choice number one was an inhaler. Lasting about an hour at a time, I didn't even look into the cost, that wasn't going to work for me. I needed to sleep. Choice number 2 was a sublingual oil. Placing a drop under your tongue, again lasting for a short period of time. That wasn't going to work either. Choice 3 was a pill. Lasting up to 8 hours and having the ability to take up to 3 pills a day. Cost? $4 per pill. That was $84 a week. Impossible. I would have to maybe just use these at night and only towards the end of the 2 week cycle. I had already ordered the frankincense and that had arrived. I now had a choice, but since I had the frankincense I decided to use this and save money. I made the right choice. These oils would be lifechanging.

Bob's frustration was increasing. He was now being blamed for the failure of this department he just took over! It was unreal! The reality was that his boss, who prior to his current position, held the director's position, the position Bob now held. The truth was that he was nothing more than a used car salesman and treated customers accordingly. So his tactics in selling may have worked initially, but his ability to resell and maintain customer relationships didn't exist. It was becoming increasingly obvious that this was just not going to work out. The owners made a point that they wanted to see people busy, always working, because that is exactly how they were. Bob would spend half the day looking for things to do. He'd ask his boss for reports. He was told he didn't need them. Bob explained he wanted to research, see what the problems were and find a solution. He was told to research it himself. Bob would argue why did he has to research it when reports told the story already? It was unreal! He started sending out resumes. Ok, here we go again. He continued there, trying to run a department he hadn't been trained, dealing with salesmen under him, all who held the same opinion of his boss. Impossible, miserable, demeaning and arrogant.

It was February, the slowest month of the year for restaurants. And here was Bob, attempting to sell. Everyone would cut back. Bob knew this! He spent 30+ years inside the restaurant. Food costs, bottom line. That was his job. Bob had the impression that Mac, his boss, was for sure undermining him and speaking negatively about him to the owners. Suddenly things started to change. He wasn't spoken to, not by Mac, not by others. Someone handed Bob a note telling him to watch his back. Knowing now that Bob was extremely unhappy, he had the feeling that he was going to get fired. He would scream at Bob when he failed to make a sale. Bob, as calm as ever, would just look at him and tell him that he couldn't force a restaurant owner trying to cut expenses during the slowest month of the year to purchase what they wouldn't use and ultimately become waste. Mac's answer to that? " You don't let the owners tell you what they need, YOU TELL THEM WHAT THEY NEED!" Well. There it was, the clear picture why this department was in trouble. He didn't care about his customers needs. So they stopped buying from him. Period. End of story.

Once again our lives seemed to be up in the air. Now what? Nothing was out there. This area was so depressed. I could see him getting depressed and stressed. I wasn't worried. With all that we had gone through and God pulled us out of, I told him not to worry. It was going to be ok. And I just didn't say it. I meant it. I just believed. No matter what, never, ever lose hope. What it did do is kick back to reality. Now what? If he was afraid of getting fired money was going to be even tighter. We were ok. We paid our bills. Bob's credit still took a huge hit, we had never gone bankrupt. We were hoping to pull ourselves out of this completely. That was Bob, no easy way out. He was responsible. The benefit my friends had given me saved us. And now with my inlaws in our house, they paid us rent so while we weren't catching up on everything, we lived. And at this point, that was all that mattered to me. Then, just then, the amazing happened! Bob walked in one night from work, on his phone, grinning ear to ear. I hadn't seen him walk in from work like that in months! I had no clue who or what was going on, all I could gather from listening that he was excited about something. He hung up the phone, saying, "You are not going to believe this!"

On his way home he received a call from a man he has known for a very long time. Bob had actually given this man his first job at Kentucky Fried Chicken when he was 16. When we moved into our home back almost 18 years ago, Bob on his way home stopped and picked up a pizza for dinner. Running into Jay after a very long time. He had bought the restaurant and was running it. Since that time, the restaurant had become very successful. Jay was a hard working, nose to the grindstone type of guy who would tell everyone who asked him about business that he had learned everything he knew from Bob. From the pizza place, he opened a small deli, very modern, very New York style with a small bar in the back. This guy had a golden touch. Don't get me wrong. He worked his tail off. And he had great instincts. From there he purchased an empty building in a growing part of town. The Varick St. area had become quite popular during these years. Our local and long time Brewery, Saranac would open its parking lot around Memorial Day weekend and have local bands every Thursday. It was SARANAC THURSDAY. 2-3 thousand people would show up. Bars started opening, the streets would be packed and it was a great way to wash away the winter blues and see everyone again. Jay had been working inside this building for nearly 3 years. Doing most of the work himself. Once again, the bar / small pizza place was an instant hit. With bands on Thursdays, Fridays and Saturdays and best of all, it was geared to our age range!

When Jay called, he informed Bob that he was in the process of purchasing yet another restaurant. This was an established restaurant with a strong following. Jay needed someone to oversee all of these businesses. He had started interviewing and then he remembered the one person who taught him everything in business. He picked up the phone immediately and asked Bob if he was happy. There it was. God's hand. They met the following week for about 5 hours. I figured at that point he had the job. Unfortunately, being the slowest month of the year and wanting to complete this sale, Jay had asked Bob to hold off for a month or so. So Bob held on. Me on the other hand felt it wouldn't be right to spend all this money on the medical marijuana pills. I'm not like that. I would always put my families needs above my own. Even now. So without saying anything, I started reading more about these essential oils. Instead of putting it on just the balls of my feet I put it all over my feet. I started putting it on my nails which were taking a beating from the chemo. I rubbed it on my thyroid, my chest and with the residue on my fingers, I used it as a moisturizer on my face. Within a few weeks I noticed a change in the pain level. Was this really relieving my neuropathy for hours and hours?

Since my thyroid results came back in December I promised myself that I would get myself back on track the beginning of the year. And I kept my promise to myself. I started eating healthier. I didn't really exercise because of the neuropathy so I tried to really focus on nutrition. My muscle tone was excellent and I knew that if I went ahead with a low fat, higher protein diet it would come off. When I lost all the weight last time, I was walking daily and it literally melted off. That wasn't happening this time. I did lose 4 pounds in about a month but that was too slow. The bloat was still there. Ok. Time to jump start myself. Back to the cleanse. Back to the Leaky Gut Syndrome cleanse.

I talked about this in a previous chapter, but to remind everyone, this is a cleanse, an all natural cleanse used to clean out the digestive track of our bodies. Sludge and bacteria build up in our system and eating the proper foods can help clean out and rid yourself of this bloat. Doing this cleanse for one week you have the ability to lose anywhere between 5-20 pounds, all depending on the amount of sludge in your system. It is a perfect way to jump start your system.

February ended on such a high note. New opportunity for Bob, the weather was gorgeous. Snow was completely gone and everything was drying up beautifully. I couldn't wait to get outside and rake, clean up, get the pool open and enjoy Spring weather! In upstate New York March is extremely unpredictable. As a matter of fact, in the 12 years that I worked at the school doing recess there were only three times in all those years that we were able to get the kids on the back playground and lawn in March. All I wanted was to get the main deck in our backyard powerwashed and stained. It was long overdue. As the weather saying goes" In like a Lion out like a Lamb. Well it certainly came in as a lion and it stayed like a lion all the way through. Mid month we got our surprise. 31 inches of snow. A nor'easter that wasn't supposed come inland suddenly changed direction and caught us by surprise at the last minute. It was hell. It takes a lot to snow-in central New Yorkers, but it did. If you live here and don't own a 4x4 you are nuts! Getting a snowstorm of that level this late in the year as tremendous effect on you mentally. Well, at least with me it did. It was so pretty, snow capped trees, everything white and clean....I hated it. I looked out my kitchen window to see the elephant cover on my pool sinking deep into the pool. Oh God, my liner. Now I had to worry if the pool liner would pop out with all the weight. The temperatures were staying rather cool so my hopes of a quick warm up to lose all this snow wasn't going to happen. It literally took 2 weeks for the snow to go. Winter refused to go away. I really wanted to beat the hell out of Mother Nature.

My next scan was due a few days after this snow storm hit. The day before my appointment, looking out the front window, I saw my visitors, my cardinals. Male and female. It never failed. They showed up every single time. The last time I saw them was December. Those 3 months would go by so quickly. I felt amazing, actually even better having lost now a total of 20 pounds. 12 from the leaky gut cleanse and the other 8 with exercise. Having been able to control the neuropathy with the essential oils, adding in another blend of oils called DEEP BLUE. This is a combination of wintergreen, peppermint, ylang ylang, champhor, blue tansy, blue chamomile, helichrysum and osmanthus, and the pain relieving effects are unbelievable. I was able to start walking on the treadmill and start up with the PIYO workouts. I stayed at the beginning level because with my injuries I didn't want to push myself. I was more interested in stretching and my overall mobility. It was working. My hair was growing in. Not as thick as it was, but looking at me you would never know, but I did. Keeping my sense of humor about it all I would laugh at myself because at first I would wake up looking like Mr. Kotter, a character from a 70's tv show. From there I progressed to Kramer, the character from Seinfeld. I didn't want to complain. There are women who pay a lot of money for the curls I had! I was anxious for my appointment for the scan/ blood work/ followup visit this time. Not scared anxious but excited. My weight down, I knew

Dr. T seeing that big of a loss would be concerning to him, the pain on my side, now knowing it was my fatty liver being inflamed stopped bothering me, I wasn't taking naps in the afternoon. I had zero pain relating to cancer. God had healed me, and while I know that my battle is and always will be for a lifetime, and that cancer could rear its ugly head, I was winning the war. Bob was able to come with me this time because he had finally given his notice at work. He was trying to hold out until this new opportunity started but like always, the sale and transfer of a business never goes as planned so it was delayed. He was so frustrated and angry because Mac just refused to even acknowledge him daily. The owners seemed a bit more distant and Bob just knew he was telling them that Bob just wasn't able to manage. Then one Wednesday in late February, Bob gets called into Mac's office and naturally he has to sit and listen to his phone conversation. Well during the conversation Mac mentions that he is being demoted to sales director, Bob's position, and they are hiring a new sales manager! And no one mentioned this to Bob? This is how you find out? By listening to a conversation? The following day, Bob walked in and spoke to a few people. He thanked them for the opportunity, wished training was available or the position he was hired for, and let them know that Mac made it impossible to work under him. Bob had come to find out that he wasn't the only one who felt that way. So now who to blame. Sometimes you have to wait for karma to take hold.

My scan and blood work went off as normal. Dr. T walks in with great news, no change! NO EVIDENCE OF METASTATIC CANCER!!!! 6 months clean! Thank you sweet Jesus! Then there was a but.....

A tiny bit of fluid was back around my lung lining. Damn it! Usually this was the first sign that I was building up a resistance to the medicine. What followed after was my heart rate would usually drop and my blood pressure would rise. I would feel some pressure and pain on my lower left side. Sometimes pressure mid chest and mid back. I had nothing of that. It was so aggravating, here I was, finally feeling and starting to look like myself again and is this the beginning of another set back? Dr. T was cautious, he scheduled me for a scan in 2 months rather than 3 to be sure, having me promise if I was having any issues at all to call Immediately. Naturally, seeing the weight loss he was concerned. I really had to almost get angry because he didn't want to listen. Yes, I am eating healthy, no, I'm not starving myself. Yes, I feel good. Yes, I am exercising. Yes, I understand considerable weight loss in a short period of time is concerning but listen to why. My thyroid is functioning, my body is responding, I'm getting rid of all the inflammation. Yes, I am using essential oils. He got quiet. He asked why. I told him, this is ancient, holistic methods. Frankincense is talked about in the Bible as a healing oil and pain relief. It is for cell regeneration. I told him I use different ones. Oregano to help my nails grow. Peppermint for digestion. Lemongrass to aid my thyroid, lavender for relaxation diffusing it at night for a more restful sleep. His eyes started to roll. This made me angry. I wasn't going to have this denied by him. I told him that the frankincense and the deep blue oil combination was relieving the neuropathy! That cannot be denied. It needs to be shared. I also explained to him that I understand that the inflammation was causing my entire body to not function correctly. That in itself aids the cancer! Inflammation in our guts cause illness. I am ridding myself of that, in effect aiding my body to be stronger to continue on my healing path. This was a direction given to me by God. Of that I am sure. My entire journey these past few years have lead me here, right here, right now. To lead. To teach, to follow the voice inside. To pay attention to the path set before me. It was my decision to follow this or not. But sometimes you know, you feel it deep inside, that you are right where you need to be. And I am.

I decided to become an advocate for DoTerra essential oils. I never in my life have done this but I am living it! How can I not spread this finding? First and foremost to me was engaging people in a conversation, telling them my story. How it helped me. Why DoTerra products are better than the others. It was simple. These oils, harvested from roots, trees, flowers, plants and bark are grown in their natural environments. This is world wide co-sourcing, grown by farmers who for generations have worked these lands. They aren't grown in a geeenhouse in someone's backyard. These are Certified Pure, Therapeutic grade oils. No fillers, no additives. Johns Hopkins is partnered with them for research and development! Why wouldn't we take a chance on a natural product, that won't cause side effects, instead of a pill? That was my argument with the pill Dr. T wanted to prescribe for neuropathy. Why take a pill that may help but cause 5 more side effects? I want off of every pill that I can. I don't want to take high blood pressure pills anymore. If I can lose the weight and take a natural approach, isn't it worth the chance? There's nothing that will harm us unless there is a specific allergy to an oil. To me there was no debate. Especially after I found that they are working! The funny thing was getting Bob to believe. Watching the surprised look on his face was priceless everytime I give him an oil blend and it worked. His faith as I told you before waivered. Not anymore. He never believed in the signs I used to talk about, now he does. Well, I must say that he listens to me a lot more than he used to!

These past few years have been a huge learning experience for not just me but my family. Standing firm, never losing faith, holding each other up in the hardest of times. It hasn't been easy. It was never without fights and harsh words that were sometimes spoken. Feelings hurt. But I never ever questioned God's plan for us all.

I never could have imagined the path my life has taken. Writing this. Holistic treatments. Stage 4 cancer patient, now a 2 time survivor. Our paths are set before us. If my eyes weren't open and I didn't accept God and believe in His path for me I can't imagine where I would be. And like I've said before. I'm not special. My strength comes from the power of our Lord, Jesus Christ. I am His child. We are all His children.

Bringing you up to speed.....

As I sit here, with the ending of the book that isn't ready to end, I can tell you that once again my treatments changed. Once again fluid built up in my lung lining and I needed it removed. I started on Ibrance(have you seen the commericals?) and Faslodex. This combination has been working beautifully for me! My Blessings continue! My determination, my prayers and positive thoughts will always be there. I will continue to live by The Serenity Prayer, keeping only positive people in my world. I will continue to pay my Blessing forward. And just now, as I sit at the game table in my living room, I looked up and noticed a framed verse I put up not too very long ago.

LIVING LIFE

Life is not a race- but indeed a journey. Be honest. Work hard. Be choosy. Say " thank you", " I love you", and " great job" to someone each day. Go to church, take time for prayer. The Lord giveth and the Lord taketh. Let your handshake mean more than pen and paper. Love your life and what you've been given, it is not accidental – search for your purpose and do it as best as you can. Dreaming does matter. It allows you to become that which you aspire to be. Laugh often. Appreciate the little things in life and enjoy them. Some of the best things really are free. Do not worry, less wrinkles are more becoming. Forgive, it frees the soul. Take time for yourself, plan for longevity. Recognize the special people you have been Blessed to know. Live for today, enjoy the moment.

Simple thoughts. Simple ideas. Why, oh why then, do we complicate life? Why is it that it usually takes a crisis for us to look at all the beauty that surrounds us? Trials are given to us for a reason. I don't believe they are to punish but to teach us life lessons. During this journey of writing this book, I often think back to how my father handled his illness. He was going to go full speed ahead, not changing a thing. When it was over it was going to be over. How I wish I had the wisdom that I have now to explain to him that just because you change, it doesn't mean you gave up, or that you are weak, or that you can't enjoy life.

MODERATION. Remember that word. Everything in moderation. I still love my wine, I may not have as much of it, but I drink it. I may follow the no gluten, no sugar, no dairy rule, but I allow for my exceptions. We have to continue to try to enjoy all that surrounds us. And then make time for it. I pray that if you were without hope that I may have given you some. I pray that I could have a positive impact in just one person's life. I pray that I come to realize all that I need to do. I pray that God's Blessing continue.

I wish everyone the peace I feel inside. It's an incredible feeling. Thank you for allowing me to tell my story.

Remember. Breathe

Have faith
Get angry
Never stop fighting

My last prayer. The last thing I prayed on. Our life is coming back into place. I will thank God everyday for the rest of my life.

Well, this is my life so far....we have to take the good with the bad. Find the balance, trust in our faith to carry us through the valleys and be thankful for the peaks. As I sit here and write the final words in this book, my hope is that you did laugh with me through the tears of life. We can never lose hope and always TRUST in a plan that God has set forth of all of us.

Whatever the future holds, it holds. But I will continue to hold Bob's hand through our journey in life. Until death do us part. God Bless you all!

94360812R10135

Made in the USA
Middletown, DE
19 October 2018